# INIGO JONES

*Vandyke's original Drawing, from which the Print by Van. Voerst was taken, in the
Book of Vandyke's Heads. Given me by the Duke of Devonshire.*

*B Burlington*

**INIGO JONES**

*From the Drawing by Vandyke in the Chatsworth Collection*
*Copyright of the Duke of Devonshire*

# INIGO JONES

## J. ALFRED GOTCH

Benjamin Blom, Inc. Publisher
New York 1968

ABIGAIL E. WEEKS MEMORIAL LIBRARY
UNION COLLEGE
BARBOURVILLE, KENTUCKY

720.92
J77g

First published 1928
Reissued 1968 by Benjamin Blom, Inc.
Bronx, N.Y. 10452

Library of Congress Catalog Card No. 68-20224

Manufactured in the United States of America

# Preface

# PREFACE

INIGO JONES is so great a figure in English art, and has attracted so much attention, that most of the facts relating to him are fairly well known. Much, however, has been taken for granted, and repeated by various writers without close investigation. The most careful accounts of his life are those by Peter Cunningham and Mr. H. P. Horne, who wrote the memoir in the *Dictionary of National Biography* ; on these sources the following pages have drawn with great advantage. But since those accounts were written a number of fresh facts have come to light, thus enabling a clearer view of the subject to be obtained. Not a few buildings have been attributed to Inigo Jones on slender authority, which recent researches show to be either inadequate or mistaken ; and although his work upon the Masques, and the duties of his office as Surveyor to the King, have by no means been overlooked, they have hardly received the amount of attention they deserve. The publication by the Walpole Society of the *Designs by Inigo Jones for Masques and Plays at Court* has enabled the proper emphasis to be laid upon the former, and a careful investigation of the State Papers has similarly helped in regard to the latter. In the result the view hitherto held of Inigo Jones requires to be modified, but without lessening—

indeed perhaps increasing—the admiration he in-
spires.

It has been thought desirable to avoid distracting
the reader's attention by numerous footnotes, and
therefore the authorities for statements in the text
are cited in the ' References and Notes ' at the end
of the book, and among the ' Notes ' and in the
Appendices will be found additional information
acceptable to all those who are interested in the
subject.

Besides the books already mentioned, the *Ben
Jonson* of Messrs. C. H. Herford and Percy Simpson,
and Miss Mary Hervey's *Life of Thomas Howard,
Earl of Arundel*, have been of great assistance.
Sincere thanks are also due to Mr. W. Grant Keith
for his help in transcribing the State Papers and in
supplying valuable references ; to Mr. Dircks, the
librarian of the Royal Institute of British Architects,
Mr. Wilkinson, librarian of Worcester College, Oxford,
and Mr. Francis Thompson, librarian at Chatsworth,
all of whom have most kindly helped in the necessary
researches. Thanks are equally due to the Duke of
Devonshire, the Royal Institute of British Architects, the Radcliffe Library, Worcester College and
the Oxford University Press, and to all others who
have given permission and assistance in connexion
with the illustrations.

J. ALFRED GOTCH

WEEKLEY RISE, KETTERING
*October, 1928*

# CONTENTS

vii

# LIST OF ILLUSTRATIONS

* Reproduced from *Designs by Inigo Jones for Masques and Plays at Court*, by permission of the Walpole Society.

*PLATE I*

A NEGRO NYMPH

FOR BEN JONSON'S 'MASQUE OF BLACKNESS,' 1605

*From the Chatsworth Collection*
*Copyright of the Duke of Devonshire*

PLATE II

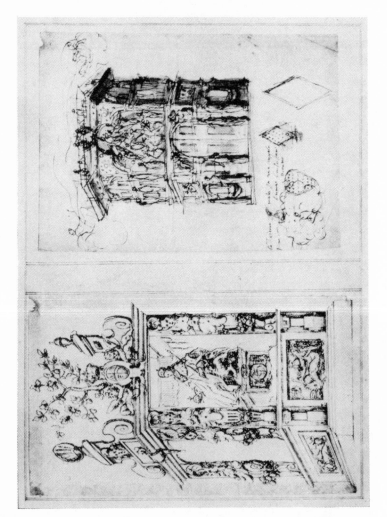

CATAFALQUE FOR A QUEEN
(See page 118)

SKETCH FOR THE HOUSE OF FAME
FOR BEN JONSON'S 'MASQUE OF QUEENS,' 1609
From the Burlington-Devonshire Collection at the Royal Institute of British Architects

*PLATE III*

TETHYS, OR A NYMPH

FOR SAMUEL DANIEL'S 'TETHYS' FESTIVAL,' 1610
*Walpole Society, from the Chatsworth Collection*
*Copyright of the Duke of Devonshire*

PLATE IV

SKETCHES FOR MEDALLIONS ON THE DESIGN FOR
TEMPLE BAR

(See page 207)

TITLE-PAGE OF INIGO JONES' SKETCH BOOK

From a facsimile copy of the Sketch Book

From the Collection at the Royal Institute of British Architects

*PLATE V*

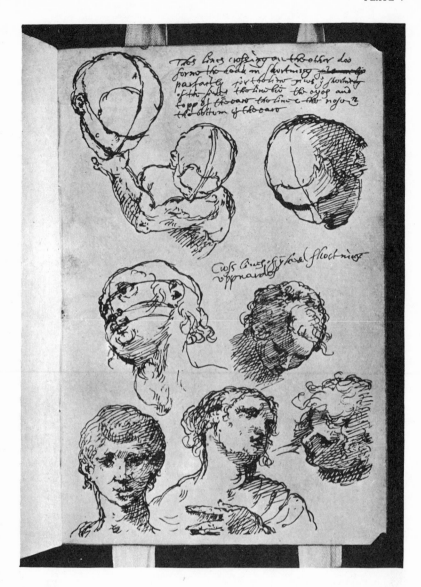

A PAGE FROM INIGO JONES' SKETCH BOOK

*PLATE VI*

JACOBEAN PORCH
1616
*From the Collection at the Royal Institute of British Architects*

*PLATE VII*

THE QUEEN'S HOUSE, GREENWICH HOSPITAL
1618–1635

*PLATE VIII*

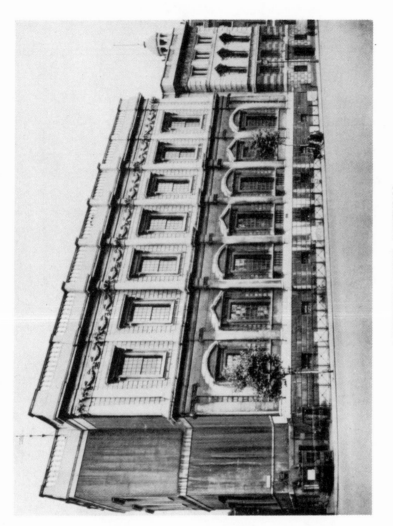

BANQUETING HOUSE, WHITEHALL

NOW USED AS THE UNITED SERVICES MUSEUM

PLATE IX

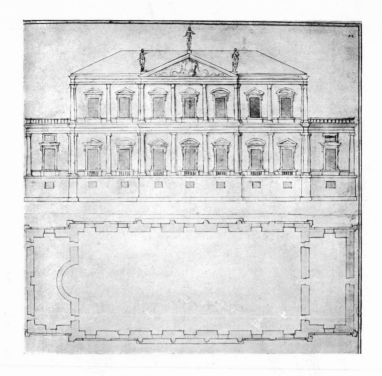

DESIGN FOR BANQUETING HOUSE, WHITEHALL

*From the Chatsworth Collection.   Copyright of the Duke of Devonshire*

PLATE X

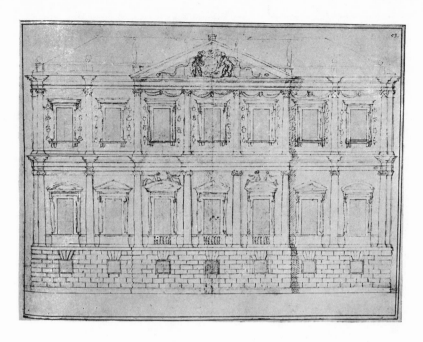

ANOTHER DESIGN FOR BANQUETING HOUSE, WHITEHALL
*From the Chatsworth Collection.   Copyright of the Duke of Devonshire*

*PLATE XI*

GATE AT BEAUFORT HOUSE
1621
*From the Collection at the Royal Institute of British Architects*

*PLATE XII*

YORK HOUSE WATER-GATE

AT BOTTOM OF BUCKINGHAM STREET, STRAND

*PLATE XIII*

CATAFALQUE FOR JAMES I
1625
*From the Collection at Worcester College, Oxford*

PLATE XIV

PROSCENIUM AND STANDING SCENE FOR A FRENCH PASTORAL
February 1626
*Walpole Society, from the Chatsworth Collection.   Copyright of the Duke of Devonshire*

PLATE XV

CEILING FOR THE DUKE OF BUCKINGHAM
*From the Collection at Worcester College, Oxford*

PLATE XVI

**CHLORIDIA (HENRIETTA MARIA)**
1631
*Walpole Society, from the Chatsworth Collection.   Copyright of the Duke of Devonshire*

*PLATE XVII*

STOKE BRUERNE PARK, NORTHAMPTONSHIRE
1630–36

*PLATE XVIII*

SOUTH FRONT

WEST FRONT

ST. PAUL'S CATHEDRAL, SHOWING INIGO JONES' WORK
*From the Engravings by Hollar, in Sir Wm. Dugdale's 'History of St. Paul's Cathedral,' 1658*

*PLATE XIX*

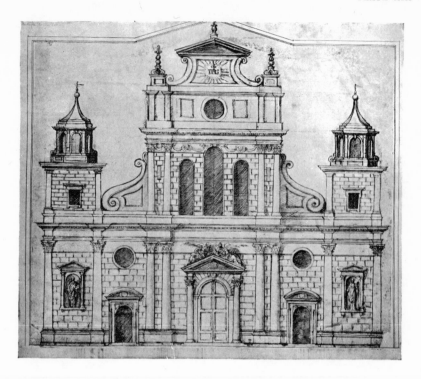

ST. PAUL'S CATHEDRAL

INIGO JONES' DRAWING FOR WEST FRONT

*From the Collection at the Royal Institute of British Architects*

PLATE XX

PROSCENIUM FOR THE QUEEN'S MASQUE OF INDIANS
1634
UTILISED IN THE 'TEMPLE OF LOVE,' 1635
*From the Collection at the Royal Institute of British Architects*

PLATE XXI

BORDER AND STANDING SCENE—'THE ISLE OF DELOS'
FOR FLORIMENE, 1635 (DEC. 31)
*Walpole Society, from the Chatsworth Collection.   Copyright of the Duke of Devonshire*

*PLATE XXII*

THE QUEEN'S HOUSE, GREENWICH HOSPITAL
CHIMNEY PIECE, 1637

*From the Collection at the Royal Institute of British Architects*

PLATE XXIII

ENGLISH HOUSES WITH LONDON AND THE THAMES AFAR OFF

FOR SIR WM. DAVENANT'S 'BRITANNIA TRIUMPHANS,' JANUARY 7, 1638

*Walpole Society, from the Chatsworth Collection. Copyright of the Duke of Devonshire*

PLATE XXIV

SCENE FOR 'LUMINALIA,' FEBRUARY 6TH, 1638

*Walpole Society, from the Chatsworth Collection.   Copyright of the Duke of Devonshire*

PLATE XXV

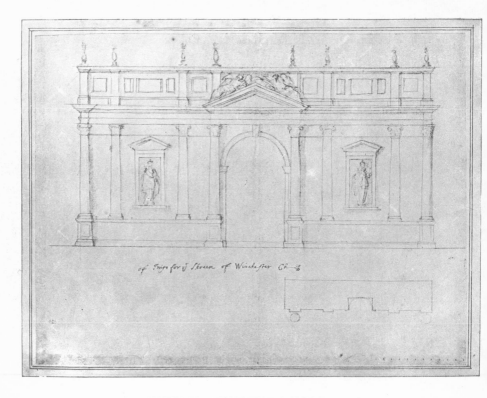

of Snip for y Skreen of Winchester Ch——

SCREEN FOR WINCHESTER CATHEDRAL, 1638

*From the Collection at the Royal Institute of British Architects*

*PLATE XXVI*

TEMPLE BAR, 1638
(Sketches for Medallions are given on plate IV, facing page 78)
*From the Collection at the Royal Institute of British Architects*

PLATE XXVII

TWO HOUSES

*From the Collection at the Royal Institute of British Architects*

*PLATE XXVIII*

GATEWAY IN OUTER COURT, KIRBY, 1640
PROBABLY BY INIGO JONES

PLATE XXIX

DRESS FOR YE KINGE
1640
IN SIR WM. DAVENANT'S 'SALMACIDA SPOLIA'
*Walpole Society, from the Chatsworth Collection.   Copyright of the Duke of Devonshire*

*PLATE XXX*

A CEILING FOR WILTON HOUSE, WILTSHIRE, 1649
*From the Gibbs Collection, Radcliffe Library, Oxford*

*PLATE XXXI*

WILTON HOUSE, WILTSHIRE—INTERIOR OF DOUBLE CUBE ROOM

# INIGO JONES

## CHAPTER I

Change in Architectural Style—Classic Style established—His Early Days—His Education—Death of His Father.

IN endeavouring to obtain a true picture of an eminent man, long dead, around whose memory, in the absence of abundant knowledge, imagination has played the more freely, it is inadvisable to place him upon a lofty pinnacle at the outset, and then look at the facts relating to him with that altitude always in mind. Rather is it advisable to marshal the facts without prejudice and help him to emerge from a scrutiny of them on his own merits. This course is particularly desirable in the case of Inigo Jones, inasmuch as from the early eighteenth century onwards he has been credited with much architectural work on evidence which was either inadequate, or liable to rejection in the light of modern inquiry. Yet when all necessary corrections have been made, it will still be found that he is one of the most interesting and notable of modern English designers in architecture and the arts allied to it.

It should not be taken for granted that Inigo Jones was a solitary and commanding figure, compared with whom, for the purpose of his biography,

all his contemporaries were of secondary importance. It must be borne in mind that he was not
always famous ; that he moved among men of
abilities equal to his own, although exerted in other
spheres than that of design ; and that by many of
those for whom he worked, persons now long con-
signed to oblivion, he was not unreasonably regarded
as an inferior. Such persons must necessarily be
taken into account, and so must be the atmosphere
of the time in which they lived. That time had
its own characteristics, but in its essentials it was
not unlike our own. There were wits and dullards
in the seventeenth century as there are in the twentieth ; there were honest men and unscrupulous,
cantankerous persons and obliging. There were
profiteers and the newly-rich striving for position
against others whose position had greater antiquity
behind it. The springs of human passion and
endeavour were the same then as now. But in
tracing the career of a remarkable man of that period
certain inherent differences must inevitably appear
and impart their flavour to the narrative.

In order to place Inigo Jones in due relation to
his surroundings it will be necessary shortly to tra-
verse a tract of well-trodden ground in explaining
the change from the Gothic style of architecture in
England to the Classic, since by so doing a clearer
view will be obtained of the leading part he played
in bringing that change about.

For some fifty years before Inigo Jones was born
this change had been affecting English architecture.
It consisted in the gradual introduction of Italian
detail and methods of design into work which was

the outcome of long-established Gothic traditions. These traditions had altered of course with the various phases of the Gothic style ; but that style can be traced step by step through a slow process of evolution, not only back to the time of the Norman invasion, but beyond that through France, Rome and Greece to the hoary antiquity of Egypt. With the Norman invasion came the Norman handling of architecture, and the earliest expressions of the Gothic style in England are closely allied to what may be found in Northern France. But English architecture developed on lines of its own, and its subsequent phases may be held as native to the soil. During more than four hundred years it produced innumerable masterpieces in all kinds of buildings, in cathedrals, churches, castles and houses. But by the time when Henry VIII came to the throne in the early years of the sixteenth century the Gothic style had lost much of its vigour and fertility of design ; it was therefore predisposed to accept a new impetus, an impetus not forthcoming in England, but which Italy was able to supply. Italy was teeming with new ideas, and so, in less degree, was the whole western world, for the Renaissance had caused an extraordinary awakening of men's faculties. In Italy the expression of the Fine Arts had been brought to a high state of perfection. Her architecture had never been dominated by the Gothic style to the same extent as that of her neighbours beyond the Alps, and so it was all the easier for her, in the revival of ancient learning and art, to take her inspiration from classic sources, abundant and close at hand. Her influence spread to France,

Germany, the Netherlands and England ; of her superabundance of enthusiasm and of her artists who were filled with it, other countries availed themselves. Several men of the first rank in the arts were invited to France by Francis I ; our Henry VIII followed his example and thus made the way easier for the invasion of classic detail as handled by the Italians.

But the Italianizing of English design was a slow process. No great number of Italian craftsmen came over ; building was still carried on by English workers, who, although with limited information, endeavoured to apply the novel methods to their work. The process was checked by the fact that each trade provided its own designs, and consequently that many different minds had to be imbued with the new spirit. The acquisition of the new knowledge was not perfect, and it was more imperfect in some craftsmen than in others. Its application to buildings resulted in a curious mixture of the old and the new, which to the mind of the modern purist was so distressing that the writers of a hundred years ago expressèd their disapproval in the term ' bastard Gothic '. But a larger sympathy than theirs delights in watching this struggle between the old and the new, in noting how ancient Gothic traditions were tempered with modern classic ideas. The men who actually did the work were alert, clever and touched with the fire of the age, and they gave us buildings that are as truly English as any that went before them, and perhaps more individually English than any that came after them.

The Italian germ grew without intentional hind-

rance ; indeed it was the desire of all concerned that
it should grow.   Wealthy and influential persons
like Lord Burghley sought after Italian detail in
several directions ;  he got correspondents to send
him books from France, he obtained drawings from
the Netherlands.   Other men in his position sent
young architects to Italy in order that they might
acquire first-hand information.   One such traveller
on his return offered his services and his foreign
knowledge to Sir John Thynne in his new building
at Longleat.   But notwithstanding all this the old
traditions were carried on, although with a large
infusion of the new spirit.   Great houses were built
in this attractive, if bastard, style all through the
reigns of Elizabeth and James I, and indeed the
style was followed by local and unlearned architects
and builders down to the end of the seventeenth
century and even into the eighteenth.

But the polite world, fortified in due course with
the powerful support of Inigo Jones, knew better
than to do this ;  to them, so great was the change
of ideas, the only architecture was Classic architecture.   Jones himself, it is true, steeped though he
was in the Italian spirit, recognized the splendid
Gothic cathedral of old St. Paul's as ' so great and
noble a work ' ;  but the cultured Evelyn held Gothic
buildings (and he cites as examples all our finest
cathedrals) to be ' Mountains of Stone, vast and
Gygantick Buildings indeed ;  but not Worthy the
Name of *Architecture*'—so completely had fashionable taste turned from Gothic to Classic by the
middle of the seventeenth century.   It had taken
more than a hundred years to effect the revolution,

and it might have taken longer still, with results
far less satisfactory, if it had not been for Inigo
Jones.

Just at the time when the new conception of
design had become so well established as to result
in a distinct style of architecture, the Elizabethan,
in the year 1573, Jones was born.  He was baptized
on the 19th July, as the register records, in the
church of St. Bartholomew-the-Less, Smithfield.
Some of the finest mansions of the period were then
in course of building.  Kirby Hall, in Northamptonshire, had been begun three years before ; Castle
Ashby, in the same county, was commenced in the
year of Jones's birth ; Burghley House was already
habitable, but was increased to what we now see
when he was four years old ; Longleat, in Wiltshire,
was in much the same case ; Knole, in Kent, had
been started ; and a few years later the first stone
was laid of Wollaton Hall, near Nottingham.  All
these buildings, upon which the best skill of the
craftsmen was expended, exhibit in varying degrees
the mixture of Gothic and Classic treatment characteristic of the time.

It was of course not only architecture that felt
the new Italian influence, although architecture
reflects it more visibly than anything ; all kinds of
decoration were affected, and not only so, but literature, music, the drama and indeed all methods of
expressing emotion were touched by it.

Architecture, however, found the most obvious
models to guide it, for there were scores of buildings
in Italy already designed according to the most
approved rules established through a study of

ancient work. But the times had not produced in England a man who had completely mastered these rules, and who had at once the ability and the opportunity to apply them with freedom and discretion to English work. The two best-known designers of the time, Thorpe and Smithson, had both ability and opportunity, but they were far too busy to go to Italy for the purpose of prolonged study, and they had to obtain what help they could from the few books which were then published on architecture. So, as the fates would have it, Inigo Jones became the first Englishman who, by long residence in Italy, familiarized himself with the rules, and not only with the rules, but with Italian methods and ways of thought, and was able subsequently to apply his knowledge under no less powerful patronage than that of the King and the Court.

But his opportunity was still far off, for it was not until he was forty-six years old that Jones produced the first truly Italian building that England had yet seen, in the shape of the Banqueting House at Whitehall. Of the first thirty years out of his forty-six, but little is known, and it is not possible to give any account of his education or early training. His father, who also bore the name of Inigo, was a clothworker, and lived at the time of his son's birth in Smithfield, a district devoted to his trade and in which was held the great cloth fair of St. Bartholomew. He appears subsequently to have moved to the parish of St. Bennet, Paul's Wharf, for it was there that he died, and in the church of St. Bennet he was buried by the side of his wife. In any case, Jones was city-bred, as also were several of the eminent men with whom he consorted in later life.   The city in those days was a pleasanter place to live in than it would be now.   It was plentifully sprinkled with dwelling-houses and gardens, and resembled, on a larger scale, many of our old-fashioned provincial towns which have not been submerged in the wave of 'industrialism'.   Rows of shops of modest frontage and quiet aspect, with houses over them, were broken by a larger house and its garden, or by a church and its burying-ground.   The shop-fronts were unpretending and displayed their contents through windows of many panes.   Ambitious tradesmen would perhaps throw out a bay-window in order to attract more attention to their goods.   But the rivalry which now expresses itself in huge sheets of plate-glass then found its vent in a way which, although less obnoxious to the eye, must have been distressing to the ear ; for the apprentices stood outside and varied their insistent cry of 'What d'ye lack ?  What d'ye lack ? ' by an interchange of jests with passers-by, a procedure which, one would imagine, must have repelled as many customers as it attracted.   Not only was the city a homely and neighbourly place to live in, but its surroundings were pleasant. There was the river, a great highway for business and pleasure ;  the Strand, with its fine mansions and gardens ; and, close at hand, the open country with its hills and woods.

Inigo Jones, the father, was not a rich man. This is made tolerably clear by an action between him and one, Richard Baker, whose trade tallied with his surname.   It would appear that Jones had become indebted to Baker for a sum of £60, which, unless he paid it by a certain date, was to become £80. He paid off part of the money and arranged with his creditor to pay the remainder by monthly instalments of ten shillings. Some dispute seems to have occurred, and Baker started an action for recovery of the debt. Jones appealed, with the result that the arrangement for paying ten shillings a month was confirmed. This no doubt was satisfactory as far as it went, and nothing more has transpired as to the event ; but a man who could only pay a debt of £60 by monthly instalments of ten shillings could not have been well-to-do. The decree of the Court is dated 18th October 1589, when Inigo the younger was sixteen years old. By this time he may be supposed to have finished his schooling, and considering the facilities then existing for obtaining education, and indeed the obligations imposed for acquiring it, he must have received sound instruction in spite of his father's want of means. He never proceeded to either of the universities as did many comparatively poor young men, and he never could have been considered a profound scholar. Indeed in such homely matters as writing and spelling he did not shine, and in both those directions his manuscripts have caused much perplexity to transcribers. Of Latin, which was then one of the principal subjects taught at school, he may have acquired a smattering, but his acquisition, whatever it was, became in after years a matter for banter, if not ridicule, to Ben Jonson, who, with much the same early opportunities, became himself an accomplished scholar. But Jones must have had great natural abilities which in due time he cultivated in his own way. He had neither the upbringing nor the wonderful mental equipment of Christopher Wren, a combination which led John Evelyn to describe him as ' that miracle of a youth '. Nothing having been recorded as to Jones's youth, we can only argue back from what we know to what we do not know, and as, despite the shortcomings already mentioned, he became the companion of wits, poets and men of letters as well as the favoured adviser of men like Lord Arundel and Lord Pembroke, it may fairly be assumed that he acquired a considerable tincture of learning and manners.

Whichever way we look for information as to his early years we are baffled. Horace Walpole thinks that the most probable account is that he was apprenticed to a joiner, but the source of the suggestion is vague, and as there is no confirmation forthcoming we are left in doubt. It is tolerably certain, however, that the career of a joiner, if ever contemplated, was never pursued, for according to his own testimony he was naturally inclined in his younger years to ' study the arts of design '. It is in this phrase that the key to the whole of his life and work is to be found. It was not architecture alone to which he was devoted, although he favoured that art above the others, but ' the arts of design ', which ultimately resolved themselves mainly into architecture, decoration in connection with it, and the scenes, scenery and costumes for the long series of masques upon which he was employed over a period of five-and-thirty years.

During this early time he must also have studied
painting and have actually produced some pictures,
for the very first mention of him that has come to
light is one in which he is described as ' Henygo
Jones, a picture-maker '.   This goes to confirm the
statement made by his earliest biographer that ' he
was particularly taken notice of for his Skill in
the Practice of Landskip-Painting '.   But this biographer is somewhat wide of the mark in his other
statements, and the only surviving picture attributed
to Jones is a small one that belonged to the Earl
of Burlington and was housed in his Chiswick villa.
Horace Walpole says of it that ' the colouring is
very indifferent, but the trees freely and masterly
imagined '.   The probability is that the unimpas-
sioned description of him as ' a picture-maker ' more
nearly conveys his relation to the world at large
than the suggestion of his biographer that he had
already made a reputation.

One undoubted fact emerges from the barren
field of conjecture as to this period of Jones's life,
and that is that his father died in the spring of 1597
when the son was three-and-twenty.   Mr. Peter
Cunningham, whose careful ' Life ' is full of well-
attested information, himself discovered the father's
will in Doctors' Commons.   It is dated 14th
February 1596–7, and it was proved by Inigo on
the 5th of the following April.   There was not much
to leave, and what there was was to be divided
equally between Inigo and his three sisters, Joan,
Judith and Mary.   The sisters forthwith fade from
the canvas, save for one shadowy reappearance, and
leave their brother, presumably with very little

means, to make his own living. How he managed to do this and at the same time contrived to study the art of painting and become a picture-maker is not known. But the time was approaching when the records become a little more generous in relation to him, and we must leave him for a time in order to say something about the principal sources from which information as to his life and work is to be derived.

# CHAPTER II

No Early Employment in Architecture—His *Stone-Heng Restored*—
Dr. Charleton's Dedication—John Webb's Dedication.

THE principal sources from which information as to Inigo Jones's life and work is derived are five in number. First in importance are his own drawings, of which a large number have been preserved ; these are supplemented by a copy of Palladio's *Four Books of Architecture,* in which he made copious marginal notes during his best-known visit to Italy, and by the sketch-book which he carried with him on that occasion. All these are the work of his own hand. The fourth source is John Webb's book *The Vindication of Stone-Heng Restored,* in which Webb, who was the pupil, assistant and ultimately the representative of Jones, as well as his kinsman by marriage, makes valuable references both to his work and to incidents in his life ; and lastly there are the State Papers (Domestic) of the time.

In addition to these some help is obtained from casual references, such as that in which he is described as a picture-maker, and it is from this direction that further assistance may perhaps be found in the future.

Jones's own drawings, notes and reports furnish the surest criterion of his personal ability in design-

13

ing and in the employment of the English language.
The allusions to him in Webb's book, which have
to be taken with caution for reasons that will be
given later, afford considerable help as to his life,
character and work ; and the State Papers furnish
unimpeachable evidence as to the manner of his
employment over a great many years, and throw
some interesting side-lights on his occupations.

It may be said at once that the evidence derived
from these sources, when carefully examined, suggests a view of him different from that hitherto
accepted. He has always been regarded as, first
and foremost, a great architect with a practice
extending over nearly the whole of England and
even into Wales and Scotland, while, supplementing
his work in this capacity, were his duties as surveyor
to the King, and the devising of masques for the
Court and sometimes for distinguished outside
bodies. But judging by the available evidence it
would appear that he was known as an ingenious
designer of masques years before he accomplished
anything great in architecture ; that his appointment as surveyor of His Majesty's Works gave him
the opportunity of displaying his architectural skill
but at the same time limited the range of possible
activity in this direction, and imposed upon him
routine work which must have absorbed much of
his time, and furthermore constrained him to devote
a large part of what remained to the business of the
masques. If this view is reasonable, as it appears
to be, he can no longer be regarded as an architect at
large with the surveyorship thrown in as a help to
his resources, but rather as the Surveyor to His

Majesty whose services were sometimes obtained by influential courtiers ; and this opinion is fortified by the titles on his drawings and by much of the work which has, more or less plausibly, been attributed to him. After all, it is not the quality, but the quantity, of his work that is affected by this change of outlook.

He was forty-two when he obtained the Surveyorship in 1615, and during the ten or fifteen years of maturity that preceded this event there is no properly authenticated building by his hand. There is nothing to connect him with any of the large houses then being built, such as Hatfield or Audley End. His architectural record is a blank. Horace Walpole, whose account of him has no doubt largely helped to establish the misunderstanding, attributes one or two Jacobean houses to him and supposes that his style was purified by his visits to Italy ; but it is much more probable that from the outset he was out of sympathy with work which fell short of the true Italian ideal, and set himself to free English architecture of its shortcomings. There is only one drawing of his that can be classed as Jacobean— part of the front of a house, signed and dated 1616, and this is very mediocre in design ; it lacks the freedom and mastery which distinguish his mature work.

The absence of evidence as to his having executed any notable architectural work during these years is undoubtedly curious, and the future may yet reveal facts, now unknown, which may modify the foregoing conclusions and add to the interest of his life.

John Webb's book *The Vindication of Stone-Heng*

*Restored* has so important a bearing on the story of Inigo Jones's life, that its origin had better be explained at this stage, although by so doing a considerable jump into the future has to be made. In the year 1620, King James I being a guest of the Earl of Pembroke at Wilton in Wiltshire, Inigo Jones was sent for by the Earl and received instructions from His Majesty to discover out of his own practice in architecture and experience in antiquities abroad, what he possibly could about the great monument of Stonehenge, a subject which has puzzled antiquaries down to our own time. Accordingly Jones proceeded to take copious measurements and make notes, but for some unknown reason he did not pursue the inquiry, and apparently it passed from recollection until a year or two after his death. Then, in 1655, John Webb, who was in turn his pupil, assistant, and deputy in the office of Surveyor after the outbreak of the Civil War, and moreover was the executor of his will, and who throughout his life was a devoted admirer of his master, revived the subject on the persuasion (he says) of several learned friends. He published the result of Jones's investigation ' from some few indigested notes ' of his which had been preserved, under the title of *The most notable Antiquity of Great Britain, vulgarly called Stone-Heng, on Salisbury Plain, Restored, by Inigo Jones, Esq; Architect General to the King*. It is quite clear that Jones himself did not write the book, but that Webb wrote it in his name : Webb says expressly that ' his (Jones's) notes were not found, much less *Stone-Heng Restored* written until long after his death '. It is to be presumed that Webb founded his theory of the

origin of Stonehenge on his master's notes, but he
elaborated the theme in his own very learned fashion
and with many more Latin quotations than would
have been possible to Jones, who, there is good reason
to believe, was no great Latin scholar. We have
therefore the rather curious phenomenon of a book
published as the work of Jones, and yet bearing in
its preface the assurance of J.W. (John Webb) that
it was compiled from some few indigested notes of
its ostensible author.

The treatise went to prove that Stonehenge was
in fact a Roman temple dedicated to Caelus, the senior
of the heathen gods. But how Inigo, who had
studied and drawn Roman remains in Italy, and was
himself a skilful designer of the revived Classic
architecture, could have led Webb to confound the
uncouth and rugged stones of Stonehenge with the
carefully wrought and well-proportioned work of the
Romans, is incomprehensible. It is equally hard to
understand how Webb, who was as serious a student
of Classic architecture as his master, could have
adopted and elaborated such a theory. But the
merits of the theory are of no importance, it is the
results of its publication that are of interest. Shortly
after the appearance of the book it was attacked
by a Dr. Walter Charleton, physician-in-ordinary to
the King, at one time President of the College of
Physicians, and a Fellow of the Royal Society, ' but
reputed to have over valued his parts and performances'. In a treatise called *Chorea Gigantum*,
which was even more learned than the object of his
attack—for he brought Greek as well as Latin to
bear upon his opponent—he demolished Jones's

theory and proved that Stonehenge should be
restored to the Danes.

The challenge was at once taken up by Webb in
his *Vindication of Stone-Heng Restored*, wherein with
further learning and a considerable infusion of
acerbity, he in his turn demolished Dr. Charleton.
The only abiding interest of the controversy lies in
the *Vindication*, and that because of its references
to Inigo Jones.  It is important, however, to take
Webb's attitude of mind into account.  Here was a
doctor who presumably knew no more about architecture than what he had gathered from his reading,
attacking a theory propounded (ostensibly) by Inigo
Jones.  Webb, therefore, had to vindicate both the
theory and the author, and it is rather amusing to
watch him eagerly defending the opinions and statements of ' Mr. Jones ', when one shrewdly surmises
that they were in reality those of Mr. Webb.  He
evidently thought that ' this doctor ', as he disdain-
fully calls him, was not fully aware of the greatness
of Inigo Jones, in spite of the admission that he ' was
one of the most famous architects of our age ' ;  upon
his greatness, consequently, he held it necessary
to insist at intervals.  Indeed his controversial
energy seems to have led him into over-emphasis
in some of his statements, and this tendency it
is that has to be borne in mind in weighing his
testimony.

A spirit of over-emphasis pervades all these old
controversies, and in this instance it finds its most
copious expression in the dedications of the several
treatises to the King, Charles II.  Dr. Charleton, for
instance, begins his dedication in this wise :

*Your Majesty's* Curiosity *to survey the Subject of this Discourse, the so much admired Antiquity of STONE-HENG, hath sometime been so great and urgent, as to find a Room in Your Royal Breast, amidst Your weightiest Cares ; and to carry You many Miles out of Your Way towards* Safety, *even at such a Time, when any Heart but Your Fearless and Invincible one, would have been wholly fill'd with Apprehensions of* Danger, *For, as I have had the Honour to hear from that Oracle of Truth and Wisdom, Your* Majesty's *own Mouth, You were pleased to visit that* Monument, *and, for many Hours together, entertain Your self with the delightful View thereof, when after the Defeat of Your Loyal Army at* Worcester, *Almighty* GOD, *in infinite Mercy to Your Three Kingdoms, miraculously delivered You out of the bloody Jaws of those* Monsters *of* Sin *and* Cruelty, *who taking Counsel only from the Heinousness of their* Crimes, *Sought* Impunity *in the highest* Aggravation *of them ; desperately hoping to secure* Rebellion *by* Regicide, *and by destroying their* Sovereign, *to continue their* Tyranny *over their Fellow-Subjects.*

The incident of the fugitive prince hiding in the oak at Boscobel is known to every one, but this visit to Stonehenge during his flight has been less loudly acclaimed. The hard words used by the doctor about his political opponents do but echo the prevailing sentiment of the dominant party, for at this period, 1662, the regicides were being relentlessly hunted ; no treachery was too shameless to be employed in their capture, and when caught they were executed with all the barbarity the times allowed.

The doctor in conclusion leaves his case

*to Your Majesty's Most Excellent* Judgment, *in which You are no less* Supreme, *than in Your* Power ; *and than which, none can be either more* Discerning, *or more* Equitable. *So that if it prove so fortunate as to receive Your* Approbation,

*I need not fear the Censure of any Understanding Reader ;
if not, I shall however gain this Advantage, to have my Mistake
rectify'd by a* King, *whose Reasons are Demonstrations, whose
Enquiries are the best Directions unto Truth, whose Assent
always is a sign of Truth, and to whose other Regal Prerogatives
an admirable Wisdom hath superadded this, that He is less
subject to be imposed upon than any other Man.*

Whatever may be thought of the doctor's attribution to Charles of all the qualities he mentions, he
was not far wrong in crediting him with shrewdness,
and no doubt this shrewdness came into play in
considering the doctor's panegyrics and his idea that
the *ipse dixit* of Charles was to solve a puzzle that
is still open for any antiquary to turn his hand to.

But Webb was not going to be outdone if unstinted
praise could move the King.   He begins his dedication thus :

AUGUSTUS CÆSAR *will be ever glorious, for leaving*
Rome *a* City *of* Marble, *which he found ignobly built.*   TITUS,
TRAJAN, ADRIAN *are Eternized for practising all liberal*
sciences.   HENRY LE GRAND, Your Heroeick Maternal
Grandfather, *designed as well* Palaces *as* Battels, *with His
own Hand.   And* YOUR MAJESTY, *without doubt, will be
no less Glorious to future* Ages ; *for* Your Delight *in* Architecture, Esteem *of* Arts, *and* Knowledge *in* Design, *which must
be confessed so great as no* Prince, *now living, understands a*
Drawing *more knowlingly :  Not of* Architecture Civil *only,
but* That *that conduceth to make* Your Empire *boundless, as*
Other Your Fame *immortal,* military *and* maritime *also.
This I deliver in the Simplicity of* Truth, *from* Experience,
*by* Your MAJESTY'S Royal Encouragement *of late.*

No doubt Webb was right in estimating the King's
ability to read a drawing, for at this time, 1664, and
during the preceding year, Webb had been designing

for the King that block of the new Palace at Greenwich known as 'King Charles's', not to mention the King's approval of one of Webb's designs for a great palace at Whitehall, a grandiose idea which never came to fruition. But as to Charles's immortal fame in exploits military and maritime, the less said the better.

The dedication proceeds in the same strain, with an allusion to Charles's visit to Stonehenge which he deigned to look upon 'with far, far more peril than Alexander the Great underwent in travelling to the remote Lybia, to behold the oracle of Jupiter Cham-mon there': and it reaches its climax in the concluding paragraph:

*The* Blessing *of GOD, that giveth all* Blessings, *pour down abundantly, beyond what can be askt, or thought,* Beatitudes *to* Infinity *upon* Your Blessed MAJESTY: *And grant* YOU *and* Your Royal Progeny *Happily, Peacably, Victoriously to* Reign *over* us, *and* our Children, *Evermore, till the* World *it self be no more.* Live *eternally,* CHARLES *the* Good. DREAD SIR, YOUR SACRED MAJESTY'S Ever Most Lowly, Ever Most Loyal *Subject* and *Vassal,*
*JOHN WEBB.*

Almost immediately after the Restoration Webb had submitted a petition to the King praying to be granted the office of surveyor in succession to Inigo Jones, but without success, that office being bestowed upon Sir John Denham, the poet. The blow was softened by his employment at Greenwich, and his effusive gratitude found expression in this Dedication.

So much for the sources of information; it is now necessary to take up the story again and apply them to its elucidation.

# CHAPTER III

IN confuting Dr. Charleton, Webb felt it incumbent upon him—for the doctor's edification and that of the world at large—to exalt the experience and knowledge of Inigo Jones in regard to architecture and antiquities. In his preface to *Stone-Heng Restored*, he had called Jones 'the Vitruvius of his age'; the unlucky doctor misquoted this as 'the English Vitruvius', a limitation which Webb rejected with scorn: 'had he so styled him, he had done him much injury: in regard Mr. Jones was not only the Vitruvius of England, but likewise, in his age, of all Christendom; and it was *Vox Europæ* that named him so, being, much more than at home, famous in remote parts, where he lived many years, designed many works, and discovered many antiquities, before unknown, with general applause.' If this were so, no echo of the applause has reached us save what Webb caught and repeated in his book; nor from any other source do we learn that Europe was ringing with his praise: and it is generally agreed that it would be vain to search abroad for buildings of his design either in Italy or anywhere else. Indeed it is remarkable that hardly any contemporary mention of him has come to light beyond such as might be made by those who came in close contact with him.   So Dr. Charleton may perhaps be excused for not being so fully aware of his greatness as Webb considered he should have been.   Elsewhere Webb says he had resided many years in Italy, especially at Venice, and although known dates rather preclude the idea that he lived there many years at a stretch, yet it is certain that he knew Italy well, that he studied its famous buildings, ancient and modern, with great discrimination and care, and that he became intimately acquainted with all the expedients and niceties of design as practised by Italian masters.   His marginal notes in his copy of *Palladio* show this conclusively.   His sketch-book would at first sight lead one to suppose, on some of its pages, that he ' discovered many antiquities ' in Rome, but as it appears that his notes were largely taken from a guide-book, he figures less as a discoverer than as a diligent student of antiquities.   In another direction his sketch-book is of paramount interest, for it is mainly devoted to sketches of drapery and of the human figure in whole or in part, as though it were in fact the sketch-book of a student of painting and drawing rather than of architecture.   This point will be dealt with more fully at a later stage.   There is no doubt that he made a reputation in Italy, for, fifty years after his death, Vertue advanced the opinion that the Italians confessed him to be ' the most skilful *Transmontani* that ever was ' ;   a phrase that excluded Italian architects from comparison.

The last definite date so far associated with Jones was April 1597, when he proved his father's will.

The next is 1601, inscribed in his *Palladio* possibly, but not certainly, as the date of its purchase.[1] By this time, therefore, he was presumably in Italy, but how he got there or when he went there is unknown. He could have had but little means of his own, and it would be interesting to know whether some wealthy patron bore the expense of his travel and maintenance. The names of the Earl of Pembroke and the Earl of Arundel, who were warm patrons of his in later life, have been mentioned in this connection, but the former did not succeed to his inheritance until early in 1601, and the latter was only a boy of sixteen in that year. Of his means of progression as little is known as of his means of living. The most usual method of travel was on horseback ; nothing was easier than to buy a horse, ride him as far as was convenient and then sell him : when the visit at the place of sale was concluded another horse was bought for the next stage of the journey. A few public vehicles were sometimes available along great highways, and a private vehicle could generally be obtained by those who could afford it. In crossing mountains (and nobody could get to Italy by land without doing so) carrying chairs, or *chaises à porteurs*, were available, and so were mules, and as a last resource there was always the alternative of walking. But this alternative was both too heroic and too eccentric to be adopted for

[1] The book was published in Venice in 1601, and on an early fly-leaf is a note, partly worn away, which, in addition to the date of 1601, appears to give two ducats as the price and either Venice or Vicenza as the place of purchase. But the evidence is hardly conclusive, for the price, ' doi doccate ', is not in Jones's writing.

any great distance. A well-known traveller of that
time, Thomas Coryat, whose acquaintance with Inigo
Jones is an interesting episode to be presently
mentioned, actually did walk from Venice to the
English Channel, a feat held to be unique and one
which he commemorated by hanging the shoes in
which he performed it in the church of his native
village of Odcombe in Somerset. Coryat indicates
the routes of his outward and inward journeys to
Italy, but nothing is known of the direction taken
by Inigo, the only fact that transpires being that on
one occasion he visited the Château de Chambord,
on the Loire, a place far distant from the shortest
way to Italy.

In that country he must have spent many months,
if not the ' many years ' of Webb, and it would be
of the greatest interest to learn how he spent his
time. Webb makes him say in the opening lines of
*Stone-Heng Restored*—' Being naturally inclined in
my younger years to study the Arts of Design, I
passed into foreign parts to converse with the great
masters thereof in Italy,' but he gives no names of
those whom he sought out. Judging by Coryat's
interviews with celebrated scholars as he tramped
across Europe, there was no great difficulty for a
stranger to gain access to them, and doubtless the
masters of design were no less courteous to young
inquirers than the men of learning. But how did
he pass his evenings, when it became difficult to study
the arts of design and in particular his favourite art
of architecture ? Did he go to spectacles, or to such
dramatic shows as there were, and pick up practical
knowledge of how the scenic effects were contrived ?

ABIGAIL E. WEEKS MEMORIAL LIBRARY
UNION COLLEGE
BARBOURVILLE, KENTUCKY

It seems clear that in some manner he acquired this knowledge which formed the basis of his own later achievements in the masques. Did he pass his time in improving his painting and drawing in some great man's studio ? Did he sometimes drop into an *albergo* and play dominoes ? or gain admittance into some *coterie* of eager young men who had been drawn to Italy on errands similar to his own ? The impression one vaguely gains is that he made friends there of earnest and accomplished men, and that he gained the reputation of a brilliant and eager student.

Reputation he must have gained, for, through some unknown channel, it came to the ears of Christianus IV, King of Denmark, who, according to Webb, sent for him out of Italy and engrossed him to himself. Webb further says that Jones attended the King on his first coming to England, but in this he was mistaken, for Christianus did not come until July 1606, and Jones had already been engaged on two masques in 1605. In connection with the visit to Denmark, it is worthy of note that it was just when the Earl of Rutland, himself a traveller, was about to proceed in 1603 to Denmark as ambassador and bearer of the Order of the Garter to Christianus on the occasion of the christening of his first son, that in the Earl's household accounts appears the entry already referred to. Among the rewards, gifts, New Year's gifts and annuities is included, ' Item, 28 Junii, to Henygo Jones, a picture maker, x li.' Possibly this gift may have had some connection with Jones's stay in Denmark—a return for some service rendered or information imparted : it is perhaps idle to conjecture. But the gift seems to point to Jones being in England to receive it in June 1603. His stay in Denmark, according to Webb, was lengthy, but nothing is said as to the nature of the services required by the King, although the inference is that they were connected with architecture. The only comment that has come down to us is that of a Danish gentleman, ' Your great architect left nothing to my country, but the fame of his presence.'

The visit to Denmark may not unreasonably be regarded as a turning-point in Jones's career, for our King James had married the sister of Christianus and to this source may perhaps be traced the Queen's patronage of Inigo and his long connection with the English Court.

On Twelfth Night 1605 was produced the first of that long series of masques for which the courts of Queen Anne and Queen Henrietta Maria were famous. Some of the most celebrated poets of the time devised them and provided the words, while to Inigo Jones was entrusted in almost every case the contrivance of the scenery, the stage effects and the costumes. The masques were a production peculiar to the age. They were an elaboration of a kind of entertainment much in vogue during the time of Elizabeth, when the guests at some great hospitable function would appear in the guise of shepherds, or Russians or other ' outlandish ' characters, would make presents to the host, go through a dance and finally dance themselves away. There was no strict co-ordination of their efforts ; the effects, such as they were, must have been largely impromptu ; what coherence there may have been was imparted by the master of the revels. The outcome resembled rather a quickly

devised charade than a carefully rehearsed come-
dietta.   But the later masques were a more serious
undertaking.   It was Ben Jonson who infused them
with a spirit of poetry, who gave them a definite aim
and well-ordered means for its achievement.   They
were necessarily slight in their nature ; they unfolded
no thrilling drama, they stirred no deep emotions
either of sorrow or mirth.   The characters were taken
by amateurs who had received no training in one of
the most difficult of accomplishments—that of the
finished actor.   The handsome gallants and beautiful
women of the Court filled the cast : but who selected
the players, who stage-managed the affair and
soothed the ruffled feelings roused by every amateur
performance is unrecorded.   It is obvious that little
plays so slight in their plot, so devoid of dramatic
situations, and so academic in their flavour as that
imparted by the learned Ben Jonson, pleasantly
though his lines read, would be greatly helped by
ingenious stage effects, and these were the very
notable contribution of Inigo Jones.   Notable they
necessarily were, for the Elizabethan stage had but
a modicum of scenery, and Jones's contrivances had
all the attraction of novelty.   ' What of his masques,'
says Webb, in a passage summing up his master's
achievements, ' what of his masques, for the delight
and pleasure of all those several great princes ; since
that for variety of scenes, machines, habits, and well
ordering of them, in the judgment of all foreign
embassadors and strangers, they exceeded whatever
of that kind were presented in any other court of
Christendom besides ? '

The masque of Twelfth Night 1605 was *The*

*Queenes Masque of Blacknesse,* inspired by Queen Anne, and her first entertainment of the kind : it was her will, says Jonson, to have them Blackmoors (Plate 1). As Jonson himself gives a long description of the stage effects, which may serve as an indication of Jones's share in this and subsequent ventures, it is worth while to quote something of what he says :

First for the scene was drawn a landtschap consisting of small woods, and here and there a void place filled with huntings ; which falling, an artificial sea was seen to shoot forth, as if it flowed to the land, raised with waves which seemed to move, and in some places the billows to break, as imitating that orderly disorder which is common in nature. In front of this sea were placed six tritons, in moving and sprightly actions, their upper parts human, save that their hairs were blue, as partaking of the sea-colour : their desinent parts fish, mounted above their heads, and all varied in disposition. . . . Behind these, a pair of sea-maids, for song, were as conspicuously seated ; between which, two great sea-horses, as big as the life, put forth themselves ; . . . The Masquers were placed in a great concave shell, like mother of pearl, curiously made to move on those waters and rise with the billow ; the top thereof was stuck with a cheveron of lights, which, indented to the proportion of the shell, struck a glorious beam upon them, as they were seated one above another. . . . On sides of the shell did swim six huge sea monsters, varied in their shapes and dis-positions, bearing on their backs the twelve torchbearers. . . . These thus presented, the scene behind seemed a vast sea, and united with this that flowed forth, from the termina-tion or horizon of which (being the level of the stage which was placed in the upper part of the Hall) was drawn by the lines of prospective, the whole work shooting downwards from the eye ; which decorum made it more conspicuous, and caught the eye afar off with a wandering beauty ; to which was added an obscure and cloudy night piece, that made the whole set off. So much for the bodily part, which was of Master Inigo Jones's design and act.

This description, whether fully illuminating or not, makes it quite apparent that here was a wonderful change from the rudimentary and stationary furnishing of the contemporary stage. There were colour, poetry and movement in the setting of the piece such as had never been seen before in England. It is equally clear that these novelties were the outcome of great ingenuity of invention and of long preparation, extending in all probability over many months. No doubt, as the years went by and continual experience was gained, the period of preparation grew less, but each new masque entailed fresh invention on the mechanical side, and in addition there were the costumes to be devised and drawn and to be submitted for the approval of the wearers. It is manifest, therefore, that these entertainments, for which Jones's services were required almost every year down to 1640, must have claimed a large proportion of his time.

It is quite certain that they completely absorbed the spare time of the performers while they were under rehearsal, for in regard to two of them the Earl of Arundel wrote to his father-in-law, the Earl of Shrewsbury, in 1608:

My wife would fayne have written, but that her practisinge of the masque, which is now deferred until Sonday nexte, will not give her leave.

This was written on the 8th January, and refers to the *Masque of Beauty*, presented at Court on the Sunday after Twelfth Night. Again on the 1st February he says :

My wife defers her writinge till she may send yo<sup>r</sup> Lo<sup>p</sup>: the booke of the Queene's masque, w<sup>ch</sup> will be shortly : and I am so troubled with another masque, as I want leisure to write any more to y<sup>r</sup> Lo<sup>p</sup>: at this time.

The other masque was *The Hue and Cry after Cupid*, presented on Shrove Tuesday on the occasion of the marriage of Viscount Haddington.  Both masques will be further mentioned when the story reaches the time of their performance.

But no doubt, in spite of the time and trouble required by the 'practisinge', these rehearsals, as in the case of amateur theatricals in the present day, provided as much amusement to the actors as the performances themselves.

Of the many drawings by Jones's own hand that have been preserved, by far the greatest number are devoted to the costumes for the masques.  These are preserved at Chatsworth and they have been catalogued, described, and in many cases illustrated, in a book published by the Walpole Society.[1]  The whole series has been critically examined and its component drawings have either been assigned to the various masques, accounted for in other ways or (in a few instances) acknowledged as unidentifiable : four of them are of costumes for the *Masque of Blackness.*  The whole subject is too wide and its details too complicated to be discussed fully in a general survey of Jones's activities, but the outstanding facts are that the collection comprises some 450 or more drawings for costumes and scenery, all from

[1] *Designs by Inigo Jones for Masques and Plays at Court,* a Descriptive Catalogue . . . with Introduction and Notes by Percy Simpson and C. F. Bell.  Oxford, 1924.

the hand of Jones, and that the work must have taken much of his time and have been as noteworthy in its way as anything he did in architecture. His architectural drawings do not exceed seventy or eighty in number, and appear to have been treasured by Webb with as much solicitude as those for the masques.

It would appear that, in all probability, during the spring of 1605 Jones, was again in Italy. The evidence is afforded by a note he made on a view of the Castle of Sant Angelo in Rome during his tour in the year 1614, to the effect that on the night of the 29th May 1614 he again saw the fireworks and procession in honour of the coronation of Pope Pius V.[1] The assumption is that he was present on the actual occasion of the Pope's enthronement, which took place on 29th May 1605 ; but although the wording leaves no doubt that he had seen this annual procession before, it is not quite conclusive that he had seen it in 1605. There would, however, have been time for his visit between the *Masque of Blackness* and his next recorded employment in England. There is nothing to indicate when he went or how long he stayed, but in any case he had returned by August, for at that time he was called to Oxford, there to help in the production of some entertainments on the occasion of a visit by the King and his Court. The results, however, were not quite so satisfactory as in the case of the *Masque of Blackness* ;

---

[1] The wording of the note is, ' Roma 29 magio 1614 this night I saw againe ye Girandolo and focci articcale, The Procession Corpus domine at Coronation di P Paulo V.' Walpole Society's *Masques*, p. 25.

the intimate atmosphere of Whitehall was lacking, the performers were all strangers, and sympathy was not extended to them in the degree it might have been to friends and acquaintances. The tale shall be told from an account of the proceedings written by an unknown eye-witness, evidently a Cambridge man, and published in pamphlet form.

In July and August of 1605 the King, accompanied by the Queen and Prince Henry, went on one of his progresses, of which the ultimate destination was to be Oxford. He made a considerable circuit on his way thither ; the itinerary, or ' Gests of his majesty's Progress ', started on 13th July with his own house at Havering in Essex, and proceeded by way of Laughton, Theobalds and Hatfield, which was then the King's house, not having yet been exchanged with Lord Salisbury for Theobalds, to Luton and Ampthill in Bedfordshire, where was another house of His Majesty's. Thence he went into Northamptonshire, where he stayed at six of the large houses, Drayton, Apethorpe, Rockingham Castle, Harroden, Castle Ashby and Grafton Regis. This brought him by way of Hanwell to his house at Woodstock, close to Oxford.

The longest day's journey was some seventeen miles, the average being about twelve, and the usual duration of his visits was three days with each host. More than half the houses at which he stayed have disappeared. His own house at Hatfield, or such part as remains, was converted into stables when the Earl of Salisbury built his fine new mansion after the exchange. But most of the Northamptonshire

houses still remain—Drayton, Apethorpe, Rockingham and Castle Ashby—and they retain enough of
their ancient work to render recognition possible,
were King James able to revisit them.

The Royal party stayed six days at Woodstock
and Langley and then made their formal entry into
Oxford on Tuesday, the 27th August : they were
lodged in some of the colleges.  Strict injunctions
were issued by the University that academic costume
was to be worn during the King's visit and that all
those concerned were to stand in order appointed
while His Majesty was passing into Christ Church.
The town was to be put in gala array ; all woodwork
such as rails, posts, windows and pumps, was to be
newly painted both in the University and the town ;
the same pains were to be bestowed on the clocks of
the town gates and on all coats-of-arms, which, in
heraldic language, were to be ' newly tricked '.  The
streets were to be finely paved and swept clean ; in
short, the ancient town was to look as new and clean
as possible.  The entertainments provided appealed
to tastes that have been greatly modified since those
times.  There was to be a Latin sermon three-
quarters of an hour long ; the days were to be given
up to public disputations conducted in the Latin
tongue, the evenings to witnessing the performance
of masques in the great hall of Christ Church.
Learned addresses were to be delivered from various
points of vantage as the royal procession wound its
way along the streets ; colleges in a prominent position were to have verses hung on their walls, as
Orlando's in praise of Rosalind were hung on the
forest trees of Arden.  This intellectual refreshment

was to be supplemented by bodily refreshment in the halls of the principal colleges.

The gentleman who recorded the proceedings says that he reached Oxford at six o'clock in the afternoon of the Thursday before the King's entry, and found certain high personages in a great state of mind about the arrangements at Christ Church. They ' utterly disliked ' the stage, and, above all, the position of the Chair of Estate ; it was too low and the audience would only be able to see the King's cheek. The Vice-Chancellor and his workmen were much troubled at these strictures, but ' stood in defence of the thing done, and maintained that by the art perspective the King should behold all better than if he sat higher '. The Chancellor himself intervened in support of the University, but after debating the matter on the following Sunday, the University gave way and the King's chair was removed to a distance of eight-and-twenty feet, with the result that many long speeches were delivered that neither the King nor anyone near him could hear. It must have been an odd form of enjoyment to listen to long speeches in a dead language at such a distance that no one could grasp their meaning.

The stage, so ' utterly disliked ', was considered well worthy of description owing to its novelty—no doubt suggested by Inigo Jones. ' The stage was built close to the upper end of the hall, as it seemed at first sight ; but indeed it was but a false wall, faire painted, and adorned with stately pillars, which pillars would turn about ; by reason whereof, with the help of other painted cloths, the stage did vary three times in the acting of one tragedy '—which

must have been a very notable innovation. The
false wall was in fact five or six paces from the end
of the Hall, thus providing a place for the assembling
of the actors.

On Tuesday, 27th August, then, the King made his
entry into the newly-painted city amid a sea of
academical costumes, and he quickly had a taste of
the entertainments provided for him. For at Carfax
the Greek Reader delivered an oration in good
familiar Greek with good action and elocution, which
the King heard with pleasure and the Queen with
delight, because, she declared, never before had she
heard Greek. But she seems to have been temperate
in her desire to listen to learned discourses, and left
that recreation to the King, who entered with zest
into the disputations which, held in St. Mary's
Church, occupied the daytime of his stay. He
followed the arguments with close attention, sometimes bringing an orator up sharp, sometimes urging
him to continue when stopped by the president ; and
on occasion he would himself settle the dispute once
for all in a Latin speech of considerable length.
When the question of tobacco came to be argued, one
disputant advanced the opinion that tobacco must
needs be good because the great ones of all nations
and countries, including kings, loved it ; whereupon
James broke in with the observation that there was
one King (himself, of course) that neither liked it nor
loved it, ' which moved great delight '.

So eager was he in following these disputations and
putting every one right, that he had no spirit left for
the masques in the evening. Here he had to be a
listener only, and that, moreover, for some four hours

on end, from nine o'clock till one in the morning.
On the first night the title of the masque was—' Alba,
whereof I never saw the reason,' says our reporter.
The rustical songs and dances made it very tedious,
and an incident that might have relieved the tedium
—the bringing of five or six men on to the stage
' almost naked '—only served to shock the Queen
and her ladies.   So dull was the performance that if
the distinguished Chancellors of both the Universities had not earnestly entreated His Majesty, he
would have left before half the comedy had been
played.

The play on the next night fared no better ; it was
the tragedy of *Ajax Flagellifer*, and here it was that
the stage was varied three times.   But in spite of the
goodly antique apparel of the actors, their performance was so bad that the weary monarch grew out of
all patience and roundly expressed his dislike.   The
third night was equally unfortunate, for although
the comedy *Vertumnus*, a learned production of Dr.
Gwynn, was much better acted, chiefly by men of St.
John's, the weary King actually fell asleep, and when
he awoke was anxious to be gone, saying, among
other hard things, he wondered what they took him
to be.   With much difficulty he was persuaded to
stay and was eventually released at one o'clock in the
morning.

It had been intended to repeat the plays after the
King's departure for the benefit of the many members
of the University who had been unable to gain
admission, but probably in view of their irritating
effect the idea fell through.   One gleam appears to
have penetrated the gloom, for an English play by Mr.

Daniel, acted on the morning of the last day before
the Queen and Prince, was well acted and greatly
applauded.   Its success may have been partly due to
its having taken place when the audience was fairly
wide awake.

On the fourth day of these diverting pastimes, after
the King had dined, there was great posting to horse
and he took his departure.   Both he and his retinue
had clearly had their fill of learned amusements, for
as they left the University no one troubled to look at
the verses hung on college walls, and those effusions
were torn down by the boys and scattered to the
winds.

Such is the story of the King's visit to Oxford, its
moral lies in a later paragraph of the report :

For the better contriving and finishing of the stages, seates
and scaffolds in St. Marie's and Christ Church, they entertained two of his Majesty's Master Carpenters, and they had
the advice of the Comptroller of his works.   They also hired
one Mr. Jones, a great traveller, who undertooke to further
them much, and furnish them with rare Devices, but performed very little to that which was expected.   He had for
his Pains, as I heard constantly reported, 50 [lib].

The failure of Inigo to fulfil expectations may perhaps be accounted for by his having found the actors
incompetent and the managers intractable : it is only
their side of the question that has been recorded ;
what Jones's views may have been has not transpired.
The writer of the account who, from the fact that he
went down to Oxford on purpose to describe the
event, may be supposed to have been familiar with
matters of public importance, evidently did not know
him.   He was merely ⋖ one Mr. Jones, a great

traveller ' and was mentioned after the King's carpenters and controller of the works. Whatever fame
he may have acquired in remote parts, Jones was,
in the year 1605, but little known in England.

# CHAPTER IV

THE next event in which Jones had a part was another masque, presented some five months later, in January 1606. It was 'Hymenaei, or the Solemnities of Masque and Barriers, magnificently performed on the eleventh and twelfth Nights, from Christmas, at Court ; To the auspicious celebrating of the Marriage-union between Robert Earle of Essex, and the Lady Frances, second daughter of the most noble Earle of Suffolke.' Ben Jonson was the poet, and Jones the deviser of the scenery and costumes, his failure to satisfy the Oxford people not having affected his prospects at the Court. Of his share in the production Jonson says, ' the design and art together with the devices and their habits, belong properly to the merit and reputation of Master Inigo Jones, whom I take modest occasion, in this fit place, to remember, lest his own worth might accuse me of an ignorant neglect, from my silence '. In later years a quarrel sprang up between the poet and the artist, arising, it is said, from the poet paying insufficient homage to the artist on a similar occasion ; but so far Jonson's tributes were adequate, albeit not so exuberant as those paid by other writers in connection with other

40

masques. The *Masque of Hymen* produced further ingenious devices for scenery, notably a globe in which the masquers sat, which appeared to hang without support in mid-air, and in the turning of which the poet himself took a hand.

The performance gave general satisfaction, according to the testimony of one of the news-writers of the day, a Mr. John Pory, who told Sir Robert Cotton :

> I have seen both the maske on Sunday and the Barriers on Munday night. The bridegroom carried himself as gravely and gracefully as if he were of his father's age. . . . Both Inigo, Ben and the actors, men and women, did their parts with great commendation . . . eight men-maskers together with Reason their moderatresse . . . sate somewhat like the Ladies in the scallop shell last year.

The letter is undated, but the scallop shell of last year was no doubt the ' great concave shell ' of the *Masque of Blackness,* and it is the fact that the eleventh and twelfth nights after Christmas fell on Sunday and Monday, the 5th and 6th January 1606.

The masquers had been trained as to dancing by Master Thomas Giles, and the music was composed by Master Alphonso Ferrabosco. The familiar way in which Mr. Pory mentions the artist and the poet argues no great awe or even deference, and doubtless Inigo Jones's claim to distinction rested, outside his skill in masques, on his being ' a great traveller '.

The comment on the serious carriage of the bridegroom was provoked by his extreme youth, for he had not yet turned fifteen. His father, the Earl of Essex, whose rebellion had ended in his death on the scaffold five years previously, would by now have been forty years of age. The bride was a year

younger than her husband ; they were little more
than children, but such early marriages were customary at the time. The auspicious celebration of the
marriage was not followed by a happy union ; a
few years of unsatisfactory wedlock were ended in
October 1613, on equally unsatisfactory grounds by
a divorce, the shameless result being achieved entirely
through the influence of the Court and determined
by a narrow majority of the commissioners appointed
to inquire. Lady Essex, in whose favour the divorce
was obtained, had, in the unwholesome atmosphere
of the Court, carried on intrigues with Robert Kerr,
or Carr, Earl of Somerset, the chief favourite of the
King, and two months after the divorce was married
to him. Thereafter ensued the Overbury tragedy,
one of the minor scandals of history. The Countess
was incensed against Sir Thomas Overbury for
endeavouring to prevent the marriage which, in
common with other respectable people, he regarded
with much disfavour. Influenced by her the Earl
procured the imprisonment of Sir Thomas in the
Tower, where he was poisoned. Two years passed
before the affair made a stir ; the governor of the
Tower and four others were then tried and executed.
The Earl and Countess were arraigned but escaped
with their lives, they were only banished from the
Court and condemned never to see the King's face
again. This was in 1616. In April of that year
another news-writer tells his correspondent that the
arraignments of Lord and Lady Somerset were
deferred, and that since the commitment of Lady
Somerset to the Tower attempts had been made to
corrupt and bribe the keeper appointed to attend

her, and to that end an anonymous letter had been sent entreating ' his furtherance to help out '. The whole incident had some effect upon the fortunes of Inigo Jones, for the disgrace of Somerset led to the advancement of George Villiers, afterwards Duke of Buckingham, who became his very good friend and patron. The power of the new favourite is mentioned in this same letter of April 1616—

S<sup>r</sup> Oliver St. John is nominated by his Ma<sup>tie</sup> to be L. Deputie for Ireland by S<sup>r</sup> Geo: Villers influence. It is somewhat opposed by some of y<sup>e</sup> Councell but all to little purpose for so great is the power of the favorite, as what he will, shalbe.

But this is anticipating the story by some ten years.

Nothing is recorded of Jones during 1606, nor was either he or Ben Jonson employed on the masque of January 1607. This was the work of Thomas Campion, who failed to reach the level of Jonson. The absence of Jones may conceivably be accounted for by his being once more in Italy. This, however, is merely a conjecture founded on an inscription in a book, preserved at Worcester College, Oxford, given to him at the New Year of 1607 by Edmund Bolton, who was then in Italy. Bolton was a year or two younger than Jones and, like him, was a Roman Catholic. He was distinguished as a profound scholar, and an indefatigable student of historical and antiquarian learning. For many years he had lived at his own charges a free commoner of Trinity Hall, Cambridge, whence he moved to the Inner Temple and ' lived in the best and choicest company of gentlemen '. To gain the close friendship of such a man shows that Jones must have been a person of considerable attainments and ambitions. What his aims were can be gathered from the inscription, of which the following is a translation from the original Latin :

30 December 1606. As an earnest and a token of a friendship which is to endure for ever with Inigo Jones, I, Edmund Bolton give this book. Mercury son of Jove to his own Inigo Jones through whom there is hope that sculpture, modelling, architecture, painting, acting and all that is praise worthy in the elegant arts of the ancients, may one day find their way across the Alps into our England.

The wording is consistent with the idea of a friendship recently formed beyond the Alps, and the idea receives some support from the fact that Jones was not employed on a masque at home at the time. But the evidence is not conclusive. In another direction the inscription is open to two constructions. It may have been quite genuine and serious and a high testimonial to Jones as a student of the arts of design. On the other hand, there is a vein of pleasantry about it, as when Bolton alludes to himself as ' Mercury the son of Jove ' and latinizes his friend's name into ' Ignatio Jonesio ', not to mention the rather large assumption that England was devoid of all the elegant arts enumerated. But in either case, whether the inscription was serious or tinged with a spirit of humour, it is evident that Jones's own idea of his mission was pretty much what Bolton indicated.

Bolton undoubtedly had a high opinion of Jones, for when, in 1617, he suggested to the King a scheme for establishing a royal academy or college, Jones was to have been one of the members, who were to be 'persons called from out of the most able and most famous lay gentlemen of England'. The idea was seriously considered. Buckingham, who interested himself in Bolton's fortunes, spoke favourably of the scheme in the House of Lords. The details were actually settled in the year 1624, but the death of James in the following year brought the conception to naught. Among the eighty-four original members selected by Bolton there were, in addition to Inigo Jones, George Chapman, Lionel Cranfield, Earl of Middlesex, Sir Kenelm Digby, Michael Drayton, Ben Jonson, Sir Thomas Lake, John Seldon, Sir Henry Spelman and Sir Henry Wotton. No one need ask for a higher testimonial to distinguished ability than to be included in such a list.

Nothing is heard of Inigo during the year 1607, and he took no part in the *Masque of Beauty* which was performed before the Court at Whitehall early in January 1608. The order of the scene, says Jonson, was skilfully contrived by the King's master carpenter, William Portington, but the scenery did no credit to the painters. The master-hand was lacking, and this probably because Jones was busy with a still more important entertainment to be given a few weeks later on Shrove Tuesday. This was a masque by Ben Jonson called *The Hue and Cry after Cupid*, in celebration of the marriage of Viscount Haddington with Elizabeth, the daughter of the Earl of Sussex. 'The great Maske intended for my L. Haddington's marriage is now the only thing thought upon at Court,' says a news-writer, Rowland White,

to Lord Shrewsbury.   There were to be five English
and seven Scottish gentlemen engaged and their
participation was expected to cost them £300 a man.
Among them were Lord Arundel and Lord Pembroke,
who both became friends and patrons of Jones.   The
Viscount himself was a Scot, a great favourite of the
King, and he had enjoyed his title now for some
eighteen months.   The royal generosity was shown
in an unusual but gratifying way at the marriage
feast.   The King pledged the health of the bride and
bridegroom in a cup of gold which he then sent to
them, and in it was the grant of a pension of £600
a year to him and to her and the longer liver of them.
He survived her and married again : she died ten
years after her marriage of smallpox, then a prevalent and devastating disease.   There were two
children, both boys, who died as infants.   The
younger had for one of his sponsors the Prince of
Wales, afterwards Charles I.   The mother, it is
pleasing to know, ' died wonderful religious, and most
well-prepared for heaven '.

There are no drawings of this masque in the Chatsworth collection, nor is there any record of how
Jones employed himself during the year 1608, but
undoubtedly much of his time must have been
occupied in preparing for his next great effort, *The
Masque of Queenes celebrated from the House of Fame*,
which was written by Ben Jonson and performed on
2nd February 1609.   There are no less than twenty-
one drawings connected with this masque, including
a rough sketch of the House of Fame (Plate II), which
must be a preliminary study, as it does not agree with
Jonson's description of the actual edifice.   The

scenic effects must have been the most remarkable
that Jones had hitherto designed, and the allegorical
figures he introduced, unless they were suggested by
Jonson himself, indicate that Jones had an acquaintance with the Latin poets and their themes. That
this was in fact the case is suggested by the observation of Jonson that the House of Fame was entirely
of Jones's invention and design. On the other hand,
among the ancient queens who figured in the masque
Jones is not always certain of the peoples who owed
them allegiance, nor of the special attributes which
mythology had assigned to them.

Jonson chose his theme on the suggestion of the
Queen, but was probably not loath to take advantage
of the galaxy of beauty that adorned the Court.
The queens were twelve in number, personages who,
even in those days when many ladies had more than
a tincture of classical learning, must have taxed the
knowledge and ingenuity of the fair players in their
endeavour to give a suitable character to the parts
they sustained, but whose names in the present day
would hardly stir a responsive chord of recollection
or interest.

The costumes of seven out of the twelve are
definitely named by Jones on his designs. They
are Penthesilea, Queen of the Amazons, Camilla of
the Volscians, Thomyris of the Scythians, Artemisia
of Caria, Berenice of the Egyptians, Candace of the
Ethiopians, and Zenobia of Palmyra. There is an
eighth, Atalanta of the Ætolians, but this part,
which was to have been played by the Countess of
Arundel, was changed for another. It would give
even Macaulay's schoolboy pause, if he were sud-

denly asked for biographical details of some of these queens. He might be excused for not recognizing the last of the twelve, Bel-anna, Queen of the Ocean, for this was an invention of Jonson's own to signify Queen Anne herself. The several parts here enumerated were taken by the Countess of Bedford, the Lady Catherine Windsor, the Countess of Montgomery, the Lady El. Guilford, the Lady Anne Clifford, Lady Wynter, a younger sister of Lady Guilford, the Countess of Derby and the Countess of Arundel. Most of these ladies were young married people. The Countess of Bedford and she of Derby had been matrons longer than the rest, having been married some fifteen years ; but the Countess of Montgomery had been married about four years, and the Countess of Arundel three ; they were both quite young, not much more than twenty, while the Lady Anne Clifford was but nineteen and still unmarried. However, a few weeks later she became the Countess of Dorset, and after the Earl died in 1624, she married in 1630 Philip, Earl of Pembroke, as his second wife. She was a bright creature and had a lively pen, with which she touched off, as quite a young girl, some of the innumerable lords and ladies who were her relatives or friends. She long outlived her second husband, and when she died at the age of eighty-seven she left a notable gap in the English aristocracy. Earl Philip was a younger brother, and at the time of the masque was the Earl of Montgomery, so both his wives took a part in it.

The intermarriages of great families of that time were numerous and far-reaching, and the Court became very largely a congregation of cousins of close

or distant degree.   It is no matter of surprise, therefore, that newly-made Peers did not always receive
a warm welcome in Court circles.   Nor need we
wonder that when any of these distinguished persons
wanted help in matters of art they should seek the
advice of the ingenious Mr. Inigo Jones, who devised
the masques and doubtless flitted about among the
masquers, advising, directing, and perhaps humour-
ing the foibles of such ladies as had any.

These performances must have been the most
splendid imaginable.   The poetic fancy of Ben Jonson was devoted to their service, his learning and his
skill in drama.   All the ingenuity, refined taste and
instinct for colour that distinguished Inigo Jones,
tempered by the sound judgment that his study of
architecture had given him, were lavished upon them.
All the youth, beauty and gallantry of the Court were
engaged in their behalf.   No expense was spared in
presenting them ;   indeed thousands and thousands
of pounds were devoted to their display, and it is not
difficult to imagine that the staid and earnest country
squire, of serious leanings, may have turned un-
sympathetic eyes upon their extravagance.

Jones seems by this time to have become well
established in the good graces of the Court, a very
fortunate circumstance for a man of thirty-six who
pursued no regular calling, and whose uncommon
gifts were of a kind that required a patron for their
due exercise.   There is no evidence that he had done
any architectural work up to this time, or that he
was trying to pursue the calling of an architect.   He
was in much the same case as most of the poets and

literary aspirants of the time, who found no sufficient market for their wares among the general public, and so looked to the influence of wealthy and powerful personages to obtain for them some kind of post that carried a regular, if not a generous, salary.

The experiences of John Donne, afterwards the well-known Dean of St. Paul's, are a case in point. He was born in the same year as Jones, and his father, too, was a merchant. His education was more extensive, and he had friends of good position. He, too, became a great traveller and spent a year or two in Italy and Spain when he was about five-and-twenty years old. On his return to England he became Secretary to Lord Chancellor Ellesmere, but eventually lost that post through a secret marriage with a niece of his employer, a daughter of Sir George More of Loseley, who was furious on hearing of the union. Thereafter for a considerable period, with a young, gently nurtured wife and a growing family to maintain, he sought employment in vain. Fortunately he had good friends, and with two of them, Sir Francis Wolly of Pirford and Sir Robert Drewry, he and his family resided for some years. In the meantime other friends lent their interest at Court towards his advancement, but without effect. The Bishop of Durham offered him a benefice if he would take orders. He knew, he told him, of Mr. Donne's expectation of State-employment and of his fitness for it, but he also knew of the many delays and contingencies that attend Court-promises, and he urged him to take his advice. But Donne did not yet feel a call to enter the Church, and so he continued to pursue his precarious life. At last came a definite and hopeful expectation in circumstances that throw a strong light on the personal power of the King and the uncertainty of hopes founded on his goodwill. The Earl of Somerset, then at the height of his power, sent for Mr. Donne to Theobalds, where the King then was. After compliments the Earl said, ' Stay in this garden till I go up to the King and bring you word that you are Clerk to the Council ; doubt not my doing this, for I know the King loves you, and know the King will not deny me.' But unfortunately the King did deny him most positively, on the ground that Mr. Donne was a learned man with all the abilities of a learned divine, and if he were qualified that way there was nothing he would deny him. It is unnecessary to follow the fortunes of Mr. Donne further than to say that in course of time he sincerely saw his way to taking orders, and the King appointed him with much cordiality to the Deanery of St. Paul's. His experiences are typical of those attending the pursuit of Court favour. He was better educated and better connected than Inigo Jones, and his abilities were of the first order, and yet so long was his success delayed that Jones must have felt himself lucky in having at the age of thirty-six a definite footing among the influential persons who formed the Court.

That he had such a footing is confirmed, if confirmation were needed, by the fact that shortly after the production of the *Masque of Queens* he was sent to carry ' letters for His Majesty's service into France ', a service of responsibility only entrusted to persons of some standing at Court. The warrant for the payment of his expenses upon his return, amounting to £13 6s. 8d., is dated the 16th June 1609, and in a copy of *Vitruvius*, wherein he wrote marginal notes after the style of those in his *Palladio*, is one mentioning the fact of his being in Paris in 1609.[1] It is of some interest to learn that forty years earlier, in October 1569, a sum of £6 13s. 8d. had been granted to Edmund Spenser, the poet, for conveying letters from the ambassador, Sir Henry Norris, who was then at Tours in France, to Queen Elizabeth.

A whole year now passed during which nothing is recorded of Jones, but he was shortly to take another step in his upward fortunes by being appointed Surveyor to the Prince of Wales. Henry, the eldest son of King James, when he was seventeen years old, was on the 30th May 1610 created Prince of Wales with much solemnity. Garter King of Arms bore the letters patent, eight great nobles bore the insignia, the Prince in his surcoat only and bareheaded was attended by twenty Knights of the Bath. He knelt before the King while the letters patent were read, and then the King, after investing him with the robes, sword, cap and coronet, the rod and the ring, kissed him upon the cheek, and the ceremony ended. After his creation he kept his Court apart, with all suitable officers.

A few days later, on 5th June, a masque was performed in honour of the occasion. Ben Jonson had no hand in it ; it was written by Samuel Daniel with the title, *Tethys' Festival or the Queen's Wake* (Plate III), and is noteworthy from the fact that little Prince Charles, then a child of nine, took part in it ; he represented Zephirus, and a drawing of his

[1] See Appendix A.

costume is preserved at Chatsworth. His elder sister,
Princess Elizabeth, made her first appearance on the
stage, as also did the newly-married Viscountess
Haddington, but most of the other ladies (who
enacted nymphs) had already taken part in other
masques. The Queen herself filled the part of
Tethys, the mother of nymphs and rivers. Daniel
gives Jones credit for the success of the performance
and expresses the view, with which this age would
probably agree, that ' in these things wherein the
only life consists in show, the art and invention of
the architect gives the greatest grace, and is of most
importance, ours the least part, and of least note in
the time of the performance thereof '. It can hardly
be gainsaid that the masques were much more notable
as spectacles than as dramatic productions, but this
view did not by any means commend itself to Ben
Jonson. Daniel refers to Jones as ' the architect ',
but he probably meant the architect of the scenery,
which could only have been devised by one who had
a competent knowledge of the art : it would be rash
to infer that he looked upon Jones as a practising
architect. Nevertheless, Inigo had qualified himself
for the post of Surveyor to the Prince, as will be
presently seen.

Prince Henry appears to have been a cheerful
youth of free and generous disposition, and even
when the courtly historian's dictum that he was
' infinitely beloved of the people ' has been dis-
counted, there can be no doubt that he was a great
favourite, and that the quenching of his early
promise by death was a severe loss to the Kingdom.
Had he lived, the history of English liberties might

have had a far less stern record. He was addicted to sports, and was fond of jewellery, pictures, music and books. The accounts of his expenses during the last two years of his life, when he had a household of his own, afford much curious and interesting information. During that time he lost £2,681 4s. in tennis, dice and cards, the exact amount not being disclosed, it is to be hoped, to his Puritan subjects. He spent £312 13s. on tennis balls ; some thousands on jewellery, and many hundreds on horses, hawks and dogs. His tilting expenses were comparatively light, only £200 or so. For a great organ, viols, lutes and music he gave something over £300 ; for medals and coins, £2,200 ; for books, about £600 ; and for pictures, over £1,200. He was clearly a Prince of cultivated, if expensive, tastes ; it must be remembered that the value of money in those days was four or five times what it is to-day.

There were now two Courts, and at Christmas-time in 1610 Jones was engaged in producing a masque for each, in conjunction with Ben Jonson. That for the Queen was called *Love Freed from Ignorance and Folly*, and, according to the detailed accounts, only cost £719 1s. 3d. The allocation of the money is interesting as indicating the value placed upon the various services rendered ; ' Mr. Benjamin Johnson,' for his invention received £40, a like sum was paid to Mr. Inigo Jones for his paynes and invention. Mr. Confesse for teaching all the dances, obtained more than Jonson or Jones, namely, £50, and a Mr. Bochen had £20 for teaching the ladies the footing of two dances. The musicians had £2 each, and the twelve ' she-fools ' that danced had £1 each.   The Prince's Masque, called *Oberon the Faery Prince*, *A Masque of Prince Henries*, was presented before the King's Majesty on 1st January 1611.   It cost twice as much as the Queen's, namely, £1,412 6s. 10d., of which amount ' Inigoe Jones devyser for the said Maske ' was paid £16 for his trouble.   Prince Henry himself took the part of Oberon, but he had no words assigned to him.   The greater part of the masque was a prelude, permeated with flattery, to his appearance : after his entrance he led the dances, in which no doubt he made a distinguished figure.

It is apparent from these matter-of-fact statements that although Inigo Jones had obtained a firm footing at the Court, both he and Ben Jonson were regarded as being little, if any, more important persons than the King's master carpenter or the teachers of music and dancing.   Their business was to provide, like the rest, entertainment for their royal and noble patrons. As we have already seen, when Jones was unable on one occasion to devise a masque, the work was undertaken, not without credit, by William Portington, the King's master carpenter.   It is only by realizing these facts that a true picture of Inigo Jones can be obtained.   But at any rate his outstanding merit was acknowledged by the Prince, for a few days after the last masque, on the 13th January 1611, he appointed Jones as his Surveyor, an office necessary for his separate establishment.   The salary was three shillings a day including Sundays, or one guinea a week ;  this was supplemented in one year by a gift of £30.   In the same account recording this gift was one to Mr. Coryat, the traveller, of £10, and another to Moun. du Caus of £157. Solomon du Caus was drawing-master to the Prince at a yearly salary of £100. Jones's emoluments amounted, it is true, to no great sum, but at any rate his office brought him in a sure income of a sort, for which he was no doubt duly thankful. It was not to last long, however, for less than two years after his appointment, on the 6th November 1612, between six and seven in the evening, the Prince died, and the surveyorship ended.

It was soon after his appointment as surveyor, in May 1611, that the first official record of his employment was dated, and that employment, although germane to his office, was not intimately connected with architecture. It is ' an Estimate of the Charge of the pyling plancking and Brickworkes for the three Islands at Richmount, xvij° die May 1611 '. It is signed by six persons, of whom three were often associated with Jones on similar occasions. The first signatory is Inigo Jones; the other three are Francis Carter, a clerk of works, Thomas Baldwin, controller of the works, and William Pottinton, who no doubt was William Portington, the King's master carpenter. It was this kind of work that occupied much of Jones's time and attention throughout his life, first as surveyor to the Prince and afterwards to the King.

Although the office of surveyor entailed many duties of this nature, it also brought with it any architectural work contemplated by royalty, and incidentally some of that undertaken by persons high in Court favour. The Prince himself does not appear to have indulged in any building-work, and some years had still to elapse before there is any authentic record of Jones being employed in architecture. But he was now definitely recognized as an architect, and there is no doubt that he had devoted himself to the study of this, his favourite art, so assiduously that when the opportunity came, he was well qualified to avail himself of it.

# CHAPTER V

IN the absence of much reliable information as to
his activities at this time, it is interesting to
learn of an incident which not only shows that
he was recognized as an architect, but throws a little
light on his private life. Thomas Coryat, whose
travels have already been mentioned, was engaged
during the year 1611 in bringing out a book of his
adventures under the title of ' Coryat's Crudities,
Hastily gobled up in five Moneths travells in France,
Savoy, Italy, Rhetia commonly called the Grisons
country, Helvetia, alias Switzerland, some parts of
high Germany and the Netherlands ; Newly digested
in the hungry aire of Odcombe in the County of
Somerset, and now dispersed to the nourishment
of the travelling members of this Kingdome.'
Although his adventures were not startling, they were
related in an easy and interesting way, and brought
before his fellow-countrymen for the first time an
intimate vision of foreign lands and an insight into
the habits of those who lived there. Coryat himself
was essentially a wag with a keen eye to the ludicrous,
and he adorned his title-page with woodcuts illustrat-
ing some of the more comical incidents of his journey.
The first of these shows him paying that tribute to
the sea and its unaccustomed movements which is

still rendered by many who cross the Channel, but as there were no stewards in those days the tribute was paid direct.   The others are conceived in the same vein of broad humour, acceptable enough to his contemporaries but appealing with less force to the public taste of to-day.   This book he commended to his readers, after the fashion of the time, by inducing some six-and-fifty of his acquaintances to contribute ' Panegyricke verses upon the Author and his Booke.' Of this number he invited ten, together with three others, to a philosophical feast on the 2nd September 1611 ; probably after the publication of his book. Included among the guests and the panegyrists was Inigo Jones, his inclusion showing him to have been reckoned among the choice spirits of the age.

The feast was held at the ' Mitre ' in Fleet Street, and Coryat indicates its purpose and touches off his guests in a series of facetious Latin verses which have found their way into the State Papers.   The entertainment was to consist of food and fun, the guests were to cast off gravity and devote themselves to drinking plenteously.   It was the kind of dinner where serious men throw aside their cares and resign themselves to those boyish impulses upon which in daily life they put a severe restraint ; a dinner such as is now held by the Sette of Odd Volumes and other *coteries* of persons having some particular tastes or pursuits in common ; but it was seasoned with deeper potations than are now customary.   The guests were all men of mark, wits, poets, lawyers, scholars or distinguished in business.   They were in the prime of life, in their thirties or forties, and were all of much the same kind of extraction, being mostly

sons of merchants or destined in their youth to
commercial careers.    Not a few of them had received
a University training, and not a few were to rise to
eminence.    There was Christopher Brooke, the poet,
' chamber fellow ' at Lincoln's Inn with another guest,
John Donne, when they were both studying the law.
Donne, as we have seen, became Dean of St. Paul's,
but at this time he had not yet taken orders.    The
punning lines in which these two are introduced by
Coryat are much of a piece with the rest of his verses :

> Veniet sed lento currens
> Christopherus vocatus Torrens
> Et Johannes Factus.

Lionel Cranfield is next on the list ;  he had been
apprenticed to a merchant adventurer of St.
Bartholomew's Lane, and became an adventurer at
home, although not of so pronounced a type as his
friend and fellow-guest, Arthur Ingram, presently to
be mentioned.    At this time he was receiver of
customs for Dorset and Somerset.    His financial
abilities eventually brought him the office of Lord
Treasurer ;  and subsequently a peerage, under the
title of Earl of Middlesex, was conferred upon him
in recognition of his reforms at the Treasury.    Reforms in that department were much needed, judging
by the length of time that Inigo Jones, among others,
had often to wait for his salary.    In later years,
when Coryat's feast was but a memory, Jones helped
his friend Cranfield in some architectural work.
Other guests were Sir Henry Neville, Sir Robert
Phillips, who, like Jones, was a member of the Prince's
household, and Richard Connok, who was his auditor.

Then followed John Hoskins, wit, lawyer and poet,
who polished Ben Jonson's verses and earned from
him the pleasant title of Father Hoskins. The law,
however, was his vocation, and in course of time he
became famous as a Serjeant-at-law. Another of the
company was Richard Martin, lawyer, member of
Parliament and eventually Recorder of London,
celebrated for his wit and ingenuity ; his fitness as a
guest, owing to his appreciation of wine, led in the
end to his undoing, for his death was hastened by
excessive drinking. Sir Henry Goodyeare, John
West and Hugo Holland, designated by Coryat as a
famous traveller and elegant linguist, together with
Arthur Ingram and Inigo Jones, complete the
list.

Ingram was in a category by himself ; he was
neither wit, scholar nor poet, but a keen man of
business who amassed a great fortune. His father
became a successful merchant in Fenchurch Street ;
he was one of the many notable persons of the time
whose nurture had been in the City. He was not
over-scrupulous and already some years before he and
Lionel Cranfield met at Coryat's table, Cranfield had
bargained with him that neither of them was to
advance his estate by the other one's loss, but they
were to join together to raise their fortunes by such
casualties as that stirring age should afford. Ingram
took advantage of all the casualties he could, chiefly
as a speculator in land, and earned the ill will of the
many whom he injured ; at the same time he gained
the good will of the King, at whose disposal he placed
his well-filled purse. He was knighted in 1613 and
two years later was made cofferer to the royal house-

hold, that is, keeper of the privy purse. But the Court, that collection of well-born cousins, would have none of him ; they ' took it to heart that such a scandalous fellow should be put over them as they paint him out to be ', and he only held the office for some two months. This reverse did not check his successful career ; he acquired property in York, near which city his father was born, and he lived in a house charming in itself and surrounded with beautiful gardens. Here he entertained Charles I more than once, the last time being shortly before his own death in 1642, when the relations between the King and parliament had reached the breaking-point. He purchased the neighbouring estate of Temple Newsam, and built the greater part of that fine house. He was not unmindful of his obligations to the poor, for he built a hospital, or almshouse, in York, which on one occasion he showed to a friend with disconcerting results. Asked how he liked it, the friend said it was not large enough. ' How so ? ' said Sir Arthur. ' It is too little to hold those you have undone,' was the reply. Such in brief was the career of Ingram, a typical profiteer, astute in taking advantage of the casualties of that stirring age ; one thing is clear, that whether his final account showed a good or an evil balance, he was at least a man of mark.

The last name on Coryat's list of his guests is that of Inigo Jones, introduced among these men of learning and of letters as

Nec indoctus nec profanus
Ignatius architectus—

' neither unlearned nor uninitiated, Inigo the architect.' This tribute of kind but hardly enthusiastic appreciation is at least a definite recognition of him as an architect ; but as the most liberal lists of buildings attributed to him (some inadvisedly) contain nothing prior to this date, the recognition must have rested on his claims as an accomplished student of architecture and the material fact of his appointment as Surveyor to the Prince.

Coryat affords a glimpse of how his guests arrived, but nothing is said as to how they departed. There is no reason to suppose that in their libations to Bacchus they fell short of the standard indicated in the numerous catches of the period, and it may safely be concluded that towards the close of the evening, in the words of one of these songs, they ' were wondrous merry '.

Coryat's ' Crudities ' have another point of interest in respect of Jones, inasmuch as he contributed to the panegyric verses that introduce Coryat's adventures. His verses are on much the same level as those of other contributors.[1] Although not very polished, they have a touch of rather grim humour, and, as far as they go, afford a glimpse of Jones when he was in a playful mood. So little is known of his private life or of his periods of relaxation that it is pleasant to learn that his eye sometimes twinkled with fun, and that he was not behind his companions in appreciating jokes, even if, after the fashion of the times, they were rather broader than those which pass current in public to-day.

A further glimpse into Jones's private diversions is obtained from letters written by Coryat on his

[1] See Appendix.

later travels, when he was staying at so distant a place as Agra. He sends messages of remembrance to some of the ' Sirenical ' gentlemen who were accustomed to meet every Friday at the ' Mermaid ' in Bread Street. Among the masculine sirens expressly mentioned was Inigo Jones ; others were Donne, Christopher Brooke, and Martin, all of whom were guests at the philosophical feast.

In his dedicatory epistle to Prince Henry, Coryat says that he was persuaded into publication chiefly by his most sincere and entire friend, Lionel Cranfield, and the learned Laurence Whitaker, that elegant linguist and worthy traveller, who must be the same Laurence Whitaker that signed many official reports in company with Inigo Jones. Coryat need not have been so diffident if the panegyric verses are at all sincere in their praises. His sponsors included many whose fame has not survived, but among them, besides the guests at his feast, were men like Michael Drayton, Thomas Campion, Henry Peacham of the *Compleat Gentleman*, Richard Corbet, poet and wit, afterwards Bishop of Oxford and of Norwich, Thomas Bastard, the divine and poet, and Thomas Farnaby, the learned schoolmaster. Ben Jonson wrote an appreciative character of the author and added an acrostic on his name : so his book came before the world with a very respectable flourish of trumpets. There is no need to linger over its diverting contents, but Coryat notes, among other things, that the Italians were very particular to use forks in eating their meals, a novelty to the author and one which, when he put it in practice on his return, exposed him to the raillery of Laurence Whitaker. Another novelty he met with in Italy was the umbrella, an article so unfamiliar to the English that his contemporary, Elias Ashmole, placed one in his museum of curiosities. Coryat is loud in his praise of Venice, and he must indeed have found it enthralling if he was really in earnest when he declared that he would rather have forgone the gift of four of the richest manors in Somerset, had they been offered him, than have forgone the sight of Venice. Indeed the English people shared Coryat's admiration of that romantic and strange city down to our own times ; it was held to be the most famous city of Italy, and the fact that Inigo Jones had resided there was preferred by Webb in testimony of his being a great architect.

It was during this year of 1611 that John Webb was born, an event, as it was to prove, of great importance to Inigo Jones and his reputation ; for it is from Webb that much information concerning him is derived, and it is from the fact that due distinction has not been made between the drawings of Inigo Jones and those of Webb that buildings have been inaccurately assigned to Jones, notably in the case of the great palace of Whitehall, of which the history will presently be set forth.

Wholly unconscious of this event Jones went about his duties as Surveyor to the Prince. There is no record of any other activities, not even of a masque at Christmas-time or the New Year. It was not until the November of 1612 that anything important happened, but early in that month Prince Henry died and Jones's office lapsed. The account of the salary he received is thus worded :

Inigoe Jones, Surveyor of the Workes
for his fee at iij⁸ per diem for one whole
yeare and a halfe and xl^tie days begonne
the 13th January 1610 (–11) and ended
at the feast of S^t Michael the Archaungel    *li.*    *s.*    *d.*
1612 .   .   .   .   .   .   .    lxxxviij ij vj

Inigoe Jones, Surveyo^r of the princes
workes for his fee by lres pattentes at iij⁸
per diem for xxxvij dayes begonne the
firste of October 1612 and ended the vjth.    *li.*    *s.*    *d.*
of November following   .   .   .    cxj

Then follows an item for wages and materials in
connection with work at Richmond, St. James's,
Woodstock and other places, as certified in monthly
books signed by Inigo Jones and Francis Carter,
amounting to £2,828 10s. As the recipients were
officers of the works and 'Moun^sr de Caus', it is
probable that Jones took a share of the payment.
From this entry it is evident that the care of a
considerable number of buildings devolved upon
Jones and occupied much of his time, and further that
Solomon de Caus was a person of particular
importance.

The untimely death of Prince Henry was a blow
to the whole nation, but to Jones it meant the end
of his employment : however, his position in Court
circles was now well assured, and a few months later
he obtained a still greater prize in the reversion
granted to him on 27th April 1613 of the office of
Surveyor of the King's Works, on the death, when it
should occur, of Simon Basil, who then held the office.
His prospects were therefore soon brightened.

In the meantime further masques gave him full
occupation. A marriage had been arranged between

the King's eldest daughter, Elizabeth, and Frederick, Count Palatine of the Rhine, and already, on the 16th October, some week or two before the Prince's death, the Count had arrived in England, and had been conducted in great state to Whitehall. The marriage was not delayed on account of the royal mourning, and it took place on St. Valentine's Day, the 14th February 1613. The ceremony was magnificent. In the words of an historian writing some sixty years later :

the Bride being led to Church by two Bacheolors, her brother Prince *Charles* and the Earl of *Northampton* Lord *Privy Seal*. She was attired all in white, having a rich Crown of Gold upon her Head, her Hair hanging down at length curiously beset with Pearls and Precious Stones, her Train supported by twelve young Ladies in white Garments. The King gave her in Marriage, the Archbishop of *Canterbury* married them, and the Bishop of *Bath* and *Wells* Preached the Bridal Sermon. Which ended, she was led home by two married Men, the Duke of *Lenox* and the Earl of *Nottingham* Lord Admiral. These Nuptials were celebrated with stately Masques. After which the Lord Mayor and Aldermen gave the Bride a Chain of Orient Pearl, valued at Two Thousand Pounds.

The feast was sumptuously maintained at Essex House until the 10th April, when the royal couple made their adieux and took their departure by way of Rochester and Flushing to Heidelberg.

The stately masques on which Jones was engaged were two, one presented in the Banqueting House on the night of the ceremony, the other at Whitehall by the Inns of Court the following evening. The first was *The Lords Maske* by Thomas Campion, the second was by George Chapman. There are four drawings

by Jones for the one and two for the other preserved
at Chatsworth. Chapman's description of his
masque shows that Jones's devices were exceedingly
ingenious. ' It was a showe at all parts so novel,
conceitful, and glorious, as hath not in this land
beene ever before beheld.' His further testimony to
Inigo is noteworthy as indicating that Jones had by
this time a definite reputation as an architect. The
masque was ' invented and fashioned, with the
ground and speciall structure of the whole worke,
by our Kingdome's most Artfull and Ingenious Architect, Innigo Jones. Supplied, aplied, digested, and
written, by Geo : Chapman.'

A letter from John Chamberlain to Alice Carleton,
written on the 18th February, fully bears out Chapman's estimate. The masque, he says, went from
the Rolls (the house of the Master of the Rolls, Sir
Edward Phelips, which had been the headquarters for
rehearsals) along Fleet Street and the Strand and
made such a gallant and glorious show that it was
highly commended, it was generally held for the best
that had been seen for many a day. The King
watched the procession from the gallery of the palace
and made them ride about the Tiltyard ; they then
went to the Hall where their devices made a glittering
show, and their dancing in particular delighted the
spectators. The King himself accompanied them at
the banquet and took care that it should be well
ordered. So great was the throng, adds the writer,
that instructions were given that no gentleman or
lady should be admitted with a farthingale, in order
' to gaine the more roome, and I hope may serve to
make them quite left off in time '. This sumptuary

reform, however, does not seem to have followed as he desired.

Some three years and a half later the learned lawyers did not meet with so much success, for the same correspondent tells Dudley Carleton that ' our Inns of Court gentlemen carried themselves but indifferently at the barriers the night of the Prince's creation '. They made up their deficiencies, however, in another direction, for ' in requital they played the men at the banquet '—therein, it seems, they showed no lack of prowess.

The cost of the masque in 1613 to the Society of Lincoln's Inn, one of the two concerned, the other being the Middle Temple, was £1,086 8s. 11d. The expense of one evening's entertainment, in terms of the present value of money, was therefore prodigious.

It is in connection with this masque that one of Jones's sisters makes her shadowy reappearance : for in the accounts relating to it, preserved at Lincoln's Inn, is a payment in 1612 of £100 to ' Mr. Inigoe Johnes ' towards the work for the Hall and street —presumably at Whitehall, as the masque was presented at Court—and a further payment of £10 to ' Mrs. Johnes for her brother Mr. Inego Johnes '. The honorary title of ' Mistress ' was of course bestowed upon spinsters in those days. It is a matter of speculation as to which of his sisters received the payment, and why it should have been made to her, unless perchance she managed his household and had more leisure than he enjoyed during the busy time of preparing and rehearsing the masque. A receipt for £110 signed by Jones and dated 20th January 1612–13, which was paid to him by Sir Edward

Phelips, is preserved at Montacute House, the home of the Phelipses.

The absence of evidence compels the assumption that Jones was not engaged on general architectural work during such of his time as was not devoted to his official duties and the preparation of masques, and it is not difficult to infer that he was ready to embrace the opportunity offered him later in this year of 1613 to pay another visit to Italy. Especially was this the case in view of his becoming at no distant date Surveyor to His Majesty, in which office a further acquaintance with the arts as practised in Italy would stand him in good stead. But as this journey was one of the most interesting and important events of his life, it deserves a chapter to itself.

# CHAPTER VI

Old and New Styles of the Calendar—His Principal Visit to Italy—
Recipes copied into his *Palladio*—His Sketch-book—Reflections on
Architecture.

IT fell to the lot of the Earl of Arundel and his
Countess to attend the Princess Elizabeth and her
husband on their journey to Heidelberg, a journey
which became a kind of triumphal progress from the
time of their arrival at Flushing on 28th April until
they reached home on 7th June. Here they invited
their escort to stay a few days, and it was not until
the 14th that the Earl and his Countess took their
departure on a tour of pleasure which they had
contemplated from the outset. They went by way
of Strasburg and Basle to Milan, where they arrived
on the 11th July. On the 9th of that month Dudley
Carleton had written to John Chamberlain from
Venice (where he was the English Ambassador) saying that some of Princess Elizabeth's train had been
in that city and had told him ' my Lord of Arundel
and his lady, whom they left with the Duke of
Lennox at Strasburg, will return through France
home, without passing any further. But I rather
believe they were so told to get rid of their companies ; and the more because I heard my lord had
Inigo Jones in his train, who will be of best use to
him, by reason of his language and experience in
these parts.'

71

From this reference it looks as though Inigo Jones had either accompanied the Earl throughout his journey, or at least that he was with him at Strasburg. It is also clear that Jones was already tolerably familiar with Italy and its language, and that his expenses in whole or in part were defrayed by the Earl. Jones nowhere mentions Lord Arundel in the records he has left of his visit, indeed he seems, notwithstanding his duties to his patron, to have had abundance of leisure for the pursuit of his own particular studies. His records are to be found in his sketch-book and in the notes in his *Palladio*. He has fortunately entered a considerable number of dates, and to some of them he has added the day of the week, a matter of much importance, as will presently appear.

There were at this period two styles of dating events in different countries. One, called the Julian, had been in general use until Pope Gregory XIII in the year 1582 reformed the calendar in order to bring it in line with astronomical facts. This reformation, which cut ten days out of the calendar, was largely adopted throughout Europe, but not by England, Russia or Greece ; it was called the New Style, to distinguish it from the old or Julian Style. But although the days of the month differed in the two styles, the days of the week were the same in both, and Sunday was Sunday throughout Europe. Sunday, the 12th June 1614, according to the Old Style, became, owing to the excision of ten days, Sunday the 22nd June in the New Style ; whereas according to the Old Style, Sunday being the 12th, the 22nd would have fallen on a Wednesday. When therefore the day of the week is given as well as the day of the month, it is an easy matter to determine which style is being employed. It becomes apparent on examining the dates recorded by Jones that when he was in Italy he adopted the New Style, as he naturally would in a country where every one else did so ; but as soon as he got back to London, he reverted to the Old Style.

Another fact liable to lead to confusion of dates is that in England the civil year began on 25th March, not 1st January, so that the change of dating the year did not take place on 1st January, but on 25th March, with the result that all dates from 1st January to 24th March in any particular year, say 1614, belong according to our present computation to the year 1615. This difficulty is now generally met by giving both years, thus, 24th January 1614–15. The confusion lasted in England until 1752 when the New Style was established by law, and the first day of the year was ordered to be 1st January.

There is no confusion, however, about the first date that Jones gives during his visit. He was at Vicenza on Monday, 23rd September 1613, according to the New Style of Italy. Vicenza was the birthplace of Palladio, and was full of buildings of his design ; no town could have suited Jones better for studying modern architecture, and among his drawings is one of the Teatro Olympico in that town designed by Palladio. In the meantime, however, Lord Arundel had left Milan, in dudgeon at the want of respect shown by its Spanish Governor, had made a stay at Padua, and thence had gone to Venice, where he still

was on 13th September.  Jones makes no mention
of dates or places until that at Vicenza ; nor can he
be followed in Lord Arundel's subsequent journeys
to Bologna, Siena and Florence during October,
although he may be supposed to have accompanied
him.  There is a link of a sort between him and
Florence, for in the Worcester College collection is
a drawing of the Pitti Palace, although not of his
handiwork.

But his party presently moved on to Rome, where
Jones, at any rate, made a long stay and became
exceedingly busy in the pursuit of knowledge both
in architecture and painting.  He was there early
in the New Year, as we learn from this rather
portentous note in his *Palladio* :

> In the name of God Amen.
> The 2 of January 1614 (new stille) I being in
> Rome compared the desine(s) following with the
> Ruins them sealves.  Inigo Jones.

Then follows a list of some score or so of the buildings,
chiefly temples, illustrated by Palladio on the
succeeding pages, his text relating to them being
annotated with innumerable marginal notes by
Jones.

But he studied other antiquities besides temples,
as appears from several pages in his sketch-book
*Of the Antiquites of Roome*, and although the notes
were probably taken from a guide-book, it is not
unreasonable to suppose that Jones went to examine
such remains as there were.  Indeed when referring
to the Forum of Nerva he says, ' The ruines of this
wear pulled down whilst I was in roome, and only to
have yᵉ marbell.'  It was the reigning Pope, Paul V,

who took down a temple of Minerva that stood in the Forum, in order to obtain marble for some new buildings.

Jones's doings can be partly followed by the dates he gives. On Sunday, 5th January, he visited the temples of 'Fortuna Virile' and Vesta ; on Tuesday, 21st January, he was sketching drapery and making notes as to its folds ; on 20th February he began his notes on the antiquities, and was continuing them on Monday the 24th. Soon after this he left Rome for a time and went on to Naples in Lord Arundel's train, examining the Via Appia on his way. On Saturday, the 8th March, he visited the Temple of Castor and Pollux at Naples, and he appears to have stayed in that city some length of time, for on the 1st May he bought a book on the title-page of which he wrote : 'Napoli, 1 Mayio, 1614, Inigo Jones.' That Lord Arundel was at Naples as well is clear from a letter of Carleton's on 25th April, in which he mentions the Earl as being there. By the end of May, however, Jones (presumably with the Arundel party) was back in Rome, for on the 29th he witnessed, as already mentioned, the procession on the anniversary of the Pope's coronation, and on the 31st he was examining the Pantheon, of which he says : ' This temple I observed exactly ye last of Maye 1614, and have noated what I found more than is in palladio.' On the 13th June he went to the Temple of Vesta at Tivoli ; and then apparently made an excursion as far as Trevi, near Spoleto, as to which his note is : ' This tempel I saw Munday, ye 16 June.' But he was back by Sunday, the 22nd, on which day he was making further notes about drapery. Of visits in

Rome to which he appended no dates was one to the
' Tempel of Marse ', and another to that of Bramante,
' This tempietto I obsearved often being in Rome
1614.'

But soon after Midsummer the Earl's party, and
possibly Jones as well, must have quitted the South
and proceeded northwards.   The Arundels, however,
found their wanderings cut short by the news of
the death of the Earl's great-uncle, the Earl of
Northampton, from whom he received an inheritance
requiring his presence in England.   But illness
detained them in Genoa, whence he wrote to his
mother on 2nd August, and it is evident that Jones
had left them for a time and had gone to Venice, for on
the 30th July he there bought another book, in which
he wrote his name, the place and the date.   Scamozzi
was then in the city, since on Friday, the 1st August,
Jones ' spoake with Scamozo in this matter and he
hath resolved me in this in the manner of volte '.
Other matters architectural they must have discussed, including Palladio's work, one design of which
Scamozzi utterly disliked.   But it would seem that
Jones was not a great admirer of Scamozzi, if only
from an observation regarding some refinement mentioned by Palladio—' this secret Scamozio being
purblind under stoode nott '.   On the 13th and 14th
August, ' new stille ', Jones was again at Vicenza, and
thenceforward he is lost to sight until he was well on
his way home, if not already there, for the next dates
to be found are Thursday and Friday, the 19th and
20th January 1614, in which he reverts to the
English calendar (thus making the actual year to
be 1615), and these are followed by three several

notes dated in London on the 26th, 27th, and 28th January.

It is quite possible that this second visit to Vicenza was paid on his way to join the Arundels at Genoa, for he has a note in regard to doorways—' The Entrate are varried according to the greatness of the house as I obsearved at Vicenza whear are the best that ever I sawe,' and this is followed by another note as to the usage at Genoa in this respect. If he did so join them he would have accompanied them on their journey homewards through Turin and perhaps over the Mt. Cenis Pass to Nîmes and ultimately to Paris. Some colour is given to this supposition by a mention he makes of the Maison Carrée at Nîmes. But no certain conclusion can be arrived at regarding the exact time and manner of his return to London.

Such is a brief itinerary of his journeys in Italy, undertaken to a large extent in the train of the Earl of Arundel, but not wholly ; for apart from the fact that he employed much of his time in studies of painting and architecture in which the Earl could have taken no share, it is certain that he parted company in order to go to Venice. His stay in Rome was probably longer than that of the Earl, whose presence there was politically inexpedient ; and during his stay he bought a number of pictures for his patron, with which transactions the latter appears to have had no personal connection and no such certain knowledge as would have been the case had he been in Rome at the time of their occurrence.

Most of Jones's architectural notes in his *Palladio* were made during his wanderings, but some of them were added after his return, and dated in London, and were further comments on the text and his own annotations. Palladio illustrates a design of his for a double staircase, somewhat after the fashion of the well-known intertwining staircase at the Château of Chambord. He says that the one at ' Sciambur ' had four sets of steps with four doorways to them. Jones has added beneath this description : ' The stairs at Shambourge I saw being in France . . . and they are but 2 wayes to ascend and ye nuell hath a waal with windowes cut into but this yt seemes was discoursed to Palladio and he Invented of himsealf this staires '—from which it would seem that some one who had been to Chambord had described the staircase to Palladio, who thereupon designed one after the same idea. The blank space left after ' being in France ' was doubtless intended for the date which unhappily Jones omitted to fill in.

But the Palladio volume was used for more than the notes on architecture. It became a kind of commonplace book in which he jotted down observations for many years and in sundry places ; among the years are 1618, 1625, 1630, 1632, 1633, 1636, 1637 and 1639 ; and among the places, London, Kingston, Greenwich and Hampton Court. He measured, by pacing them, the courtyards of Windsor on 5th December 1619, and of Theobalds on 20th June 1621. He has a note that in the year 1625 the ' bras train ' of the portico of the Pantheon was taken off to cast into ordnance by Barbarini Pipo, and ' train of timber ' was put in its stead. This was told him by Will Smith, painter of burnished work, who was present at the time.

At the top of the same early fly-leaf that gives the possible date of purchase is an inscription comparable to that on the first page of his sketch-book. It has been very assiduously scored through with strokes of a pen, but appears to be decipherable as, 'Basta quell che contenta, Inigo Jones.' But the relevancy is not quite apparent of saying that what satisfies is enough, or as one might put it, 'Enough is as good as a feast.'

At the end of the book he leaves architecture altogether, and records a number of miscellaneous prescriptions obtained from various sources and in relief of various ailments. One, obtained from ' my la : Penbrooke ', was for the stone. Other prescriptions are of the robust nature which distinguished those of the seventeenth and eighteenth centuries. Some of them were effectual, others failed, notably one to comfort his stomach and head which he tried at Hampton Court. Another of more attractive nature was successful. It began by the advice to ' eate and drinke claratt wine exteroudinary much at dinner '. Jones followed the advice on Thursday, 8th September 1631, with good effect, he says, ' but I do youse to sleep before I vommit '. The trouble here indicated, ' the spleene and vomiting mellencholy ', had afflicted him seriously for thirty-six years, but a remedy of his own (approved by my Lord Newcastle and others) was happily efficacious. He was subject to colds in the head, but found that to sneeze with a feather in the nose before meat helped to purge the brain by the nose and mouth, and it relieved a pain in his neck. A remedy of ' my lo. of hungtington ' was to fill a pipe with tobacco, wrap it in linen, and when well alight, to inhale the smoke

through the nose.  Jones tried this on one occasion
with unfortunate results, for going abroad too soon
he took a great cold and rheum.  Other remedies
were good for comforting and strengthening the brain,
and among the last to be mentioned were yet others
for ' sharpness of vison ' and ' dimnesse of sight '—a
pathetic indication of advancing age.

So much for his *Palladio*.  His other companion
during his stay in Rome was his sketch-book, which,
as already said, was chiefly devoted to the study of
painting.  The title-page is occupied by this note in
bold lettering (Plate IV) :

Roma.  Altro diletto che Imparar non trovo—Inigo
Jones.  1614.

The statement that his only delight was in learning
is certainly justified both by the contents of the book
and by the notes in his *Palladio*, but the prominence
of the announcement, together with the terms in
which his friends Edmund Bolton and Tom Coryat
referred to him, induce a suspicion that perhaps he
took himself more seriously than did his acquaintances.  But this foible, if foible it were, did nothing
to lessen the earnestness of his studies.  The sketch-
book is devoted largely to sketches taken from
pictures or prints by celebrated masters, among
whom he names Raphael, Michelangelo, Parmegiano,
Baccio (Fra Bartolommeo), Andrea Schiavone and
Polidor (Polidoro Caldora da Caravaggio).  At least
four of his figures are sketched from Michelangelo's
' Last Judgment ' in the Sistine Chapel.  There are
pages devoted to studies of drapery, to innumerable
heads in various positions, in profile, looking up, look-

ing down, looking sideways and straight forward
(Plate V) : heads with abundance of hair and beard,
heads of shaven men and of women.   There are
studies of muscular men and round-limbed children ;
of legs, arms, mouths, noses and eyes.   All these are
supplemented by notes (many from Lomazzo) as to
drapery, ancient costume, the proportions of children,
colouring and the treatment of hair.   All the sketches
are rendered in masterly fashion.   Indeed the impression created by a study of Jones's drawings, both
these and those of subsequent years, is that he
enjoyed drawing the decoration of his architecture,
especially where the human figure played a part,
even more than the architecture itself.

The sketch-book has only two direct references to
architecture, both of which occur towards the end
and are dated Thursday, 19th January 1614, and
Friday the 20th, but, as already pointed out, the
1614 in connection with these dates is in reality 1615.
These reflections about architecture are worth giving
as an example of his sentiments as well as of his
manner of expressing them :

Friday ye 20 January 1614.

In all inuencions of Capresious ornaments, on must first
designe ye Ground, or ye thing plaine, as yt is for youse,
and on that varry yt, addorne yt.   Compose yt w$^{th}$ decorum
according to the youse and ye order yt is of, as in the Cartouses
I sawe of Tarquinio Ligustri of Vittorbo.

and to saie trew all thes composed ornaments the w$^{ch}$
Proceed out of ye aboundance of dessigners and wear brought
in by Michill Angell and his followers in my oppignion do
not well in sollid Architecture and ye fasciati of houses,
but in gardens loggis stucco or ornaments of chimnies peeces
or in the inner parts of houses thos compositiones are of

neccessety to be youused. For as outwarly every wyse
mā carrieth a graviti in Publicke Places, whear ther is
nothing els looked for, yet inwardly hath his immaginacy
set on fire, and sumtimes licenciously flying out, as nature
hir sealf doeth often tymes stravagantly, to dellight, amase
us sumtimes moufe us to laughter, sumtimes to contemplation and horror, so in architecture ye outward ornaments
oft [ought] to be sollid, proporsionable according to the
rulles, masculine and unaffected.

Whear within the Cimeras youused by the ansients the
varried and composed ornaments both of the house yt sealf
and the mouables within yt are most commendable.

Thursday ye 19 January 1614.

As in dessigne first on sttudies the parts of the boddy
of man as Eyes noses mouths eares and so of the rest to
bee practicke in the parts sepperat ear on comm to put
them toggethear to muak a hoole figgure and cloath yt and
consequently a hoole storry w$^{th}$ all ye ornaments. So in
Architecture on must studdy the Parts as loges Entranses
Haales chambers staires doures windowes, and then addorne
them w$^{th}$ colloms cornishes sfondati, stattues, paintings,
compartiments, quadratues, Cartochi, tearmi, festoni, armes,
Emprese, maskquati, folliami, vasi, harpes, Puttini sera-
fini (?), strats, scroules, baccinenti, balustri, Risialti, lions
or eagls claws (?) converted into folliami, sattires, serpents,
victories or angels : antike heads in shells, cherubins heads
w$^{th}$ winges : heads of beasts, Pedistals, Cornucopias, baskets
of fruites, trofies, Juels and agates, medalie, draperies,
frontispices Broken and Composed.

Then he indicates a bad habit into which he had
fallen :

### Noate.

I must ever remember to ciure the deffecte of wrighting
and drawinge awaye upwards to ye right hande and rather
sinn in the contrary.

If in addition to this defect he had cured those of careless writing and inconsistent spelling it would have saved students of his work much time and trouble.

It is obvious from these reflections and the notes in his *Palladio* that Jones had made a close and systematic study of Italian architecture, and his conclusion that the handling of architecture should be ' masculine and unaffected ' is one that cannot be too insistently recommended or too faithfully followed.

# CHAPTER VII

**B**Y the end of January 1615, then, Jones was back in London after an absence of nearly eighteen months, which had been largely devoted to the study of buildings and pictures.

His position with Lord Arundel was by now well established, and the Earl was using his influence to obtain the personal interest of the King in him and his work. In July the King was in Wiltshire, and on Sunday the 30th of that month Lord Arundel wrote from Salisbury :

To my most deere wife the Countesse of Arundell at Arundell House, London.

My deerest Hart,

I thank you for y$^r$ letter. . . . Upon Thursday nexte the Kinge dineth at Wilton, by which time my lo. of Pembroke hopes Mr. Jones will be come hither. I tell him I hope he will, but I cannot promise, because I spake not with him of it when I came out of towne. I meane (by God his grace) to be at Arundell on Tuesday or Wednesday, come seavennight, w$^{ch}$ is the eighth or ninthe of Auguste : if Mr. Jones come hither, I will bring him w$^{th}$ me ; if not, you must w$^{th}$ you.

As there is no reason to suppose that Jones was too full of work to comply with Lord Pembroke's wish,

it may be presumed that he waited on the King at
Wilton, and that in due course he accompanied Lord
Arundel to his home in Sussex. A postscript to the
letter refers to the business that Jones undertook in
Rome :

I pray comend me to my James, Han and little Mr. Bill,
whoe the queene says is a very proper gentleman. I make
noe question but Mr. Jones will soone speake w<sup>th</sup> Mr. Old-
borough, and have under his hand some certainty of his
disbursements and employment in Rome, consideringe his
Mr (Master). I am sure Mr. Jones will, in his bargayne
with Cimandio, include that picture of his father and uncle
w<sup>ch</sup> hanges amonge the rest.

There is no information regarding the sequel to this
letter, either as to the meeting with the King, if it
actually took place, or to Inigo's reimbursement for
his work in Rome. But the time was now approaching when the records became fuller, for in the following September Simon Basil died, and Inigo Jones
succeeded to the office of Surveyor of His Majesty's
Works, his pay commencing on 1st October. He thus
comes within the scope of the State Papers.

He had now succeeded in obtaining what many of
his acquaintances of corresponding gifts were aiming
at—an official appointment for life. The salary was
not large, but it was more than he had received as
surveyor to the Prince ; it was at the rate of eight
shillings a day for his entertainment, eighty pounds
a year for his ' recompense of availes ', and two
shillings and eight pence a day for his riding and
travelling expenses, in round figures £275 a year.
This was a sort of retaining fee for routine work, and
was supplemented by payments for special work in

preparing designs for buildings and their decoration, and by such fees as were payable to him in his official capacity.   He had in addition a livery cloak which presumably he wore as a sign of his office.   The warrant granting it to him was issued in March 1616, the Master of the Great Wardrobe being instructed to deliver ' unto our well beloved servant, Inigo Jones, whom we have appointed to be Surveyor of our Works, in the roome and place of Simon Basill, deceased, the parcels hereafter following for his Livery'. The parcels consisted of five yards of broadcloth for a gown at twenty-six shillings and eightpence the yard, four and a half yards of baize to line it at five shillings the yard, one fur of budge (that is, lamb's wool) price four pounds, and a pound for making the whole. Such a cloak, or its equivalent in money of £12 15s., was to be delivered yearly on 1st November, the Feast of All Saints, to Jones during his natural life. The surveyors of the works had formerly had a house in the palace of Westminster as part of their emoluments, but its use had for some reason lapsed. Simon Basil had a house in the Office of Works ' called Scotland Yard ', which he had pulled down and, having procured a lease of the site, had built several houses for his own benefit.   His successor appears to have been liable to a yearly rent of forty-six pounds, an encumbrance from which Jones was relieved by warrant in 1629, the wording of which is more cordial than that of the grant of his livery. King Charles is made to say ' that of our special grace and favour unto our trusty and well beloved servant, Inigo Jones, Esqr, now Surveyor of our Works, as well in consideration of his good and faithful service done both to our said dear father and to us, as for diverse other good considerations us hereunto moving, we are pleased to give and grant unto him the sum of forty-six pounds ' for the rent of his house. Jones, who was a bachelor, lived in fact in Scotland Yard, and John Webb after him had his office there.

The effect of Jones's appointment becomes at once apparent in his drawings. Hitherto they had been wholly concerned with scenery and costumes for masques, now they include architectural features such as doorways, and some buildings. The earliest one is of a porch, or rather of a projection from the façade of a house containing the entrance (Plate VI). It is dated 1616 and signed in full. In general treatment it conforms with that usually adopted at the time, of bringing forward a comparatively slight projection the full height of the house, having the entrance on the ground floor and a small room on each floor over it. The windows have mullions, the thickness of which shows them to be of wood; the string-courses are of Classic profile, there is a Classic gable of flat pitch with bold carving in its tympanum, and a rather discordant finial on its summit, and the doorway is circular-headed of plain but solid design. It has none of the columns and carving which generally emphasized the principal doorway of a Jacobean house. It is an interesting piece of design, neither so clever nor so attractive as the work of the more skilful of Jacobean architects and masons, but it shows how Jones was endeavouring to comply with the prevailing taste in spite of his own insistent leaning towards a more rigidly classic handling. He was sufficiently satisfied with it to append his signature,

'Inigo Jones *fecit* 1616'. From this example and from the style of the buildings in his masques, which show hardly any Jacobean feeling, it may be concluded that he had no sympathy with the Jacobean rendering of Classic architecture, that his aim was to purify design of what he considered its shortcomings, and to establish firmly the unadulterated Classic which he had studied in Italy. Webb's observation goes to confirm this ; ' for I must tell you,' says he to Dr. Charleton, ' that what was truly meant by the Art of Design, was scarcely known in this Kingdom, until he, under the Protection of his late sacred Majesty, and that famous *Mæcenas* of Arts, the Right Honourable *Thomas* Earl of *Arundel* and *Surry*, brought it in Use and Esteem among us here.' If this conclusion be just it rules out all such buildings as Heriot's Hospital in Edinburgh, and Walpole's suggestion that Jones had two manners, one before he went to Italy and another, of greater purity, after his return.

Now that Jones had received an official appointment more information is available as to his doings and a clearer insight is gained as to his occupations. There is a letter from a news-writer, Edward Sherburn, to Sir Dudley Carleton, ambassador at The Hague, dated the 9th April 1616 (to which reference has already been made), which is full of interesting gossip. The writer had gone with Lord Arundel to the house of a Mr. Hartry to see some pictures which the Earl and Mr. Inigo Jones had fully reviewed. They were twelve in number, and were to be divided between Lord Arundel and Lord Danvers. The writer asks for directions as to price, for the pictures

were some which Carleton had bought from Daniel
Nys, of Venice, on behalf of the Earl of Somerset,
but owing to the disgrace of the favourite they were
left on Carleton's hands, who, as it appeared, wanted
£200 for them.  As Lord Arundel had determined
to buy, he now felt free to accept from Carleton a
certain Jupiter's head which Carleton was anxious
to give him, but as to which Arundel had hitherto
hesitated owing to a feeling of delicacy in increasing
the obligations he was already under to Sir Dudley.
His acceptance of the gift is announced later in
Sherburn's letter, who says that the Jupiter's head
had been placed in Lord Arundel's garden at the end
of a vista exactly opposite the doors of the gallery.
Then the writer mentions the arraignments of Lord
and Lady Somerset and Sir Thomas Monson, which
took place, it will be remembered, in connection with
the death of Sir Thomas Overbury.  A warrant is
mentioned by Horace Walpole for the payment
of £20 to Inigo Jones, Thomas Baldwin, William
Portington and George Meale, officers of His Majesty's
works, for certain scaffolds made by them against
these arraignments.

A further piece of news, which throws some light
on the condition of the times and the dislike of the
English for their new countrymen, the Scotch, was
to the effect that a certain Sir John Gryme (probably
Graham, as he was a Scotsman), a favourite of Sir
George Villiers, had died and had been buried with
great solemnity in Westminster Abbey.  But certain
butchers and shoemakers, in scorn and derision of
Sir John and generally of all the Scots, had the
following night killed a mastiff dog and carried the

body in a procession of some three score persons with
links, and in mockery of Sir John's funeral, to Tuthill
Fields and there buried it solemnly, saying that the
soul of a dog was as good as a Scottishman's soul.
This done, they had repaired to an alehouse where
each man had his can in imitation of the accustomed
ceremony after funerals. Divers of them had been
apprehended and were to be punished by whipping
and such-like correction.

Three months later, on July 11th, the same correspondent tells the ambassador that Lord Arundel
had that day instructed Mr. Inigo Jones to pay the
agreed £200 for the pictures during the week. But
as Mr. Chamberlain (another correspondent) had
heard a rumour that Carleton had already given the
pictures to the Earl of Somerset, Sherburn was resolved that if the money were not paid during the
week he would remove the pictures to some other
place, pending further instructions.

He then relates how on the preceding Sunday the
Earl of Rutland, Sir George Villiers (soon to be Duke
of Buckingham) and Lord Lisle had been installed
at Windsor as Knights of the Garter, and on the
following Tuesday Sir John Roper and Sir John
Hollys had been created Barons, or, as a contemporary diarist puts it, ' lorded at £10,000 a piece '.
Sir John Roper, we are told, ' parts with his great
office, which is said is conferred upon Sir George
Villiers' brother, the last supplies my L. Hay for his
Ambassage into France (being to depart from here
to-morrow) with a matter of £10,000 '. Thus went
on the struggle for position and office ; these great
personages, now mostly forgotten, being able and

willing to pay in a single transaction a sum of which the interest would have maintained Inigo Jones in comfort for the rest of his life.

Carleton was kept well informed of what went on in England during his absence.    In December of the same year, 1616, his constant correspondent, John Chamberlain, a gentleman of easy means and good position, tells him among other things, that the King is contemplating a journey into Scotland.    The people there are making great preparations to be in their best equipage.    Many things are being sent from London, including a pair of organs that cost £400, and all manner of furniture for a chapel, of which Inigo Jones tells him he has the charge.    There are to be pictures of the Apostles, Faith, Hope and Charity and such other religious representations, but how welcome these things will be in Scotland God knows.    All the difficulty, however, will be to find money for the journey.

The money was found, however, and the King started on his progress on the 15th March 1617, accompanied by a retinue of some five hundred persons.    Somewhere on their way they witnessed a dramatic entertainment, for by a warrant of the 11th July 1617, a sum of £30 was granted to John Townsend and Joseph Moore, stage players, 'for acting three severall playes before his Ma^{tye} in his Jorney towardes Scotland'.

The details of the King's visit need not here be related, particularly as, notwithstanding suggestions to the contrary, it is highly improbable that Inigo Jones was of the party.    It is certain, in any case, that he did not start with the royal expedition, for

it so happened that another consignment of pictures
for Lord Arundel was in question.  It had been
obtained from Daniel Nys by Sir Dudley Carleton
and was to be shared between Arundel and Lord
Pembroke.  On the 29th March Sherburn wrote to
Carleton :

I have acquainted my L : of Arundell w<sup>th</sup> Mr. Nys his lre
(letter), and I have direccon from his Lo : when ye shipp
doth arrive here, to deliver ye pictures to Mr. Inego Jones in
his absence his Lo :  being nowe gon after the King.

Lord Arundel had stayed to hear Dr. Donne's sermon
at Paul's Cross on Accession Day, the 24th March,
and had followed the King, who had got as far as
Lincoln on the 27th, that is, two days before Sherburn's letter.  It is clear that during Arundel's
absence, Jones was left behind to act for him in
relation to the pictures.  In view of this and of the
absence of any express mention of Jones being in
Scotland, the presumption is that he did not go, and
this supposition is strengthened by some lines written
by Jones ' To his false friend Mr. Ben Jonson ' (of
which more hereafter), in which he says :

> For though with tired pace and sweaty feete
> I never went to Scotland,

the qualifying circumstances being an allusion to
Jonson's journey on foot to that country.

In June of this year we get the first definite and
authentic information as to Jones being employed as
an architect, for on the 22nd Chamberlain wrote to
Sir Dudley Carleton :

The Queene removed on Teusday from Greenwich to
Oatlands and the Prince to Richmond :  she is building

somewhat at Greenwich w<sup>ch</sup> must be finished this sommer, yt it saide to be some curious devise of Inigo Jones, and will cost above 4000<sup>li</sup>, but he hath another modell or platforme for a new starchamber w<sup>ch</sup> the Kyng wold faine have don yf we could find monie ; (after good wishes) from London this 22nd. of June 1617.

In explanation of this letter it should be said that there was an ancient royal palace at Greenwich, another royal house at Oatlands, where Jones subsequently carried out some work, and a palace at Richmond which had been built by Henry VII. The ' curious devise ' of Inigo was in all probability, in view of its great cost, the Queen's House, which still exists as one of the few examples of his architectural work (Plate VII). But far from being finished that summer, it was not finally completed until 1635. It is quite possible, however, that the house was soon made habitable and that the work of later years was in the nature of embellishment, such as the insertion of chimney-pieces, of which the original designs are still preserved. The device was no doubt considered ' curious ', because it departed entirely from English tradition in its design, and was in fact extremely like an Italian villa both as to its plan and its appearance. It is necessary to bear this change in mind if the full significance of Jones's work is to be grasped. Neither the Queen's House nor the Banqueting House at Whitehall, which was the next important work of his, appears out of the common to us, but to Jones's contemporaries they must have been entirely strange and new, and might well be termed curious devices.

In later years Charles II resumed the idea of rebuilding Greenwich Palace ; John Webb made a plan for a large new building with the Queen's House as its determining feature. This scheme was never carried out, but Webb designed and built one half of the block known as ' King Charles's ' in 1663–66, and placed it in such a position as to form part of a great lay-out of which the Queen's House was the central object. Charles II subsequently abandoned the idea of rebuilding the place as a palace and turned it instead into a palatial hospital, the completion being carried out by Wren and his successors.

The ' modell or platforme for a new star-chamber ' (that is the plan) is preserved at Worcester College, Oxford. It is drawn to a large scale on two sheets, half on each, and is endorsed in Jones's own hand ' for the Modell of the Starr Chamber, 1617 '. The words ' platforme ' and ' platte ' were used at this period for ' plan ', and the word ' model ' was used in the sense of ' design ', which included certainly a plan and probably an elevation as well. There is no elevation accompanying this particular plan, but there are three supplementary drawings to a smaller scale, comprising plan, elevation and section, which are almost certainly of Webb's draughtsmanship. As Webb was at this time only six years old, and did not go to Jones as his pupil until 1628, it looks as though these three drawings were either an exercise of his or a preparation for a resuscitated idea of building the Star Chamber in later years. The building was to have been a large one, about the same width and height as the Banqueting House, but nearly half as long again : it was, however, never carried out.

Jones was doing at this time other and smaller

work than these two substantial buildings. He had introduced some Italian features into the town house of his patron, Lord Arundel, a fact that has only recently come to light. Among his drawings are a number of doorways, quite simple affairs without any titles ; it was impossible to say what particular doorways they represented. In the Smithson collection are also a number of doorways. Smithson was an architect hailing from Nottinghamshire, and in the years 1618 and 1619 he appears to have paid a visit to London to see what was being done there in the way of architecture, for certain of his drawings are entitled after this manner : ' The newe Bulding at Sant Jeames 1619 ', and ' My Ladye Cookes house in Houlborn at London 1619 '. There are also several relating to Arundel House : ' The uprighte draughte of an Italyan wyndowe at Arendell House ', ' A newe Italyan windowe, the gallerye at arrundell house ', one being the interior view and the other the exterior ; ' A chymnye Peece at Arundelle House 1619 ', ' The newe Italyan gate at Arundell House in the garden there ', with the date 1618 in a panel. On comparing this last drawing with those of Inigo Jones it became evident that Smithson had made an inaccurate but quite recognizable drawing of a doorway designed by Jones. Again, a doorway of Smithson's entitled ' An Italyan gate in my Lo : of Arundelles garden at London : at Arundell house ', agrees with another drawing by Jones, but Smithson has added three finials at the top. Smithson has also a survey, ' The Plateforme of the garden at Arendell house ', with the two gateways at either end of a long straight walk. Another identification is Smithson's doorway of ' Coronall Sissells House in the Strande ' with another of Jones's unnamed designs. ' Coronall Sissell ' is Colonel Cecil, otherwise Sir Edward Cecil, brother of the second Earl of Exeter. The town house of the Cecils was in the Strand, and another branch of the family also had a house in the same thoroughfare.

During this visit of Smithson's he went to Theobalds, where he made a drawing of a rather elaborate panel of woodwork, which he noted as ' The Platte of the Seelinge of the greate Chamber at Thyballes taken the 8th. of November : 1618 : By Jo : S: ', ' Seeling ' being the contemporary word for panelling : and he made a ' platforme ' of the stables there, with standing for ninety-nine horses. He made drawings of the Banqueting House, to which further reference will be made, and not content with modern work, he made a plan of Henry VII's Chapel at Westminster and diagrams of some of its complicated vaulting. But it is clear that amid all his activities of measuring and sketching, he was particularly interested in the ' newe Italyan ' work of Inigo Jones.

Jones was now busy, more or less, with architectural work, but in January 1618 he returned, after an interval of five years, to the designing of a masque in conjunction with Ben Jonson, called *Pleasure Reconciled to Virtue*. Of this there is but one drawing at Chatsworth, and the venture was not very successful. Two of Carleton's correspondents make severe comments. Sherburn, writing on 10th January, says:

The Maske wᶜʰ wee had on Twelveth night where-in the Prince was one, yoʳ L : will perceave the conceipt by perusing this little booke. I must tell yoʳ L : it came far short of the expectacõn and Mr. Inego Jones hath lost in his reputacõn in regard some extraordinary devise was looked for (it being the Prince his first Mask) and a poorer was never seene.

It was no doubt Prince Charles's first masque since he grew up, but it will be remembered that as a child of nine he had appeared in *Tethys' Festival*, when his brother was created Prince of Wales.

The other correspondent, Nathaniel Brent, was equally uncomplimentary ; he did not think it even worth while to send a book of the words :

The Maske on 12th. night is not comended of any. ye poet is growen so dul yt his devise is not worth ye relating, much lesse ye copiing out. divers thinke fit he should returne to his ould trade of brick laying againe. The actors were ye prince, marquis Buck : and marquis Hamelton, ye Earle of Montgomery, two of ye Ld Threasorers sons and others minorū gentium to make them twelve.

The gibe about bricklaying refers to the fact that Jonson's mother after the death of her first husband, a clergyman and father of Ben, married a bricklayer, who caused his young stepson to help him for a time in his respectable but hardly intellectual occupation.

The remainder of the year 1618 was uneventful ; Jones was in all likelihood busy with the Queen's House at Greenwich ; the only drawing of his known to be of this time is a sheet of sketches for windows, which he dated April 1618, but they have no connection with the Queen's House. They are studies founded on illustrations of Serlio's. There is also a rough sketch of a fountain with the title ' ffontana di Giovanni Maggi Romano 1618 ', but as the writing is Webb's and the sketch is of the roughest, the evidence it affords is of little value.

The autumn provides a touch of purely domestic interest, but it goes to show the easy footing upon which Jones stood with Lord Arundel, and how well informed Sir Dudley Carleton's correspondents kept him on even trivial matters. On the 14th October Chamberlain writes :

The Earl of Arundel with Inigo Jones the Surveyor made a step from Theobalds to Ware Park, where they were so well pleased with the grapes and peaches that ever since their being there the King hath sent duly twice a week for that kind of provision.

It was a step of nine or ten miles from Theobalds to Ware Park, which was the home of Sir Henry Fanshaw, whose garden there was praised by Sir Henry Wotton in his *Elements of Architecture*, written soon after this time.

The following year, 1619, saw the commencement of Jones's best known building, the Banqueting House at Whitehall, but this opens up so large a question that a fresh chapter must be devoted to it.

# CHAPTER VIII

Drawings for the Whitehall Palace—The Banqueting House—John Webb and the Whitehall Drawings—John Webb and Greenwich Palace—Jones and Webb.

ALMOST every one who has hitherto written about Inigo Jones and his work has taken it for granted, on the authority of his predecessors, that Jones designed a vast palace for James I at Whitehall, of which, however, only a very small portion, namely the Banqueting House, was ever built. But researches carried out some fifteen years ago tended to show that this idea was erroneous. There was no doubt about Jones having designed the Banqueting House itself ; but the design for the great palace was actually an affair of many years later; it was devised to include Jones's building, and he had little if anything to do with it, the credit being due to John Webb ; the idea of erecting it never came to fruition, and never had a chance of doing so.

The circumstances that produced the error and those that led to its correction are quite simple, and provide a story that is not uninteresting.

Inigo Jones was a collector of drawings ; he obtained possession of many by Palladio and a few by other Italian architects when on his visits to Italy. He also preserved a large number of his own, of which the larger portion were made for the masques and a smaller were architectural designs. On his death these drawings passed to John Webb, and when Webb died he left instructions that the collection, which by this time included many of Webb's own designs, was to be preserved intact. These instructions were observed for a time, but it appears that the widow of a son of Webb eventually sold them. The greater number passed into the possession of Lord Burlington, the great patron of architecture in the early years of the eighteenth century, and himself an amateur architect. Nearly all the remainder became the property of a Dr. Clarke, who bequeathed them to Worcester College, Oxford. A few others were later in the possession of a Mr. William Emmet of Bromley, one of whose descendants presented them to the British Museum; these will be dealt with in due course. The Burlington collection was inherited by the Duke of Devonshire and was preserved at Chatsworth, this, together with the collection at Worcester College, comprising nearly the whole number of the drawings left by Webb.

In the year 1727 the architect William Kent, with the encouragement and help of Lord Burlington, published a large number of the drawings as a book entitled *Designs of Inigo Jones*. The illustrations were selected without critical examination as to which were by Jones and which by Webb; indeed Jones was credited with the whole collection, and Webb was ignored. Among the designs by far the largest and most important were those for the Palace at Whitehall, in which the Banqueting House was included as a subsidiary feature. The date of the erection of the Banqueting House was known,

namely 1619–22, and it was taken for granted that
this building was the only portion (and a very small
one) that was actually built of the huge building
contemplated at that time. The inference was quite
natural in view of the information that was then
available.

Kent's illustrations were taken from drawings now
at Worcester College ; but all this while there were
other drawings at Chatsworth to which little or no
attention had been directed, and in any case the two
collections were so far apart that it was impossible
to collate them, and although it was recognized that
they were related to each other, it was impossible to
judge how close the relationship might be. But there
came a time when it was necessary to go deeper into
the matter, and in order to effect this photography
was called in aid. The whole of the drawings at
Worcester College, and those at Chatsworth relating
to architecture, were photographed, and it became
possible to examine the two sets at leisure and
together, a procedure which so far had been im-
practicable owing to their location and the difficulty
of devoting the requisite time at places so distant
as Chatsworth and Oxford. Ample time could now
be spent in deciphering the writing and in examining
and classifying the drawings, with results that were
not only interesting but surprising.

But before enlarging on these results it is desirable
to carry the history of the drawings a little further.
The drawings which came into Mr. Emmet's possession had been utilized by Colen Campbell in his
*Vitruvius Britannicus*, published about 1720. The
scheme there illustrated differed entirely from that

in Kent's book, the only point the two had in common
being the inclusion of the Banqueting House.  This
scheme, like the other, was attributed to Jones, and
thus the public had before them two designs, a large
one fathered by Kent and a smaller and entirely
different one fathered by Campbell.  There was some
difficulty in accounting for the existence of two
separate designs for the same building, but as they
differed very greatly in the size of the building, the
plausible explanation offered itself that they were
alternative schemes ;  and while some writers held
that the smaller, illustrated by Campbell, came first
and was superseded by the more magnificent scheme
illustrated by Kent, others held the view that the
larger scheme was abandoned in favour of the other
on account of the cost.  This latter opinion, as it
happens, was the more reasonable, for the assumption
was that the Kent design was prepared for James I
prior to the erection of the Banqueting House in
1619, whereas Campbell entitles his illustrations
(with slight variations) as being those of a design
' as it was presented to His Majesty King Charles I
by the celebrated Inigo Jones Anno 1639'.  This
date was evidently given on the authority of Mr.
William Emmet, to whom Campbell pays a handsome
acknowledgment in the text of his book, and from
whom, he says, ' I have at last procured these
excellent designs of Inigo Jones.'  But Campbell's
version of these excellent designs does not entirely
agree with the originals.  This set of drawings, preserved at the British Museum, comprises a certain
number which may be regarded as originals, and a
corresponding number which are described, by notes

made on them, as ' lineal copy ' and ' spurious lineal
copy '.   The so-called ' copies ' are not, in fact, exact
copies ; in some cases they differ so much from the
originals as to be variations, and, oddly enough, it
is the copies that Campbell utilized, so far as the
elevations are concerned, while as to the plan, the
original shows one half entirely different from the
other, presumably because one half was to be used
for purposes of State and the other for domestic
purposes, whereas Campbell's plan shows both halves
exactly alike.   His plan and elevations do not
exactly agree in their dimensions with those he
utilized, nor do his dimensions tally among themselves ; in fact, he took considerable liberties with his
sources of information.

His authority for the date 1639 was derived from
a note of Emmet's on one of the elevations which
runs thus :

The Incomparable Architect Inigo Jones, having in the
year 1639 presented these his Designs for the Building of
White Hall, to King Charles the First : which through the
Iniquity of the Times, could not be put in Execution.   It
has unfortunately happened that (as one Evil is often the
Cause of more) that the North Front of this designe having
been loste—I have to the best of my Judgment Erected this
Front, from the Original Plan of Mr. Jones, in his stile, to
make the Designe Compleat.   W^m Emmet of Bromley in
the County of Kent, An^o 1717.

Leaving Campbell and his discrepancies out of the
question, it is difficult to harmonize the various
drawings of the British Museum set and to arrive
at their true significance.   Mr. Emmet quotes no
authority for his statement that they were presented

in 1639, and his attribution of them to Inigo Jones rests, for anything that is known to the contrary, upon the same foundation as the similar attribution of the Kent design. On the whole the evidence is against him, but the complete solution of this particular puzzle has not been reached. It is otherwise with the Kent design, as will now be shown.

The royal palace at Whitehall had been acquired by Henry VIII after the fall of Cardinal Wolsey in 1529. It had been for centuries the town house of the Archbishops of York, and had been largely rebuilt by Wolsey, of whose work there are still some remains under the offices of the Board of Trade in Whitehall Gardens. Queen Elizabeth had built a Banqueting House of wood, distinct from the Great Hall, in 1581, and in the year 1607 James I had replaced this building by another and better one. On 16th September 1607, Dudley Carleton had written to John Chamberlain :

The King in his crossing from Windsore to Whitehall for no greater business than to see his new building, w<sup>ch</sup> when he came into it he could scarce see by reason of certain pillars w<sup>ch</sup> are sett up before the windowes, and he is nothing pleased with his L<sup>d</sup> architect for that device.

Curiously enough Smithson has a plan of this very building, with the pillars in front of the windows. It had no long life, however, for on 12th January 1619 it was burnt down, owing to the carelessness of a joiner who was repairing the scenery, of a masque. He left his glue-pot heating during a short absence, and on his return found the scenery, of oiled paper and dry fir, all ablaze and beyond the possibility of extinction. The fire was so furious that in the space of two hours the whole place was destroyed.   Inigo Jones, as surveyor of the King's buildings, was instructed to prepare designs for a new Banqueting House to replace it, which he at once proceeded to do, and three months later, on 19th April, he, together with his usual colleagues, Thomas Baldwin, Wm. Portinton, Fr. Carter and Geo. Meale, submitted an estimate for a new building :

The whole Charge of the Banqueting howse to be newe builte according to a modell thereof made, beinge in Lengthe 110 foote, and in breadth 55 foote, the under story beinge arched 16 foote in height, the upper story 55 foote highe, the masons worck, Carpenters worcke, Bricklayers worck, plombers, plastorers, Joyners, Smithes worcke glasinge, Ramminge and making ye foundations with scaffouldinge to all the saide worcks, will amount unto the some of .   9850[11]

The ' model ' is in the Chatsworth collection and consists of a preliminary plan and elevation (Plate IX), and a more carefully considered elevation (Plate X), all drawn by Jones's own hand ;  the revised design was actually carried out, with a few modifications, and is, in fact, the beautiful building which still stands on the east side of Whitehall, and is now the Royal United Services Museum (Plate VIII).

As far as any reliable evidence goes, this is the most important piece of architecture that Jones designed, its only rival being the Queen's House at Greenwich.  Upon these two buildings must his reputation as an architect chiefly rest ;  but it may rest in security, for they will hold their own with any other buildings of like degree.

The new Banqueting House was begun on 1st June

on the site of the old one : Smithson's plan shows the surroundings of the latter which can readily be identified with those of Jones's new building. Smithson appears to have been so much struck with the new work when it had risen a few feet out of the ground, that he made a measured elevation of the basement story. It is quite clear that at this time there was no thought of the Banqueting House being an incident in the long façade of a large palace, for Jones's ' model ' shows an annexe at each end somewhat narrower and lower than the main room, which would have been quite incompatible with its forming part of a façade ; and although the annexes were abandoned there could have been no intention to build anything adjoining it, for according to the official description upon its completion it had ' one great window in the upper end '. There was but one room, and its dimensions are stated as 110 feet long, 55 feet wide and 55 feet high, that is, a double cube. This proportion was much favoured in the Classic buildings of Italy, but had never been adopted in England prior to Jones's time.[1] The length was 10 feet less than that of the building that was burnt, but the width was 2 feet more.

Jones's Banqueting House, therefore, was built as a practically isolated building, merely to replace the old one and on the same site, but it was designed in a more correct and stately manner, according to the precedents that Jones had studied in Italy. If confirmation were required of the simple and limited intention regarding it, it would be found in the fact

[1] The actual dimensions, ascertained from measurement, are 111 feet 10 inches long, and 55 feet 2 inches wide.

that neither in the official nor private papers of the time is any mention made of a projected palace or other building at Whitehall. The Banqueting House alone is mentioned, the estimate for it, its final cost (which was very much in excess of the estimate) and a payment, 'To Inigo Jones upon the Councells Warr$^t$ dated 27th June 1619 for making two several models the one for the Star Chamber, the other for the Banqueting House, £37.'

It is obvious that during the three months' interval between the burning of the old building on 12th January and the submission of the estimate for the new building on 19th April, there would not have been time enough to devise the huge scheme fathered by Kent and to get it approved by the King ; but it is unnecessary to labour the point, for Webb expressly says that he it was who designed the Palace.

His testimony is quite clear and is contained in a brief of his case attached to a petition which he presented to Charles II shortly after the Restoration, probably in June 1660. He was applying for the position of Surveyor of His Majesty's Works, which had been, or was about to be, given to the poet John Denham, afterwards Sir John. In the petition he prays Charles II to ' settle upon him the Surveyo$^{rs}$ office of yo$^r$ Ma$^{ties}$ Works, whereunto yo$^r$ Royal Father assigned him, and to that end only ordered his Education ', and he says that ' he was by Mr. Jones, upon his leaving his house at the beginning of the late unhappy warrs appointed his Deputy to execute the said place in his absence '.

In the brief he says :

That he was Mr. Jones Deputy and in actuall possession
of the office upon his leaving London, and attended his
Ma<sup>tie</sup> in that Capacity at Hampton Court and in ye Isle
of Wight, where he received his Ma<sup>ties</sup> comand to designe
a Pallace for Whitehall, w<sup>ch</sup> he did untill his Ma<sup>ties</sup> unfortunate calamity caused him to desist.

The drawings themselves confirm this claim : indeed,
a study of the drawings had already led to this precise
conclusion before attention had been directed to the
claim.

When the two collections at Worcester College and
Chatsworth were collated, it became clear that
originally they had formed one collection, and that
the Chatsworth drawings provided an explanation
of the whole series. Instead of there being two
schemes, as hitherto supposed, there were seven, all
more or less worked out ; and apart from Jones's
' model ' of the Banqueting House, the drawings
were all attributable to Webb. They were in all
stages of development : some were preliminary
sketches, in some the ideas were further worked out.
It became possible to trace the designs from their
inception to their completion, both as to the plans
and the elevations. There were alternative render-
ings of the façades ; some special features, such as
the principal staircase, the chapel and the courts, were
elaborated on separate drawings to a larger scale than
that of the drawings in general. In fact, here could
be seen the gradual working out of several schemes
from the very outset, with alternative ideas jotted
down, to be afterwards adopted or rejected. All
these drawings are by Webb ; there is only one that
may possibly, although not certainly, be by Jones,

and that is an isolated drawing unconnected with the others. But so far as the various designs for the Palace are concerned that are housed at Chatsworth and Worcester College, there is nothing to show that Jones had anything to do with them. On the other hand, Webb's ideas can be followed in their development, their ramifications, their elaborations and their final results.

It is doubtful whether Webb had the opportunity of submitting any of his designs to the King who ordered them ; but if not, he submitted some of them to Charles II, for he has notes on the plan and the elevation of one of them—not the Kent scheme —to the following effect : ' Ground Plant for the Pallace of Whitehall for King Charles ye first, taken, John Webb Archit.' And, ' M$^e$, I design'd these uprights for the King at $\frac{3}{4}$ of an inch to tenn feete,' and, ' Upright for the Pallace of Whitehall for King Charles ye first, taken, but ye ffront is to bee encreased according to ye ground platt John Webb.' In regard to these notes it is to be observed that Webb claims the design as his own ; that Charles II must have been on the throne before his father could have been mentioned as ' Charles ye first ' ; and that as the front was ' to bee encreased ', it must have been Charles II by whom the design was ' taken ' and at whose suggestion the front was to be increased. It is certain that Charles II was considering plans for a palace at Whitehall early in his reign, for in addition to the numerous drawings connected with the designs already mentioned, Webb has a block plan of an entirely different scheme dated 17th October 1661, below which he has sketched

the central feature of an elevation. There are, however, no drawings showing how the scheme was to
be elaborated.

With regard to the set of drawings at the British
Museum, were it not for Emmet's statement that
they were made in 1639, they would fall naturally
into the remainder of the series prepared by Webb
upon the command of Charles I. Emmet's statement is unsupported, and it is reasonable to suppose
that had so important an event occurred as the
consideration by the King of a great palace, so
splendid that the celebrated Banqueting House was
to be but an incidental feature of it, some allusion
to it would have found its way into correspondence
or other documents of the time. But no such
allusion has yet come to light. The question of the
British Museum drawings must therefore be left in
some uncertainty, but with the balance of evidence
against the idea that Jones prepared them.

The whole idea of building the Palace fell through.
Charles II had not money enough, and what he had
he spent in other directions.

The story of the so-called Inigo Jones drawings
is not yet quite finished. Apart from those relating
to the Palace, there is a large number of designs for
houses, gateways, fountains, and other things. Some
of these are unmistakably drawn by Jones, but most
of them are equally unmistakably drawn by Webb,
who was an indefatigable student and occupied much
of his time in copying some of the designs by Palladio
which Jones had brought from Italy, and in making
use of the knowledge thus gained by drawing designs
of his own as an exercise. When the drawings came

to be published, they were all assumed to be designs by Inigo Jones and as such were given to the world by Kent, Isaac Ware, Vardy and others during the eighteenth century. The consequence is that the greatest caution is necessary in accepting the attributions of that period. Some are right, but more are wrong.

The Palace at Greenwich is a case in point, or rather that portion of it known as King Charles's Block. This has always been attributed to Jones, but nothing can be clearer than the fact that Webb was the architect. His appointment, dated 21st November 1666, runs thus :

Whereas wee have thought fit to employ you for the erecting and building of Our palace at Greenwich, Wee doe hereby require and authorize you to execute, act, and proceed there to your best skill and judgment in Architecture, as our Surveyor Assistant unto S$^r$ John Denham, K$^{nt}$ of the Bath, Surveyor General of Our Works, etc.

The salary was to be £200 per year with travelling expenses, and arrears were to be paid as from January 1663. The very contingency that Webb had foreseen and to which he had called attention in the Brief attached to his Petition, namely that if Sir John Denham were appointed Surveyor, ' he must of necessity have another at his Ma$^{ties}$ charge to doe his business ', had now arisen, and Webb may be forgiven if he secretly chuckled over his own appointment. The original drawings for the work are by Webb's hand. Some are actually signed by him, and nearly all of them bear titles and dates in his handwriting. The dates range from 1663 on the plan, to March ye 10th. 1669–70 on the drawing of the

Chapel; a few are dated 1665, but the greater number are of 1666. One design, the alcove in His Majesty's bedchamber, Vardy published as Inigo Jones's, but not only is it of a character wholly foreign to Jones's genius, and to his style of drawing, but it is unmistakably drawn by Webb, and the title and date, 1665, are in Webb's handwriting. Jones, it will be remembered, had died in 1652.

There is no wonder, therefore, that with such a want of discrimination on the part of publishers in the eighteenth century, the public were misled into attributing to Jones a great amount of work to which he had no claim and to which he never made any.

The conclusions which a careful examination of the drawings force upon an unbiased judgment must necessarily affect the popular estimate of Inigo Jones as a great creative architect, dealing with vast schemes, but they leave a residue of smaller work which itself is enough to show him to have been a designer of architecture of extraordinary skill, judgment and taste.

The suggestion that Jones was behind Webb in these schemes has no support; for in regard to Whitehall, it was not until Jones had gone away and left Webb as his deputy that the latter received the command to design the palace; and in regard to Greenwich, Jones had been dead fourteen years before Webb received his appointment. There are no preliminary sketches by Jones; if there had been there is every reason to believe that Webb would have jealously preserved them; and having regard to the multiplicity of the designs for Whitehall a sketch or two would have served little or no purpose.

The story of Webb's part in the design of these two palaces has yet to be told in its details and would be well worth the telling. It has been touched upon here in so far as it affected Inigo Jones, but its consideration has taken us many years in advance of the subject, and a return must be made to the building of the Banqueting House.

# CHAPTER IX

The Banqueting House—Death of the Queen—Lincoln's Inn
Fields—Lincoln's Inn Chapel—Letter to Lord Arundel—Report on
Quality of Glass—Alterations to New Hall—Festivities at Court—
Visit from the Infanta expected—York House Water-Gate—
Jones and Gerbier.

ON 1st June 1619 the new Banqueting House
was begun, and it took nearly three years to
complete, being finished on 31st March 1622.
In addition to his original design for the whole building there are two drawings by Jones for its details,
one entitled ' Scizo of the great doure Ban Ho
1619 I.J.', the other a ' window of ye Modell '. There
is now no door that resembles Jones's sketch, but the
window can be identified as the pattern of those in
the upper story. The master mason, to whose skill
and knowledge of detail the building doubtless owes
much of its character, was the well-known Nicholas
Stone. There are no large-scale profiles of the
mouldings among the drawings that have been preserved, and it is quite possible that the mason may
have submitted patterns from his own stock for the
approval of Inigo. As to this there is no evidence
either way, but it is certain that some of the skilled
masons of the time were in possession of admirable
profiles, and it is equally certain that Jones was
thoroughly acquainted with examples to be found
in Italy, and that if he did not draw the profiles
himself he was well able to judge of the effect of any
that might be submitted to him.

As already mentioned, the cost of the building far exceeded the estimate; it was rather more than half as much again.   This is shown in an account of the ' charges in building a Banqueting House at Whitehall, and erecting a new pier in the Isle of Portland, for conveyance of stone from thence to Whitehall '. The Banqueting House cost £14,940 4s. 1d. and the pier £712 19s. 2d.   There is a full description in the Declared Account, which is worth quoting at some length, as it can be checked from the building itself. It is described as

a new building, with a vault under same, in length 110 feet, and in width 55 feet within ;  the wall of the foundation being in thickness 14 feet, and in depth 10 feet within ground, brought up with brick ;  the first story to the height of 16 feet, wrought of Oxfordshire stone, cut into rustique on the outside and brick on the inside ;  the walls 8 feet thick, with a vault turned over on great square pillars of brick, and paved in the bottom with Purbeck stone ;  the walls and vaulting laid with finishing mortar ;  the upper story being the Banqueting House, 55 feet in height, to the laying on of the roof ;  the walls 5 feet thick, and wrought of Northamptonshire stone, cut in rustique, with two orders of columns and pilasters, Ionic and Composite, with their architrave, frieze, and cornice, and other ornaments ;  also rails and ballasters round about the top of the building, all of Portland stone, with fourteen windows on each side, and one great window at the upper end, and five doors of stone with frontispiece and cartoozes ;  the inside brought up with brick, finished over with two orders of columns and pilasters, part of stone and part of brick, with their architectural frieze and cornice, with a gallery upon the two sides, and the lower end borne upon great cartoozes of timber carved, with rails and ballasters of timber, and the floor laid with  spruce  deals ;  a  strong  timber  roof  covered with lead, and under it a ceiling divided into a fret made of great cornices enriched with carving; with painting, glazing, &c.

The date of this document is 29th June 1633, more than eleven years after the building was completed, an eloquent commentary on the state of the royal coffers.

During the building of the new Banqueting House there is no record of any masques being produced for the Court. The last had been in 1618, and, as already mentioned, it was far from being a success ; both Ben Jonson and Inigo Jones were at fault. It may have been this misfortune that was the first cause of the disagreement that arose between them and that ultimately developed into a serious quarrel, although some authorities hold that it started as far back as 1612. The first signs of it are to be found in the *Notes of Ben Jonson's Conversations with William Drummond of Hawthornden, January, M.DC.XIX.* Towards the close of the year 1618 Jonson paid a visit to Drummond at his house in Scotland whither he went the whole way on foot. While with his host he talked about his acquaintances and seems to have vented his spleen in regard to many of them. These outpourings of a fellow-poet so well known as Jonson, Drummond recorded in these 'Notes'. As to Inigo Jones he says that Jonson told him he had ' said to Prince Charles, of Inigo Jones, that when he wanted to express the greatest villaine in the world, he would call him ane Inigo '. Again, somebody must have told Jones that Jonson had been calling him a fool, for another note of a conversation says that ' Jones having accused him for naming him, behind his back, a fool, he denied it ; but says he, I said, He was ane arrant knave, and I avouch it.'

This opinion, which Jonson was then ready to affirm and maintain, he held for the remainder of his life, although he suppressed it for a number of years during which he and Jones collaborated in the production of further Court masques. But it seems to have been an abiding conviction which found expression in many bitter lines in after years. These must be touched upon in due course, for they cannot be wholly ignored in forming an estimate of Jones's character.

Meanwhile Jones himself was busy in London with other matters besides the Banqueting House. The idea of a new Star Chamber had fallen through, but repairs were required at the old one, and payments to him and some of his colleagues are recorded for work done there in February 1616–17, January and February 1618–19 and April and May 1619. His official duties also called him to report, in conjunction with Thomas Baldwin, on the gatehouse of the prison at St. Albans, which was to be repaired at the King's charges.

But an event which must have affected him deeply occurred at this time in the death of the Queen on the 2nd March. Anne of Denmark was the sister of his earliest patron, the King of Denmark, and although there is no record of any particular effort she made in his favour, there is no reason to doubt that her influence had much to do with the strength of his position at Court. To him was entrusted the melancholy duty of designing the hearse for her funeral, which took place on the 13th May. She had died at Hampton Court and her body had been brought thence to Somerset House, where it lay ' with all the state and magnificence of so great a queen ' until it was conveyed with much pomp to Westminster Abbey. There is a sketch by Jones of a queen with orb and sceptre seated under a substantial canopy on which are arms identifiable as those of England (Plate II); this may perhaps have been prepared in connection with the funeral of Queen Anne. For the making of the hearse and for repairs at the Star Chamber a payment of £50 was made to Inigo Jones and his usual colleagues, the comptroller (Thomas Baldwin), the carpenter and the clerk of works, in November of the following year.

Another work upon which Jones was now engaged was the laying out of Lincoln's Inn Fields and the building of the chapel there. A commission had been appointed on 16th November 1618, on which, among many others, William, Earl of Pembroke, ' Chamberlain of Our Household ', the Earl of Arundel, the Earl of Northampton, Sir Henry Spiller and ' Inigo Jones Our Surveyor Generall of Our Works ', were nominated. The documents set forth that there had been more public works near and about Our City of London within these sixteen years of our reign than in ages before. There were in the west part of Our suburbs of London certain grounds known by the the name of Lincoln's Inn Fields, which if reduced to fair and goodly walks would be a matter of great ornament to the city, pleasure and freshness for the health and recreation of the inhabitants thereabouts, and for the sight and delight of Embassadors and strangers coming to Our Court and City, and a memorable work of Our time to all posterity.

The Commission was instructed to repress all nuisances and inconveniences, and leave was given to clear away houses after compensating the owners. The grounds ' according to your Wisdomes and Discretions, may be framed and reduced both for Sweetness Uniformitie and Comelines into such Walkes, Partitions or other Plottes, and in such sorte, manner and forme, both for publique Health and Pleasure, as by the said Inigo Jones is or shall be accordingly drawne by way of Mapp or Ground Plot, exhibited plained and set out and approved by Us '.   Lists of persons living in adjacent parishes who could well afford to contribute to the expense, and of such as were refractory and denied to contribute were to be submitted, and a collector in each parish was to be appointed.

The scheme was carried out, but the western side of Lincoln's Inn Fields, as we know it, appears to have been the only one upon which houses were then erected, and Lindsey House is the sole remnant of Jones's work.   It has been considerably altered, but the front and the handsome pillars of the forecourt may be credited to his design.

Already for more than a year before the appointment of this commission the building of a chapel had been in contemplation by the Benchers of Lincoln's Inn.  The contemporary accounts throw some interesting light on the inception and progress of the work.   The idea of building having been accepted, it was ordered on 25th November 1617 that certain benchers ' or any two of them ' should consider the materials and how much would be necessary.   On the 27th of the following January—

The consideracion of a fitt modull for the Chappell is commended to Mr. Indicho Jones and Mr. Brooke one of the Mr^s of the Bench is requested to move him concerninge the same : and consideracion is to be had of the recompence that shall be given to the said Mr. Indicho Jones for his paynes therein.

The Mr. Brooke here mentioned is none other than the Christopher Brooke who was present at Coryat's Feast, and was also one of the Sirenical gentlemen greeted by him from the far-distant Agra. It will be observed that Jones was not approached by the clerk or secretary of the committee, as open to be employed by anyone who chose to ask him ; he was to be ' moved ' by his old friend, Mr. Brooke.

In May 1618 it was resolved to put the question of building the chapel at a cost of £2,000 to the ' gent. of the House ' ; the proposition was carried and it was ordered ' that a faire Chappell w^th all convenient speede shalbe erected and built w^th in this House ', but it was more than a month before it was resolved to decide where the chapel should stand ; and on the 12th November it was resolved that

The modull of the Chappell agreed upon by the Committees of the Chappell is approved by the Mr^s of the Bench, and the platforme of the same modull is appointed to be drawne by Mr. Clarcke who hath undertaken the buildinge of the said Chappell.

From this it would appear that Jones had supplied a sketch design or ' modull ' and that for working purposes the ' platforme ', or plan, was to be drawn out by the builder, John Clarke, who, as the ' free mason and workeman of the Chapple ', petitioned for payment in the following May (1619).

The work, however, was so slow in progress that in February 1620 it was resolved that, owing to the number of committees concerned and their slackness in meeting, a smaller committee, consisting of Mr. Jasper Selwyn, Mr. Christopher Brooke and Mr. Thomas Saunderson, should take charge and proceed as to them should seem good.

This arrangement had beneficial effects, but even so it took three years to finish the building, which was not ready for consecration until the spring of 1623.

John Clarke, the mason, together with Nicholas Smyth and others, the joiners, had some difficulties with their accounts—a state of affairs not unknown in the present day. These were referred to Thomas Baldwin, whose name appears so frequently as Jones's co-signatory of official reports, and it is to be hoped that the parties came to an amicable settlement. But there may have been good reason for investigation, because subsequent records of repairs and partial rebuilding go to show that the Chapel was very badly built, a fact which indicates that Jones's connection with it could hardly have gone beyond supplying a preliminary sketch.

The screen or frontispiece—for it is only worked on one face—of the Hall at Lincoln's Inn may not improbably owe to Inigo Jones its general design, that is, its proportions, its spacing and the relation of its voids to solids ; but the character of the detail and its thoroughly Jacobean handling point to the ornament having been designed and carried out by a skilful joiner, well versed in the ordinary methods then in vogue.

The chapel has been so much altered from time to time as to remove it from the category of buildings which throw any light upon Jones's work. The vaulted undercroft is of conventional late Gothic character, with pillars, arches and a few bosses showing touches of the seventeenth century : but in the superstructure it would be hard to recognize Inigo's hand. The chapel was consecrated on Ascension Day in 1623, when Dr. Donne, who had been a fellow-guest of Jones's at Coryat's Philosophical Feast, preached the consecration sermon.

They had summary ways in connection with works of a public character in those days. Workmen were pressed into the service of the Crown, the Knight Marshal's man having a yearly gratuity for apprehending such as obstinately refused to come into His Majesty's Works, while in connection with the lay-out of Lincoln's Inn Fields, the powers of inquisition given to the Commissioners (or any four of them) have already been mentioned. Horace Walpole, too, mentions a Commission on which Jones served, to prevent building on new foundations within two miles of London, and under its powers it caused twenty houses newly erected in St. Martin's Lane to be pulled down. Acts which, on the face of them, were so arbitrary as these, may have helped to swell the tide of dissatisfaction and resentment which eventually overwhelmed the monarchy.

Inigo makes a suggestion in the same spirit to Lord Arundel in a letter of 17th August 1620. Some masons had quitted their work without leave, apparently at the Banqueting House, but, says he, if his lordship would show some exemplary punishment and send the masons up as malefactors it would deter the others from doing the like.  The letter is of considerable interest as it is the only one of a private nature, and written by his own hand, that has been preserved :

To the Right Ho<sup>ble</sup> the Earle of Arundell and Surre, of his Ma<sup>s</sup> most ho<sup>ble</sup> Privi Councell.

Right Ho<sup>ble</sup>,

In my jorney to London, I went to Hā. Courte, whear I hearde that the Spanish imbassador came to Kingson, and sent his stewarde to Hā. Courte, who looked on the loginges intended the imbassador, w<sup>ch</sup> weare in M<sup>r</sup>. Hugines his roomes, but the steward utterly dislyked thos roomes, sainge that the imbassador wold not lye but in the house : besides, ther was no furnitur in thos roomes, of bedding, or otherwyse, nether for the imbassador or his followers, so the stewarde retorning to his lorde, he resolved only to hunt in the parke, and so retorne.  But the keeper answered, he might not suffer that, he having received no order for it ; so the imbassador went bake discontented, having had sum smaul sporte in the warrine.  But since, my lo. of Nottinghā hearing of this, sent to the imbassador, to excuse the matter, w<sup>ch</sup> the imbassador tooke verry well, and promised to cō and lie at Hā. Courte before his ma<sup>ties</sup> retorne ; but in my opinion, the fault was chiefly in the imbassador, in not sending a day or two before, to see how he was provided for, and give notice what wold please him.

Wee have satt on the comsion for buildinges, on Monday last, to put in mynde thos w<sup>h</sup> are bound by recognizance, or otherwyse, to conforme.

The plan of all the incroachments about Paules is fully finished.  I heear that the masons do begin to mak up that part of the east end w<sup>ch</sup> they have demolished, not well— but with uneven courses of stone.  I am now going to the m<sup>r</sup>. of the wardes, to tell him of itt.

M<sup>r</sup>. William was verry merry at his departure, and the busshope and he are the ' greatest ' friends that may be.

After my departure frō London, many of the masons went awaye w^{th}out leave, but since, some of thē ar retorned ; and, for the rest, yf your lo^p do shewe sum exemplary punishment, causing thē to be sent up as malyfactors, it will detter the rest frō ever doing the lyke.

The Banqueting-house goith on now well, though the going of the masons awaye have byne a great henderance to it.

Thus, with my humbel dutye, I rest

Your Honours ever to be commanded,

INIGO JONES.

Ye 17 of August, 1620.

It is hardly a matter of wonder that the Spanish Ambassador was dissatisfied with lodgings that were devoid of all furniture, and although he was afterwards sufficiently placated to promise to lie at Hampton Court, his headquarters were in fact established at Ely House in Holborn, for by a warrant dated the last day of December 1620, a sum of £20 was paid to Inigo Jones, Thomas Baldwin and William Portington, the master carpenter, for making ready and repairing that residence for him.

The Commission for Buildings mentioned in the letter was probably the same which, as already said, caused twenty newly-built houses to be pulled down : and the references to St. Paul's indicate the beginning of those repairs and rebuilding which took up much of Jones's time, and of which the architectural work constituted, according to Webb, one of his chief claims to fame as an architect.

The Mr. William who was so merry and so great a friend of the bishop, was no doubt the ' little Mr. Bill ' of Lord Arundel's letter to his wife already quoted, the boy who was described by the Queen as a ' proper gentleman '.

It is also obvious from this letter of Jones's that he was busy in looking after the Banqueting House, and it was during this year that he received the King's instructions to investigate the origin of Stonehenge, the results of which have already been dealt with in a previous chapter.   His official duties must have kept him fully employed, and among them in the early part of the year was the reporting upon the quality of some glass submitted by Sir Robert Mansfield, an admiral, who was interested in its manufacture and in the monopoly of which he first obtained a share in the year 1615.   Jones and Baldwin signed the report, which pointed out that they found three sorts of glass, some made since Christmas (the report being dated 29th March), some before that time, and some which were broken pieces and of a lower price.   The general quality of each lot was alike, as the best and worst were mixed together, and they were all very thin.   These points were brought to the notice of the glaziers, who, however, showed no desire for amendment, as it would not redound to their benefit.   The signatories then suggest that if the glass were blown to a reasonable thickness, and the best and worst separated into distinct grades suitably priced, it would be much better both for the King's service and for his subjects.   'Which we humbly leave to your lordships' consideration.'   Whether their lordships took this sensible advice or not, there is nothing to show.

During the year 1621 the records afford no information of any particular activity, with the exception of a drawing by Jones of a gateway 'for the M. of the Wardes at Chelsey, 1621' (Plate XI).

This gateway was built for Lionel Cranfield at a house known at one time as Buckingham House and subsequently as Beaufort House. There is a plan of the house in the Thorpe Collection at the Soane Museum (Fol. 63, 64), and Kip gives a view of it on his Plate 13, in which the gateway appears to be identifiable as one leading into the fields at the back of the house. Beaufort House was bought by Sir Hans Sloane in 1736 and pulled down four years later, when the gateway was given to the Earl of Burlington, who re-erected it at his villa of Chiswick with a tablet recording its first building in 1621. It is of no great size, and is one of a series of gateways for which the original drawings by Jones have been preserved, a series which forms a substantial portion of the architectural drawings which can be assigned to him beyond question. Lionel Cranfield, it will be remembered, was a guest at Coryat's Feast : in the year following the erection of the gateway he succeeded Lord Mandeville as Treasurer and was shortly afterwards created Earl of Middlesex.

Although the Banqueting House was not completed until the end of March in 1622, it was so far advanced in January as to allow of a masque being performed there on the 6th of that month. This was the *Masque of Augurs*, written by Ben Jonson, and staged by Inigo Jones, and was the first entertainment of the kind to be given in the new building. There had been an interval of four years since the last of these performances, which may be partly accounted for by the fact that there was no Banqueting House in which to produce them : there was, however, the Great Hall of the palace, which was used for similar purposes, much to the disturbance, one would suppose, of its ordinary daily uses as an eating-place.  Jonson had either recovered for the time from his ill-humour in regard to Jones or had wisely suppressed it, for they worked together in this masque and in those of the two following years.

Later in the year Jones was occupied in altering New Hall in Essex for the Marquis of Buckingham, as George Villiers then was—he did not receive his Dukedom until the following year.  A letter from John Chamberlain to Dudley Carleton of 5th September 1622 mentions the purchase of the house and the alterations then in progress, and throws some light on the visits paid by the King to his great subjects.

The King removed, on Sunday after dinner, from Theobalds to Havering, and so, the next day to dinner at New Hall, the lord Marquis's late purchase, where he confined his number to fifty, for fear of overcharging the owner. This day he comes to town, and to-morrow to Hampton Court.  The purchase of New Hall is accounted a great bargain, when for £20,000 there is £1,200 land a year, besides the value of £7,000 or £5,000 in wood, and house that cost £14,000 in building, which is now altering and translating, according to the modern fashion, by the direction of Inigo Jones, the King's surveyor.

It will be noted that Chamberlain still thinks it well to let Carleton know who Inigo Jones was.

New Hall was a large Elizabethan mansion that must have vied in extent with palaces like Holdenby House and Audley End, if the accounts are anywhere near the truth which say that John Olmius, who

bought the estate in 1737, pulled down nine-tenths
of it and yet reserved enough to make a noble and
commodious country seat for himself. He undoubtedly demolished a large part of the house, and
the demolition must have included whatever work
Jones may have added to it, for there appears to be
nothing left that can be attributed to him.

The only other work that can be definitely assigned
to this year is a drawing of a gateway by Jones
entitled ' for my lo. Stuard for Hatton House 1622,
1623 '.

In January 1623 the King was indisposed and
quitted Whitehall for a time. The Prince, Charles,
was to have had a masque on Twelfth Night, but it
was postponed and in its place the ' Prince's
servants ', a company of professional actors, gave
the play, *A Vowe and a good One.* Chamberlain in
a letter to Carleton of 25th January excuses a long
silence on the ground of the often deferring of the
masque, and indeed, he says, there had been nothing
to record except dancing and feasting which, notwithstanding the King's illness, had never within his
recollection been so frequent, and it still continued.
The soul of the gaiety appears to have been a niece
of the French Ambassador's wife, a Mlle St. Luc, and
as she and her aunt were now due to return home,
the masque could no longer be deferred, and it had
been performed on the previous Sunday. The
French and Venetian ambassadors were spectators
and they said it was ' performed reasonably well '.
Ben Jonson composed the speeches and songs, and
for the ' handsome conveyance and variety of the
scenes ' Inigo Jones had the whole commendation.

The variety was a development of the scenic art due to the ingenuity of Jones. In this masque, *Time vindicated to Himself and to his Honours*, the scene was changed three times ; first there was a view of Whitehall and the new Banqueting House, then the masquers in a cloud, and lastly a forest—a variety of setting that evidently both surprised and pleased the onlookers. The antimasques, which were interludes providing the desirable comic relief, were on this occasion tumblers and jugglers. Then followed dancing among the whole company, both actors and spectators. 'The Prince did lead the measures with the French Ambassador's wife. The measures, branles, corrantos and galliards being ended, the masquers with the ladies did dance two country dances, namely, the Soldiers' Marche and Huff Hamukin, where the French Ambassador's wife and Mademoysala St. Luke did dance.' The exact differences between these dances may be left to the curious in such matters, but they were all bright, gay and brisk, and the gossiping letters which give an account of them afford a glimpse into the happy and careless life of the Court of King James, to which Ben Jonson and Inigo Jones, in the background, gave a touch of abiding interest.

Ben Jonson, who had a considerable tinge of sourness in his disposition, seemed likely to get into trouble over his part of the business, for, says Chamberlain, he ' is like to hear of it on both sides of the head, for personating George Withers, a poet, or poetaster he terms him, as hunting after some, by being a *chronomastix*, or whipper of the time, which is become so tender an argument, that it must not

be admitted either in jest or earnest '.[1]   Only one
drawing by Jones for this masque has been preserved.

Some three weeks later, Prince Charles quitted
these scenes of gaiety on an errand at once serious
in regard to politics and of the first importance to
him personally.   This was his visit to Spain in
furtherance of the proposed alliance between him
and the Infanta, ' the Lady Mary of Spain '.   He
travelled incognito, attended by the Duke of Buckingham and a few others.   By way of Boulogne he
posted to Paris, ' where staying one day, he had a
transient view of that excellent Lady, the Princess
Henrietta Maria at a Mask '.   In this casual manner
he seems to have made the acquaintance of the lady
who subsequently became his Queen.

There is no need here to enter upon the reasons of
state which prompted the Spanish Alliance, nor the
delays that hindered it, nor its final abandonment.
Charles stayed nearly eight months in pursuit of his
object, and in the meantime great preparations were
made in England for the reception of his expected
bride, preparations which entailed much work upon
Inigo Jones.   In May the Spanish Ambassador was
busy in arranging for her lodgings at St. James's and
Denmark (otherwise Somerset) House, where many
alterations were required, and in particular a new
chapel was to be built at each place, ' for which order
is taken with the surveyor, Inigo Jones, to have
them done out of hand and yet with great state and
costliness.   The Savoy chapel, likewise, shall be

[1] George Wither, author of the charming song, ' Shall I, wasting
in despair,' had written a satire, ' Abuses stript and whipt,' for
which he was imprisoned.

converted to the use of her household.' By the
16th of the month the foundation of the new chapel
at St. James's was laid, and on that day the Spanish
Ambassador was present and ' made a cross on the
first stone, laid it in mortar, made a prayer in French,
that God would dispose of that foundation to his glory,
and the good of the church and universal good of
all Christians, and gave £80. to the workmen ; his
son laid the second stone, and gave them £80 '.

In spite of the tolerant nature of the Ambassador's
sentiments, there was among the English a profound
dislike and mistrust of Spain and of Roman Catholics
generally, and when the Prince eventually returned
from his abortive mission all the people went wild
with joy.   In the meantime, however, the arrival of
the Infanta had been expected, and in June some half-
dozen great lords were sent as a deputation to receive
her at Southampton, and to arrange suitable lodgings
for her.   She was to be welcomed with shows and
pageants, to which end Inigo Jones and ' Allen the
old player ' accompanied their lordships.   Jones no
doubt was also expected to supervise the mending
of the highways, which was another, and probably
highly desirable, form of welcome.   Chamberlain,
who conveys all this information, expresses the
opinion that Jones and Allen ' alone (with two or
three herbingers or such like officers) might have
performed all this as well as so many prime coun-
saillors, but that we must show how diligent and
obsequious we are in any thing that concernes her '.
All these preparations, however, came to nothing, as
the Infanta did not pay her contemplated visit to
these shores.   But the visit to Southampton was

not altogether barren of results to Inigo, for opportunity was taken of his presence to confer the
freedom of the city upon him.

The work that Jones did at the various chapels
has disappeared ; the best of it—that at Somerset
House—being destroyed when Sir William Chambers
rebuilt that palace as Government offices.

It was during the busy time entailed by the
Infanta's expected arrival that the chapel at
Lincoln's Inn Fields was consecrated, and it is to
this period that the water-gate of York House is
assigned, one of the few undoubtedly genuine works
of Inigo's design that has survived (Plate XII). It
was the river entrance to the residence of the Duke of
Buckingham. All the large houses that then lined
the south side of the Strand had gardens running
down to the Thames, with stairs leading to the water.
The river was a much used highway in those days
for places contiguous to it, and although there were
many stairs along its course, there could have been
none so finely designed as those of York House. But
there were few owners so wealthy as the Duke of
Buckingham or of so much influence at Court as to
obtain the services of the King's surveyor. When it
was built the gate led down to the foreshore, and,
when the tide was up, to the water itself : but since
the formation of the Embankment, the river is
severed from the water-gate by gardens and the
broad roadway. The level of the ground also has
been so much raised as to leave the building in a
hole as seen from the river side, and only six steps
of descent remain out of the many that were requisite.
On the landward side the few steps of ascent that led

to the archway have been swallowed up in the floor of the present passage.

The gateway itself is a solid, handsome work of excellent proportion conceived in the correct Italian manner, but with some originality of treatment. The principal, or river front, displays the arms of Villiers, the Duke's family name, on a cartouche surrounded by the garter and beneath a ducal coronet. The charge from the shield, an escallop or shell, is used as an ornament in several places. On the landward side are the arms of Villiers impaling those of his wife, a daughter of the Earl of Rutland. Other shields and cartouches bear an anchor in recognition of his office as Lord High Admiral of England. On the frieze at the back is incised his motto, ' Fidei Coticula Crux '—the Cross is the touchstone of faith. Although it is difficult to imagine the ' Steenie ' of James I enduring any kind of cross with patience, yet his pet-name having been suggested by his beautiful face, which resembled the pictures of St. Stephen, a motto with a suggestion of martyrdom about it was perhaps not inappropriate.

York House itself has long been destroyed and its site covered with buildings and streets, but the water-gate escaped destruction and still stands at the lower end of Buckingham Street. The Duke appears to have been contemplating a new house, for which probably he would have obtained the assistance of Jones, but such intentions as he may have had never came to fruition. He had on his staff, as many great people had besides the King, a surveyor (or architect), Balthazar Gerbier, a man of considerable gifts, but, if Horace Walpole is right, of indifferent character. His ability in one direction or another was at any rate enough to bring him a knighthood in later years. According to his own account, Gerbier designed a house for the Duke on the site of the old residence, and so admirable was it that when Jones went to see it in the year 1624 he was both astonished and abashed, and filled with jealousy.

Later in his life Gerbier wrote a book about building, in which, among much that borders on the ridiculous, he criticizes the new Banqueting House. He takes exception to the columns, the weight of which might draw down the wall on the heads of those that pass by. He says the room is too vast, the King and his retinue being lost in it. It was, moreover, unsuitable for the display of masques, which, in his opinion, had become too elaborate in their stage effects. So unsuitable was it that Inigo Jones had been constrained to build a wooden house in the courtyard for their production. He himself had designed a room near York Gate not above thirty-five feet square which Charles I of blessed memory had declared in the year 1648 to be as suitable for masques as the Banqueting House, and there were people still alive who remembered the incident.

However jealous Jones may have been of Gerbier, it is obvious that Gerbier was jealous of Jones : yet in regard to the size, and especially the height, of the Banqueting House there may have been a substratum of justification for his carping.

In the summer of this year, 1623, Jones was building a stable at Theobalds, the favourite house of

James I, and he says in a letter of the 16th August
that the work was so well forward that it would be
finished in three weeks' time. He himself had been
there on the previous Thursday to look at the building and at the repairs of the coping of the (park) wall.
If these could be carried as far as the ' six mile stone '
by the end of the month, which the workmen had
promised to do, that was as much as could be safely
done that year ; ' this your honour may be pleased
to signify also unto his Majesty '. It was doubtless
a wise precaution not to build late in the year
anything so much exposed to the weather as the
coping of a wall, but to cease building-work altogether
so early as the end of August would hardly suit the
exigencies of the present day.

# CHAPTER X

**P**RINCE CHARLES having returned from Spain
in the October of 1623 a masque was prepared
in the following January by Ben Jonson and
Inigo Jones in celebration of the event, entitled
*Neptune's Triumph for the Return of Albion*. It is
said to have been performed on Twelfth Night, but
this is not quite certain ; in any case, the scene
designed by Jones, a Maritime Palace, was used a
year later in another masque of Jonson's, *The Fortunate Isles and their Union*. The only other incident
recorded during the year 1624 is a settlement between
the Lord Treasurer and Inigo Jones for the payment
of £1,901 9s. 8d. expended by the latter on ' Maskes
for Queene Anne, and Prince Henry, and at the
marriage of the lady Elizabeth, and for the Barriers
for the said Prince '. Most of this money had no
doubt been paid to the workmen, and Jones had
apparently received instalments, but the final settlement had drifted on for more than twelve years, for
the Prince had died in November 1612, and the Lady
Elizabeth had been married in the following
February.

By the beginning of 1625 King James's infirmities
had so much increased upon him that he removed

from Whitehall to Theobalds ; but his indisposition
put little check upon the gaieties of the Court, which
entailed upon Jones further designs for the masque
of *The Fortunate Isles* on the 9th January.

But the gaiety was soon changed to mourning, for
on the 27th March the King died at Theobalds.
About a month later his body was conveyed by
torch-light, ' for the greater state ', to Somerset
House, where it lay until the 7th May, when it was
carried to Westminster and there interred with great
solemnity.   The historian who recounts these events
mentions more than once the hearse, which indeed
seems to have excited universal admiration, for
Chamberlain tells Dudley Carleton that the funeral
was ' the greatest ever known in England, there being
blacks distributed to over nine thousand persons ;
the hearse, likewise, being the fairest and best
fashioned that hath been seen, wherein Inigo Jones,
the surveyor, did his part.'   The whole charge, he
adds, is said to arise above £50,000.

Fortunately Jones's own drawings for the hearse
are preserved at Worcester College, Oxford ; they
comprise a drawing to scale (Plate XIII) and a perspective sketch of the dome.   It was indeed a
remarkable structure, a kind of octagonal temple
with a dome carried on columns, the whole resting
on a square base.   At each of the four corners was
a large female figure bearing an emblem, and at the
base of the dome each angle held a smaller figure
with hands folded on her bosom.   The royal arms,
the royal initials, crowned, and numerous small flags
together with panels bearing inscriptions, all combined to produce a rich effect.   The figures are

admirably rendered, as is nearly always the case with
Inigo Jones ; indeed he seems, as already said, to
have taken greater delight in drawing the human
figure than architectural details.

The news of the King's demise came to Whitehall
while Bishop Laud was preaching a sermon, the day
being Sunday, and the service was abandoned ' in
compliance with the sadness of the congregation ' ;
but the melancholy event did not interrupt the
arrangements that were in hand for Charles's marriage to Henrietta Maria.   On the 1st May his proxy
espoused her at the church of Notre Dame in Paris,
soon after which she crossed from Boulogne to Dover,
where Charles met her with a magnificent train and
conducted her to Canterbury, where ' the royal
nuptials were most gloriously accomplished '.   From
Canterbury the royal pair went to Gravesend and
thence by barge to Somerset House, but as the plague
was prevalent in London they removed after a few
days to Hampton Court.

The death of the King was naturally a matter of
much concern to the Court and its officials, but upon
Inigo Jones it seems to have had little effect, unless
indeed to strengthen his position, for he was, if
anything, more of a *persona grata* with Charles than
with his father.

During the next five years there is very little on
record concerning Inigo Jones and his work, but,
unless a Commission which was now appointed was
less busy than it appears to have been, many duties
of an official kind must have devolved upon him.   On
30th May 1625, a commission was appointed to carry

out the terms of a Royal Proclamation recently published concerning buildings and inmates within the city of London and confines of the same. King Charles was resolved to pursue the course begun by Elizabeth and continued by James for reducing the houses of the city and its confines to a more orderly and uniform manner of building with Brick for more ornament, strength, safety and continuance. He was also resolved to reduce the number of undesirable inmates, for the city, which, being his Chamber and Seat of his Empire, should be kept with most state and honour, had become more pestered with indigent and base people, who lived by begging, filching, gaming and other unlawful courses, than the meanest of other towns in the Kingdom. Power was accordingly given to any four or more of the Commissioners, who numbered over fifty and included the Earl of Arundel, the Earl of Clare, Lord Maltravers, Sir Henry Spiller, Laurence Whitaker and Inigo Jones, to inquire what buildings had been set up since the 13th year of King James within the city or suburbs or ' within the distance of two miles to be taken from any gate of the said city or from our palace of Westminster'. The Commission was also to ascertain what cellars were used for lodgings or victualling places, and what houses, buildings, street doors and windows were being built in any other way than that directed by the Proclamation. Power was given to the Commissioners or any four of them to commit to prison owners and workmen who presumed to proceed after being ordered to cease.

Other inquiries to be made were as to defaults by brickmakers in the quality of their wares or in sell-

ing them at unreasonable prices : also as to overcrowding in the Commission's area, and as to the
possible slackness of inferior officers in laying
informations, and of justices or aldermen in not
enforcing the regulations. In order that the work
of the Commission should be effective, the members
were to meet and report, so that those persons who
conformed to the regulations might be encouraged,
and those who were refractory and contemptuous
might be punished.

This kind of paternal and autocratic administra-
tion, which placed the liberty of the subject (under
certain conditions) at the mercy of any four out of
some fifty commissioners, selected by the King and
his immediate advisers, was little likely to commend
itself to that growing body of opinion which regarded
such high-handed actions as the negation of liberty.
The aim of the King—to improve the conditions and
the appearance of the City—was admirable, but his
methods were exasperating.

All the practical work of the Commission in relation
to houses and their doors, windows and cellars—a
long and laborious undertaking—would naturally fall
upon Jones, and another instruction to the Commission affected him in particular and was calculated
to throw duties upon him that must have occupied
much of his time. This was to the effect that any
four of its members ' whereof the Surveyor of Our
Workes to be one ' were to allot, in cases of rebuilding
within the City and the four adjoining counties
of Middlesex, Surrey, Essex and Kent, so much
ground for the foundations of a house as might
best be suitable for the uniformity and decency of

the buildings, the convenience of the place and the width of the street. It is evident that the office of surveyor of His Majesty's works was no sinecure.

The matter-of-fact duties imposed by this Commission must have involved him in much dull work ; and but little alleviation was afforded by the preparation of masques, for these were discontinued until 1631, except that in February 1626 a French Pastoral was performed at Somerset House, for which a drawing of the scene by Jones is preserved in the Chatsworth Collection (Plate XIV). The author is unknown, from which it may be inferred that it was not Ben Jonson. The scene is a charming piece of work with a vista of thatched cottages interrupted near the foreground by a Classic temple on one side and on the other by a small country house with an open pergola on the upper floor, the kind of house which Jones may have met with in his Italian journeys. The proscenium (with its side curtains) consists of a Classic cornice broken in the centre by a cartouche, supported by two amorini armed with shepherd's crooks. The title is written at the side in Jones's hand, ' Pastoral sceane Som : House, 1625 ' (i.e. Feb. 1626).

There are no other drawings that can be definitely assigned to this year, but his name appears in quite another connection. It is the second on a list of persons living in the Parish of St. Martin who refused to pay towards mending the highways. The reasons for this refusal do not appear, but the objection was widespread and was supported by the more important inhabitants, including many persons of title.

Whether the objection was upheld or overruled is unknown.

The gap in the series of drawings, whether of architecture or of masques, is broken by an elevation of a plain and simple archway entitled ' for the Park St James 1627 ', and by a clock-turret for Whitehall —' June 1 1627 for the clokehouse whight hale '— a well-proportioned design showing a large cubical base for the clock, surmounted by an arched and domed covering for the bell, against which can be seen the head of the hammer for striking the hours.

Some fortnight later than the date of the turret the routine side of Jones's duties comes in evidence in the shape of a certificate signed by him and his customary colleagues, condemning the continued use of a stove in a house in St. Martin's Lane, as being too dangerous in a place largely built of wood. It had been installed by a Frenchman, who, however, promised to dismantle it. This incident brings forcibly to mind that London was at that time largely composed of wooden houses, and that vigilance was required of all officials to minimize the risk of fire. Bearing these facts in mind, it is not difficult to understand the rapidity with which the Great Fire spread in 1666, or the vast size of the devastated area.

The year 1628 was, as it happens, an important one for Inigo Jones, although the records are silent as to his work. For it was in this year that John Webb, a youth of seventeen, came to him as a pupil. He came under august patronage, for in his petition and brief, already mentioned, as being presented to Charles II in the year 1660 in furtherance of his suit for the office of Surveyor of the Works, Webb says

he ' was by the especiall comand of yo$^r$ Ma$^{ties}$ Royall
Father of ever blessed memory, brought up by Inigo
Jones Esq$^r$, Yo$^r$ Ma$^{ties}$ late Surveyor of the works in
y$^e$ study of Architecture, for enabling him to do yo$^r$
Royall Father and yo$^r$ Ma$^{tie}$ service in y$^e$ said office ' :
and again, ' that he was brought up by his Unckle
Mr. Inigo Jones upon his late Maiestyes com̃and in
the study of Architecture, as well that w$^{ch}$ relates
to building as for masques Tryumphs and the like '.

This very interesting statement, which could not
have been made under the circumstances unless it
were substantially true, suggests several matters for
consideration. Did the King's command refer to
Webb in particular, or was Jones instructed to train
up some one of his own choice to carry on his work ?
In either case it is clear that Charles I regarded
Jones's work of so much value that he was anxious
to have it continued by a carefully trained successor.
Then, how did Jones hear of Webb, if the selection
lay with him ? Webb speaks of him as his uncle ;
some confusion has existed as to the relationship
between the two, and Webb has been spoken of as
Jones's son-in-law. But Jones was never married,
and Webb's wife was a kinswoman of his of the same
family name, Anne Jones. The kinship may have
been that of a niece, which would account for Webb's
use of the term uncle, Jones being the wife's uncle.[1]
On the whole this seems the most likely explanation,
as there is no reason for supposing that any blood
relationship existed between Jones and Webb. In
any case, no master ever had a more devoted pupil.

[1] Vertue, in mentioning Webb's wife, calls her Jones's daughter,
which, however, he corrects to ' niece '.

The connection was lifelong, with affection on one side and unbounded admiration on the other. It is hardly too much to say that to his pupil Jones owes much of his fame, partly from Webb's writings and partly from his drawings which became mistakenly attributed to his master.

Another matter of interest in Webb's ' Brief ' is the coupling of Masques and Triumphs with architecture, as being equally important items in the Surveyor's duties. Unless this point of view is fully realized, no true picture of Inigo Jones as an artist can be obtained.

Another event of this year, 1628, was of the first concern to Inigo Jones, and that was the assassination of the Duke of Buckingham on the 23rd August. Buckingham was heartily hated by the people at large. He was a prime favourite at Court, he was a supporter of the arbitrary measures of the King, and was held to be a friend to Popery. The ill-feeling he inspired was in no way lessened by brilliance in the conduct of affairs ; on the contrary, the disastrous result of his expedition to the Island of Rhé in relief of the besieged at Rochelle was the culmination of his misdeeds, and it was while he was busy in completing the arrangements for retrieving the disaster, that he was slain by John Felton, a Lieutenant of Foot. He was at Portsmouth, and as he was coming downstairs from his chamber and passing to his parlour, he was stabbed to the heart by Felton, who at once fled, leaving the knife sticking in his victim's back. Felton was speedily secured and was executed at Tyburn, declaring in extenuation that he did the deed ' For the cause of God and his country '. Bucking-

ham was but thirty-six years old when he died, and
with him Inigo Jones lost a powerful patron and
friend.

It was at some time during the preceding five years,
that is between Buckingham's creation as a Duke
and his death, that Jones made one of his most
beautiful drawings, an elaborate ceiling for an un-
identified room of the Duke's (Plate XV). It is in the
Worcester College collection, and comprises four
panels and a length of cornice. The panels are filled
with the same design, but the colours, gold, silver and
blue, are varied. In the frieze of the cornice,
opposite the ribs of the ceiling, are shields of arms
similar to those on the water-gate, his own arms
within a garter and surmounted by a ducal coronet,
and his own arms impaling those of his wife. Below
the cornice on a plain, white member is his motto,
' Fidei Coticula Crux.' Beneath all is the top of
an architrave of an arch. The whole is admirably
drawn and coloured, and it is a misfortune that the
house for which it was intended, and where it may
possibly have been in fact executed, cannot be
identified.

Much as Jones must have mourned the death of
the Duke, that event does not seem to have lessened
his activities, for although the next two years do not
afford much evidence of what he was doing, the time
was shortly to come in which the records are more
abundant. Meanwhile his routine duties involved,
during 1629, the preparation of a report from the
Commissioners of Buildings, which is of considerable
interest from several points of view. It appears that
Sir Kenelm Digby was proposing to erect some new

buildings on an open space at the back of Drury Lane, an exemplification of the prevalent custom of persons building very much according to their own fancies. In London, however, restrictions on this habit had been established, and the report states that already various persons who had attempted to build on this particular site had been committed to Newgate by the Justices of the Peace for Middlesex 'until they had demolished an enclosure there begun'. It then goes on to say that the court threatened by Sir Kenelm's enclosure had been intended to be planted with trees 'for pleasant and wholesome walkes for the comoditie' of the inhabitants, who were still wedded to the idea : and therefore the Commissioners humbly certified to His Majesty that the erecting of any building on this open space would tend to the defeating of His Majesty's serious purpose declared both by his Proclamation and Commission for Buildings. As it should not be for a moment supposed that a measure of justice could be meted out to Sir Kenelm different from that which the justices had applied to insignificant persons, it can only be concluded that he had not incurred the risk of being committed to Newgate by actually starting his building.

The report is signed by five persons in addition to Inigo Jones, whose name comes second on the list ; four of these are of no particular interest, but the fifth, who signs first, is Laurence Whitaker, presumably the same learned person and elegant linguist who was instrumental in persuading Coryat to give his 'Crudities' to the world.

By this time Jones had been made a Justice of the

Peace for Westminster, the date of his appointment, however, not transpiring.  The duties, although honourable, were attended with unpleasant risks, as may be gathered from a report issued by the justices to the Privy Council, dated 2nd November 1630, and signed by Jones and others.  It deals with the measures taken by the justices to prevent the spread of the plague, a visitation to which London was constantly subject.  It will be remembered that a few years earlier King Charles and his bride had proceeded by barge from Gravesend to London, but had speedily retired to Hampton Court as the plague (to use the word of the old chronicler) was so ' hot ' in London.

The measures taken by the Westminster Justices were fairly thorough.  Not entirely trusting their searchers in cases where a patient had died, they appointed others of good judgment, and a view was taken where necessary in the presence of some of the justices themselves, thus rendering deceit impossible. All suspected houses were searched, shut up and guarded, and on such as had been the scene of a death was placed a red cross.  All burials were con- ducted at fixed hours, at 11 p.m. and 4 a.m. in the summer, and ' now in winter ' about 10 at night and before 6 in the morning.  Burial followed death almost immediately, and ' some of us ever present to prevent such fond persons as would accompany the corpse ' from so doing ; a rule which had become rather grudgingly accepted by those concerned.

In houses where a death had occurred the occu- pants were isolated and locked in, and it was not until a personal inspection by some of the justices had satisfied them that quarantine had been effectual, that those in detention were liberated.

Then follows a list of delinquents against the regulations, some of whom were put in the stocks for their offences. One of these, a widow woman of Westminster, Elizabeth Stangley by name, was punished as a vagrant, and set in the stocks in the market during market time with a paper inscription on her head to the effect that she had quite recently broken out of an infected house and had mingled with a large congregation in the Abbey.

From all of which it appears that the segregation and isolation insisted upon in the present day were already recognized as necessary for the reduction of infectious diseases, and that the unpleasant duties now performed by the medical officer and his staff were carried out by Inigo Jones and his fellow-justices.

Jones's colleague, Thomas Baldwin, had likewise been made a justice, for in company with Inigo he signed a report at this time on the action taken by the justices in respect of the sale of grain, with a view to preventing and remedying a dearth of it. The regulations had been strictly enforced and various persons had been committed for offences against them.

It is evident, therefore, that in addition to his official duties, Jones had now to spend much of his time in public work of a useful if unprofitable kind, and some of it at no little risk to his health.

Just at this time his official duties must have kept him fully occupied, for he was preparing designs for the costumes and scenery of two masques, both written by Ben Jonson. One of these was *Love's Triumph through Callipolis*, performed on 6th January 1631, for which there are preserved some thirteen of Inigo's drawings, mostly of lovers with particular characteristics indicated by him with his customary disregard of accurate spelling. Among them are the jelious lover, the sordod lover and the melancholi lover. The other masque, entitled *Chloridia*, was performed on the 22nd of the ensuing February, and was a more important and elaborate affair. It was important both in itself, for the Queen took the principal part, and in the fact that it was the last in which Jonson and Jones worked together. It was elaborate, for no less than twenty-six drawings by Jones are assigned to it in the Walpole Society's book, among them being a masterly sketch for part of the proscenium.

This masque has a somewhat pathetic interest, for its immediate predecessor, *Love's Triumph*, when published, fanned into flames those fires of disagreement which had long been smouldering, and had now become an impassable barrier between the two great artists.

The actual breath which caused the blaze seems trivial enough and it might have dissipated itself harmlessly in space had not the materials for the outbreak been ready. It is thus indicated by Mr. Pory in a letter to Sir John Puckering, written a year later, on 12th January 1632 :

The last Sunday, at night, the King's Masque was acted in the Banqueting House, the Queen's being suspended till another time, by reason of a soreness which fell into one of her delicate eyes. The inventor or poet of this Masque was Mr. Aurelian Townshend, sometime steward to the Lord Treasurer Salisbury ; Ben Jonson being for this time discarded, by reason of the predominant power of his antagonist, Inigo Jones, who, this time twelvemonth, was angry with him for putting his own name before his in the title-page ; which Ben Jonson has made the subject of a bitter satire or two against Inigo.

Jones was so firmly fixed in Court favour, and had so good an opinion of his share in these entertainments, that he was both ready and able to assert himself. His ascendancy was complete and never again did Jonson take part in the production of masques for the Court, although they were continued for several years. His inventions were supplanted by those of others who were more ready to pay a suitable tribute to the artist. But, on the whole, at this distance of time and judging by Jones's own drawings and the opinions expressed by contemporary observers, the scales would appear to dip, as regards the attraction of the production, in favour of the deviser of the scenery, machinery and costumes.

The blow must have been a shrewd one to Jonson, who took it by no means meekly. He expressed his opinion of Jones both obliquely in his *Tale of a Tub*, and directly in good round terms, in an *Expostulation with Inigo Jones* and one or two epigrams, of which more hereafter.

The footing upon which Jones stood with royalty is indicated in the tone of a note of his written on a sketch of the Queen's dress for *Chloridia* (Plate XVI), which was sent to her for approval ; it is respectful, but by no means servile :

The dessigne I conceaue to bee fitt for the inuention and if it please hir Ma^y to add or alter anything I desier to receave hir ma^{ls} comand and the dessigne again by this bearer. The collors allso are in hir Ma^{ls} choise ; but my oppinion is that seueral fresh greenes mix with gould and siluer will bee most propper.

It is worth noting that in the draft of this note the words ' but I should humbly ' are struck out in favour of ' but my opinion is '. There are three or four sketches for the royal dress, in all of which the figure drawn is that of a lady inclining to portliness. As an example of how Jones expressed himself, and of the inconsistency of his spelling, the following note on another sketch may be cited, certain words which he struck out being omitted :

The sceane Zefferus appeares and Cals fourth the springe and tells hir the decree of Jupiter to adorne the yearth with stares as well as the heuen the Spring descendes and Zefyr passeth a way.

# CHAPTER XI

FROM the many official duties which devolved upon Jones, there emerge durng this year of 1631 several of considerable interest. It appears that Mr. Scipio Le Squyer Gent. had during the month of May erected a building upon new foundations in Long Acre, contrary to His Majesty's proclamation already mentioned. The building was faced with brick and had a frontage to the road of 24 feet and a depth into the garden of 33 feet or thereabouts. The matter was referred to Inigo Jones and two of his colleagues, Sir Henry Spiller and Laurence Whitaker, who reported to the Commissioners for Building, for transmission to the Privy Council, that they had viewed the building of Mr. Scipio Squire, which, he told them, was for himself to dwell in. It was of brick and practically of the size mentioned in the reference. There was an acre of ground adjoining the house enclosed with a brick wall and planted with fruit trees, ' whereby the same is made a fitt and convenyent habitation for a person of qualitie '. Mr. Squire does not deny that it is built upon a new foundation, and the signatories humbly leave the further consideration to their Lordships' good pleasure. It will be remembered

152

that at the instance of the same Commission twenty new houses were pulled down in the neighbouring street of St. Martin's Lane, but as to whether their Lordships meted out the same measure to a person of quality like Mr. Squire the records are silent.

About the same time the Commissioners reported to the Privy Council on another and more flagrant breach of regulations. One William Cooke, stationer, had built a shed of timber in the open street in High Holborn, close to Furnival's Inn, with the consent, he alleged, of the Society. About nine weeks before this report, he had been committed to Newgate until he should demolish the shed ; there he still lay and the shed continued. The Commissioners suggest that the Council should order either the Principal of the Society or the Sheriffs of London to take it down. This suggestion, signed by Jones, Whitaker, and G. Longe, had much to commend it in view of the restriction already imposed upon the activities of the prisoner ; but curiosity as to the result is balked by the absence of information.

So again with a third case, even more flagrant than the last, in which one David Mallard was the delinquent. It seems that a year or two previously a certain Frenchman named John Bonneall had taken some ground in St. James's field under pretence of making a Pall Mall. Instead of doing this, he proceeded to enclose a piece of ground with boards on part of the ditch that divided the field from His Majesty's highway, and to build a shed, contrary to the instructions of the Commissioners for Building. He pretended that this shed, together with other hovels, was merely a store-place for gardener's tools, whereas they were actually used as a 'tippling house', and one, it was said, of very ill fame. In the midst of his malpractices it would seem that the Frenchman died, whereupon David Mallard, pretending that it was the work of the widow, had proceeded with the building and had now begun the foundations of a brick dwelling-house, 16 feet wide and 84 feet long, which would greatly deface the prospect of His Majesty's house 'as you come to Charing Cross'. But this was not the end of his ill-doings, for he had stopped up the ditch that should carry away the water, and had built offensive back-premises near the highway. All this was a bad example and against His Majesty's proclamation, and as he was still bringing materials to continue the house, would their Lordships be pleased to order the sheriffs of London to take it down.

This report, signed by Inigo Jones, L. Whitaker, Tho: Baldwin and Jenner, shows that there was as woeful a disregard of the landscape in those days as there is in our own; for David Mallard was responsible for buildings which were not only likely to create a nuisance, but were an eyesore to the public in general and the King's household in particular.

The report on William Cooke's building is dated 28th May 1631, that on Mr. Scipio Squire's 13th June. Within the same fortnight, on 31st May, there started a business which was destined to bring Inigo Jones into more trouble than any other affair with which he was concerned, and one which, more than anything else, made him obnoxious to the fiercer Puritans—the business of St. Gregory's Church in the City. On

the last day of May a warrant was directed to him
by the Commissioners for Pious Uses, under which
he was to proceed with all convenient speed to survey
the church of St. Gregory in regard to a matter
whereof he was held able to make good judgment
by his long experience and practice in things of that
nature. The church actually adjoined St. Paul's
Cathedral, which was now to be repaired and restored to its ancient dignity, a work which involved
the removal of certain houses which were disgraces
and even profanations to a place of that importance.
Jones was instructed to report as to whether any
prejudice arose to the Cathedral or its foundations
from the fact that St. Gregory's adjoined it, and as
to what disgrace or inconvenience the church would
be when the Cathedral had been renovated. If he
found it undesirable to retain the church as a lean-to
to so goodly a fabric, he was to suggest some other
site for the church, or alternatively a scheme for
allotting the parishioners to other parishes.

Such was the gist of the warrant ; his report in
answer to it is interesting as expressing his views as
an artist in relation to a question of æsthetics, and
his care as a practical man for the safety of the
Cathedral. The report, which is in his own words,
and is not the joint production of himself and others,
runs thus :

According to yo$^r$ L'ps order I have viewed S$^t$ Gregories
church neer S$^t$ Paules, and doe finde, that the said church,
being in some danger of ruyne, by reason of an Arch w$^{ch}$
was decayed, and much of the timbers perished, the
parishioners are now in repairing of the same.

As for the neerness of the Situacon Joyning to the walls

of S<sup>t</sup> Paules : I conceave it no way hurtfull to the foundačon, or walls of the said church, nor stopping of any lights ; they intending to cover with lead the said church, w<sup>ch</sup> before was tiled, and so to leave the roofe flatt and lower.

Touching the taking away the beauty of thaspect of S<sup>t</sup> Paules, when it shalbe repaired and the howses demolished ; it butteth on an auntient Tower, called the Lollards Tower, the w<sup>ch</sup> is answered on the other side w<sup>th</sup> an other Tower, unto w<sup>ch</sup> my lo : Bishopps hall doth adioyne : And I doe conceave, that neither of them are any hinderance to the beauty of thaspect of the said Church ; neither can I finde any more convenient place thereabouts for the said Church of S<sup>t</sup> Gregories to stand in then where it now doeth.

Lastly, I finding a vault now digging for burialls (as the p'shioners say) close to the foundačon of S<sup>t</sup> Paules Church, have forbidden them the pr'ceding therein, and ordered them to fill in the earth again and make their vault (if they will have it) on the other side, w<sup>ch</sup> they are willing to doe.

All w<sup>ch</sup> I humbly leave to yo<sup>r</sup> Lo'ps further consideračon.

INIGO JONES.

xiiij Junii 1631.

The concurrence of the parishioners with Jones's prohibition in regard to the vault was not so complete as he imagined, for they shortly afterwards submitted a petition to the Privy Council in which they set forth that having had occasion to repair their church and having intended to make a vault for the interment of their dead, they had been stopped by Inigo Jones Esqr. on the ground of prejudice arising to the foundations of the Cathedral. Some of them had assented to making the vault on the other side of the church, but as divers skilful workmen had certified that the intended vault would do no harm to St. Paul's, whereas if moved to the other situation it would endanger their own church, they prayed to be allowed to go on with the vault as originally intended. The churchyard was small and the parish had much increased. The matter called for expedition as they had no certain place to repair to for divine service until the church was finished.

The Privy Council, however, considered that they had not made out their case and accordingly ordered them to desist from digging the vault and to find out some other expedient for interring their dead.

This was in July ; a report having been received that the parishioners were paying no attention to the somewhat arbitrary order, but were still persisting in excavating the vault, the Commissioners for Pious Uses instructed Inigo Jones in the following January to repair to St. Gregory's and renew the former prohibition. Jones complied with the instruction and reported on 25th February 1632, as follows :

May it please y$^r$ lord$^{pps}$ accordinge to y$^r$ orders of the 13$^{th}$. of January 1631, I wente unto the church of S$^t$ Gregoryes nere unto S$^t$ Paules London to viewe a vaulte w$^{ch}$ was formerly begunne to be digged by the p̄ishioners there for the buriall of the Dead, w$^{ch}$ I find to be stopped up accordinge to an order made by y$^r$ Lord:$^{ps}$ at the counsell Table, I also find that the sayd parishioners have made a newe vaulte for the use aforesayd, w$^{ch}$ goeth outwharte the church from the South of S$^t$ Paules toward the streete nere to Lollards Tower ; 50$^{tie}$ foote in length, and 14 : foote in breadth or thereabouts, And this I caused two sufficiente workemen of his Ma$^{ts}$ to viewe and searche ; And they found that in digginge they had bared 3. settings of from the South side of the cathedrall church of S$^t$ Paules, And upon the East and South side of Lollordes Tower. 5. foote deepe from the fixte setting of above the ground, The w$^{ch}$ although I cannot say there is any presente danger to ye church or tower by digginge the sayd vaulte, yet in my

opinion I hold it not fitte that the foundacͬon of soe great
and noble a worke should be underwroughte upon any
occasion whatsoeer, seeinge the parishioners might have
digged their vaulte towards their churchyard, And not have
come nere to the walles of the sayd churche or the Tower,
All wᶜʰ I leave to yʳ Lordᵖˢ consideracͬon.

INIGO JONES.

Jones's desire to avoid anything that could even
remotely endanger the stability of old St. Paul's was
admirable, and it commended itself so much to the
Commissioners for Pious Uses that in the following
April they ordered him to view certain cellars under
the houses at the west end of the Cathedral, to
consider what danger might be caused to its foundations, and thereupon to take effectual measures to
have the cellars firmly filled up at the expense of the
owners, and to report to the Board when the work
was completed.

Here again Jones found himself engaged upon
work of an arbitrary nature, but which no doubt
he thoroughly approved : his own disposition
would lead him to obey his orders without much
scruple.

The subsequent history of the St. Gregory's affair
goes to confirm this estimate of his disposition, and
although it anticipates the general course of events
by nearly ten years, it may as well be told here. In
December 1641 Jones was cited to appear before the
House of Lords to hear a Declaration read which had
been brought up against him from the House of
Commons, concerning a complaint of the parishioners
of St. Gregory's against him. Their church, adjoining St. Paul's, had always been the parish church,

and the population of the parish had been lately computed to be 3,000.

The said Inigo Jones, being Surveyor of His Majestie's Works, and particularly those to be designed for the re-edifying of the said Church of St. Paul's, would not undertake the work, unless he might be, as he termed it, the Sole Monarch, or might have the Principality thereof, conceiving that the work would not be well done, without pulling down the said Church of St. Gregorie's, presented a Plott to his Majesty accordingly.

The King concurred in the suggestion, and orders were issued by the Council for the pulling down. The parishioners refused to obey, and then, in or about March 1639, Inigo Jones

did pull down and caused to be pulled down part of the Church, and threatened that if the parishioners would not take down the rest of it, then the Galleries should be sawed down, and with skrews the materials of the said Church should be thrown down into the street . . . that if they did not take down the said Church they should be laid by the heels.

The parishioners, so they said, were frightened and were obliged to take down some part of the church, thus rendering it useless, and they were destitute of any place in the parish for the public exercise of Religion. The cost of rebuilding and reinstating would be at least £3,000, and it was desired that proceedings should be taken to compel its restoration at the charge of him and them by whom it was taken down.

On the reading being concluded Inigo Jones desired that he might have some time to answer by his counsel, and it was ordered that he should have

a copy of the Declaration and that he should put in
his answer ' on Tuesday come seven-night '.   In his
answer he denied that he was guilty of the offence
in the manner and form in which it was expressed
—a somewhat vague and incomplete defence.   But
there the matter was allowed to rest, for the Commons
declined to carry the matter forward ' by way of
impeachment '.   Ultimately in March 1643 the Lords
granted to the parishioners part of the materials
intended for St. Paul's, in order that they might
restore their church.

It is evident that in the interval between his first
report on the church, when he held it to be no
hindrance to the beauty of the aspect of the
Cathedral, and his carrying out of the works of
renovation to St. Paul's, he had completely changed
his mind as to the retention of St. Gregory's.   The
change may have been induced by the development
of the situation in regard to the Cathedral, or it may
have been partly prompted by the rebuff he had
received from the parishioners ;  but in any case it
is not a matter for surprise that the parishioners
resented having their church pulled down about their
ears at the bidding of an autocratic Commission.
The incident rankled deeply, and was referred to in
pamphlets of the time after Jones was taken prisoner
on the fall of Basing House during the Civil War.

Work of an entirely different nature devolved upon
him in January 1631–32, when a warrant was issued
to Patrick Young, William Boswell and Inigo Jones
Esq[rs] to put in good order the King's ancient coins
and medals, both Greek and Roman, in gold, silver
and brass.   They were to be arranged in a manner

fittest for the ready knowledge and use of them, and
the Commission was empowered to call to their aid
any persons likely to be of service to them. The
King's collection no doubt included the coins and
medals which, it will be remembered, his brother,
Prince Henry, had purchased for the large sum (in
those days) of £2,200. Of Jones's two colleagues,
Patrick Young was librarian to the King, as he had
been to James I and Prince Henry ; he was one of
the learned men selected by Selden for the examination of the Arundelian marbles. William Boswell,
who was knighted in the following year, was a
diplomatist, a man of letters and a scholar of wide
range. He succeeded Dudley Carleton, whose secretary he had been, as Ambassador at The Hague. It
was a high tribute to Jones's ability that he should
have been deputed to such special work along with
colleagues so accomplished.

About this time and during the preceding months,
Jones was busy with more familiar work in preparing
two masques in collaboration with Aurelian Townshend. One of these was *Albion's Triumph*, acted
in the Banqueting House on Sunday, the 8th January
1632 ; the other was *Tempe Restor'd*, produced on
14th February. It was the former that gave rise
to Mr. Pory's letter mentioning the quarrel between
Jones and Ben Jonson. In both of them there were
more representations of architecture than usual, and
it is needless to say that they were expressed with
his customary skill. It is, indeed, a great delight
to look at Jones's drawings for the masques, they
are so spontaneous and masterly. For some of them,
it is true, he made preliminary sketches, but for the

most part, especially those depicting architecture, they are touched in with a sureness and a grace that indicate a complete mastery of technique. The indefatigable authors of the Walpole Society's book have discovered in many cases the sources of Jones's inspiration, but no reflection is thereby cast, or intended to be cast, on his skill in adapting suggestions and in conveying them to those concerned, whether they were the elegant persons who were to portray the characters, or the craftsmen who were to fabricate the scenery and costumes.

Architecture was called upon in *Albion's Triumph* to provide two scenes, a Roman Atrium and an Amphitheatre, and it inspired part of the decoration of the proscenium. The lower part of the sides was occupied by two figures, named ' on compertiments of a new composition ', as the printed description has it, as Theorica and Practica, ' showing that by these two, all works of Architecture and Ingining have their perfection '. Theory stands to the left and is depicted as a young woman, looking upwards ; the pose of the figure suggests unmistakably a searching for inspiration. Practice stands to the right, and is represented as an old woman, looking downwards, and intent on the practical work of spacing something out with a pair of compasses nearly three feet in length. The figures are quite lightly touched in, but they convey their meaning with singular aptitude. In *Tempe Restor'd* the first scene is also of pronounced architectural character. There are thirty-one drawings preserved at Chatsworth for the first of these masques, and twenty-three for the second. On one is written a note by Jones which helps to bring before the mind the reality of his work. It runs thus : ' Dec. 31. 1631. May it please your honour to giue order for thes lightes for the firnature of his ma meske to bee deliuered on on munday by 6 of the cloke in the afternoone.' Then follows a list of the lights required, showing how the Banqueting House was to be illuminated ; it comprises 4 dozen torches, 16 dozen good wax lights, 3 dozen ordinary torches, and 2 hundred ' sises '. As may be supposed, these illuminants produced much smoke, so much indeed that in later years the masques were transferred to a temporary wooden building, in order that the ceiling of the Banqueting House, which had been painted by Rubens, might not be injured.

It would appear that Jones was engaged upon work at Somerset House during this year, for there is a drawing of a window for the Queen's Chapel, dated 1632, and of like date a rough sketch for a small water tower or ' sestern ', as he calls it, which was ' to bee made in the outer or base courte for the youse of the garden '. One other drawing for the chapel has been preserved, a sketch for a niche on the outside, and it may be that the Queen had taken over the chapel designed for the Infanta nine years before, and that the window and niche were to have been inserted by way of improvement.[1]

The year 1633 opened with a masque written by Walter Montagu ; it was called *The Shepherd's Paradise*, and was performed on 8th January. The

---

[1] The careful writer of the Life of Inigo Jones in the *Dictionary of National Biography* suggests that the Queen's Chapel was a new building, distinct from that which was begun for the Infanta.

only special comment that need be made upon it is that as many as seventeen drawings for it are preserved at Chatsworth, which must again have occupied a large amount of time and attention on the part of Jones.

In the following May Ben Jonson sought to deliver an indirect blow at Jones in pursuance of the open quarrel between them. Application was made by him, or on his behalf, to allow his new play *The Tale of the Tub*. The application was granted by the Lord Chamberlain, but only on condition that the part of Vitruvius Hoop should be wholly struck out, ' exceptions being taken against it by Inigo Jones, surveyor of the Kings Workes, as a personal injury to him '. Jones was now an important official at Court, and probably heard of the nature of the play from the Lord Chamberlain's office ; it would not be difficult for him to lodge his objections and get them respected. But a softened version of the part was included in the play as published, which must, one would suppose, have run the gauntlet in like manner with its predecessor. The details of the banned part are not known, but in its substitute, ' In and In Medlay,' Jonson pokes fun at his old associate in a fashion not wholly devoid of acerbity. The particulars of his satire may well be deferred until his general estimate of Jones has to be considered. But in this fresh encounter Jonson again came off halting.

One of the few country houses that can with any assurance be attributed to Inigo Jones is Stoke Bruerne Park in Northamptonshire. It was built

by Sir Francis Crane, who established the manufacture of tapestry at Mortlake in the reign of James I
and was aided and encouraged by Prince Charles
and the Marquis of Buckingham, as he then was.
Crane nearly ruined himself by his enterprise, and
there are several letters of his to the King and
Buckingham, praying for help and returning thanks
after it was given. The business became in the end
very successful. Among the grants made to Crane
in recognition of his services was the manor of Stoke
Bruerne, which was given in the year 1629. According to the county historian, Bridges, who was a
careful chronicler, ' the house was built by Sir
Francis Crane, who brought the design from Italy,
and in the execution of it received the assistance of
Inigo Jones. . . . The house was begun about 1630,
and finished before 1636, during which interval he
gave an entertainment here to the King and Queen.'
The building is illustrated by Colen Campbell in his
*Vitruvius Britannicus*, and he says of it that it ' was
begun by Inigo Jones : the Wings and Collonades,
and all the Foundations were made by him ; but the
Front of the House was designed by another
Architect, the Civil Wars having also interrupted this
Work '. Jones's share of the work is, according to
both authorities, a little uncertain, but Bridges'
statement as to dates is supported by the fact that
Sir Francis died in 1635.

The house was the earliest example to be found in
England of that particular disposition, derived from
Italy, which provided a central block and carried a
curved colonnade on either side to a smaller terminal
block. The mansion was altered and ' improved '

from time to time, but at length it was consumed by a fire which left nothing standing but the two terminal blocks, which still remain.   To one of these Plate XVII) has been added a considerable house in modern times and the combination forms the present residence.   The original work can easily be distinguished, in spite of certain alterations, and, subject to the intrusion of Campbell's ' other architect ', may fairly be credited to Inigo Jones.   The assistance which, according to Bridges, he rendered may have had limitations, but as Crane was, like Jones, a protégé of Buckingham, he was probably well known to His Majesty's surveyor and comes within the category of those who may have been able to obtain his help in building.

In February 1634, two masques were produced, which again must have imposed much work upon Inigo Jones, especially as his collaborators were new to him.   One of these was James Shirley, whose masque, *The Triumph of Peace*, was performed on 3rd February ; the other was Thomas Carew, whose *Cœlum Britannicum* was produced on the 18th of the same month.   The drawing of the proscenium for the former is sketched in Jones's usually masterly manner, and a note on it says that it was for a masque at the Inns of Court.   The *Cœlum Britannicum* called for three scenes of architectural composition, which, it may be said with safety, could only have been composed by Inigo.   This masque was one of the finest that had yet been devised.   The King himself took part in it, his royal person being attired in a rich masquing suit of aurora colour and white satin embroidered with silver, which cost, for patterns, materials and making, between £90 and £100. The Master of the Revels, Sir Henry Herbert, has a note in his office book to the effect that on the night of Shrove Tuesday, 18th February 1633(–34), the King danced his masque in company with eleven lords and ten pages. It was the noblest masque of Sir Henry's time; the best poetry, the best scenes and the best dresses. So pleased was the Queen that she told him, ' Pour les habits, elle n'avoit jamais rien vue de si brave.' Once again is a lively impression conveyed of the gorgeousness of these spectacles, of the consummate art that went to the grouping, the scenery, the design and colour of the dresses : and the notes made by Jones on his own drawings lead to the same conclusion.

From this splendour it is somewhat of an anticlimax to come down to the only architectural drawing by Jones dated during this year—a plain and simple gateway leading from Channel Row to the Palace Yard.

# CHAPTER XII

### Restoration of St. Paul's Cathedral.

IT was at this time that Jones began one of the most important pieces of architectural work that can with certainty be attributed to him—the renovation of old St. Paul's Cathedral. The history of the old building is complicated and there is no need to enter here upon its intricacies; they have been well set forth by Mr. William Longman in his *Three Cathedrals dedicated to St. Paul, in London.* The state of the building at this period was deplorable both inside and out. The body of the Cathedral was given over to all kinds of secular uses; the nave, under the name of Paul's Walk, was the fashionable lounge and news-mart of the day; lawyers would meet their clients at some specified pillar and there transact their business; children made it their playground; the noise made by them and by all manner of grown-up persons interfered with the services and drowned the voice of the preacher. Strenuous but vain attempts had been made to abate the scandal, but the building still continued to be put to these incongruous uses. The exterior had suffered grievous damage from a conflagration in the time of Elizabeth. The lofty spire, which was constructed of wood and covered with lead, had collapsed amid streams of flaming metal, and the fire had spread to all the wooden roofs over the four arms of the building. The damage had been repaired at considerable cost, but it requires no great exercise of the imagination to conclude that the repairs were hardly in keeping with the original character of the building. The spire had not been rebuilt, and although new roofs had replaced those that were destroyed, it must have been a sadly mutilated pile that remained. Nevertheless, much fine work had escaped injury. There was the central tower, there were the walls with their buttresses and windows, and there was the magnificent vaulted interior. The Cathedral still was, in the words of Inigo Jones, 'a great and noble work'. But mean houses had been built adjoining it, and the general effect must have been one of squalor and decay. The evil conditions so stirred a private citizen—one Master Farley—that for eight years he petitioned James I to remedy them, and at length the princely heart of the King was so moved that he set himself to attempt the work of restoration, and a Royal Commission was appointed in November 1620. This body was widely representative ; it numbered nearly seventy and was comprised of great officers of state, bishops, the Dean of St. Paul's, citizens and others of light and leading. William, Earl of Pembroke, the Lord Chamberlain, was a member, so were the Earl of Arundel and Jones's old friend, Sir Lionel Cranfield, Master of the Court of Wards and Liveries. The forty-ninth on the list was Inigo Jones Esquire, surveyor of His Majesty's works. But the project was not heartily supported ; the money came in

slowly, and although the Bishop of London, Dr.
George Mountaine, had caused a large amount of
stone to be brought from Portland, the work became
wholly neglected.   So complete was the indifference,
that after a time part of the stone which was lying
useless was borrowed by the Duke of Buckingham
in order to build his water-gate at York House.

The idea of restoration was, however, kept alive,
and when Laud became Bishop, it was resuscitated
through his zeal.   Another Commission, of the same
constitution as the former, was appointed in April
1631, but Jones's name was not included.   Among
those who served were the Earl of Arundel, Earl
Marshal, Philip, Earl of Pembroke and Montgomery,
Lord Chamberlain, Dudley Carleton, Viscount Dor-
chester, Sir Henry Spiller, Alderman of London (who
was an occasional co-signatory with Jones of official
reports), and a new Dean of St. Paul's.   The Commission soon got to work, for in May Jones received
the instructions already mentioned to report upon
' what disgrace or other inconvenience ' both St.
Gregory's church and the houses adjoining would
have upon the ' Cathedrall Church when it shall be
repaired and reduced to the auncient dignitie '.

St. Gregory's was built up against the south wall
of the Cathedral at its west end in line with which
was its tower, called the ' Lollards' Tower '.   It may
conceivably have been originally a chapel added to
the great church; in any case, it was no more of an
eyesore than are the scores of chapels which have
been built on to cathedrals and churches.   Jones
recognized this at first, especially as it was balanced
by part of the bishop's quarters on the north, but

when he came to renovate the Cathedral in the Classic manner he may well have found that such a projection not only interfered with the symmetry of his scheme, but presented a difficulty in the welding of it with the main building. The devoting of this part of the ancient Cathedral, if part it were, to the purposes of a parish church, had its counterpart in another portion of the great building, for in the undercroft beneath the choir was the church of St. Faith, space having been granted to the parishioners in compensation for the demolition of their original church consequent on the enlargement in ancient times of the Cathedral. Humorous old Thomas Fuller remarked of these two churches that St. Paul's was ' truly the mother church, having one babe in her body—St. Faith's, and another in her arms—St. Gregory's '.

The renovation seems still to have held fire for a year or two, but on 4th February 1633(–34) the Commission for Pious Uses met and ' upon consideraͨon and debate this day had of the best wayes and meanes for the aduancing the worke intended for the reparaͨon of the Cathedrall Church of St. Paule and upon conference thereof had wᵗʰ Inigo Jones Esqʳ Surveyor of his maᵗˢ work It was resolved ', among other things, that Inigo Jones should be appointed Surveyor, an office which he was willing to fill, in connection ' with soe good a worke ', without payment. He was to nominate a substitute from time to time, and he began by nominating Edward Carter, who was a joint signatory with him of several reports. Carter was to be paid 5s. per day. Jones was also to appoint the clerk of works and other minor officials.

A survey was to be taken of the old stones already provided for the work, and any that had been borrowed were to be called for and restored. (But how was the dead Buckingham to restore those in the water-gate ?)

The repairs were to begin at the south-east end and to proceed along the south front as far as the west end. The west end was to be ' sett upon ' when the King should so order.

New stone was to come from quarries selected by Inigo Jones, especially from the ' third Bed of Oxfordshire stone or of the soft Quarry of Portland stone '.

The work was not to be begun until £10,000 had been placed in the bank.

There seems now to have been little difficulty in obtaining money enough to start the work. ' Contributions from all parts of the country,' says Longman, ' then flowed in with a spirit worthy of emulation on every like occasion.' Among the most generous donors was the well-known merchant, Sir Paul Pindar, who for one special purpose or another subscribed as much as £10,000.

Difficulties presently arose in regard to the ships employed in conveying the stone from Portland, and to masons engaged upon the work. The Admiralty had a way of pressing into the service of the Navy both ships and men, in the autocratic manner so general at the time. This was frequently a matter of annoyance and concern to Jones. In April 1635 he prepared lists of ships and their crews that were engaged in carrying the stone ; and two years later, in April 1637, so great was the hindrance that Jones appealed to Archbishop Laud. He certified that two men who had been working from the outset in the quarry at Portland about the stone ' for the west end of the Cathedrall Church of St. Paul in London ', had been pressed into the Navy, thus hindering the work. Furthermore, ships that were conveying the stone had had their men pressed out of them during the preceding year, and no effort to get them back had succeeded. This much discouraged the ship-masters and was a great hindrance. Jones therefore prayed the Archbishop to give such order to Mr. Nicholas that sufficient warrants might be given to secure both the men at the quarry and those that brought the stone by sea.

The appeal was successful, for the Archbishop signed the following note on the certificate : ' Mr. Nicholas, it is his Ma$^{ts}$ expresse pleasure that sufficient warr$^t$ be given to secure both y$^e$ one and the other as is here desired.'

This was followed by an order of the Privy Council, dated 16th April 1637, to the effect that the two men mentioned by Jones, and all men that were or should be employed for working in the quarry on stone for St. Paul's, together with all masters and mariners engaged in carrying the stone, were to be free from being impressed to serve in the great fleet or other-wise. Inigo Jones was to send lists of all such persons to Edward Nicholas Esq$^r$, Clerk of the Council. Effectual order was to be taken to set at liberty all those lately impressed. On the same day Jones issued his certificate in relation to the barque *The Grace of Weymouth*, adding a list of her master and crew.

In spite of all hindrances the work went on and
Jones put new and Classic fronts to the south and
north sides and the west end.   This we know on the
authority of Webb, who says :

For the Magnificence of which Cathedral of St. *Paul*, all
Posterity will be grateful to Mr. *Jones*, who was sole
Architect, and solely, by that ever-glorious Monarch King
*Charles* the Martyr, entrusted with the Repair thereof ;
and who, in faithful Discharge of that Trust, reduced the
Body of it, from the Steeple to the *West* End, into that
Order and Uniformity we now behold ; and by adding that
magnificent Portico there, hath contracted the Envy of all
*Christendom* upon our Nation, for a Piece of Architecture,
not to be parallell'd in these last Ages of the World.

Unfortunately all Posterity was balked of its admiration owing to the Great Fire of 1666.   The west end
undoubtedly excited admiration as long as it lasted,
and the loss of ' that beautiful portico ' was deplored
by Evelyn among others.   But if, as may be taken for
granted, Hollar's views of the Cathedral in 1656–7
are correct as to its general appearance, any admiration of Jones's work on the south front must have
arisen from the fact of its being Classic and regular ', instead of Gothic and irregular (Plate XVIII)
The design is of quite an ordinary description ;   the
old traceried windows were replaced by large round-
headed openings surmounted by a cornice ;   the
buttresses gave way to shallow pilasters prolonged
upwards to carry a ball ;   over the large windows
were circular openings surrounded by an architrave.
Against the south end of the transept he placed two
tall, plain buttresses of large projection, reduced at
the top by means of a curve to a size sufficient to
support a square pinnacle.

Between the buttresses was a Classic doorway in which detail of a less uncompromising character may be detected. This new work was, of course, quite out of harmony with the old, but much of the old was left practically untouched ; nothing was done east of the transepts, the lofty choir and its appurtenances remained as they had been. Thus the play of fancy in the Gothic work, its delicacies of light and shade, its mixture of plain surfaces and intricate detail, were brought into harsh contrast with the severity and even, if one may say so, the clumsiness of some of the Classic work.

At the west end, where Jones was less hampered by constructional facts, he was able to add a façade which, while it had very little relation to the internal disposition of the building, was in itself a noble design (Plate XVIII), or, as Webb calls it, an unparalleled ' piece of architecture '. This phrase throws much light on the attitude of the seventeenth century towards architecture. Gothic buildings were not worthy of that name, Classic alone came within the category, and a piece of architecture was admirable in itself, no matter how incongruous it might be with its surroundings.

Jones's original drawing for the west end has been preserved (Plate XIX), but when making it he had not yet conceived the portico, and in several respects it falls below the standard that we are accustomed to associate with his name.

According to Dugdale, the work was started in April 1633. The houses adjoining the Cathedral were pulled down, the owners receiving compensation. The churchyard was enclosed for the use of the masons, in consequence of which the sermons formerly preached at the Cross were now delivered in the choir. In June, Jones was instructed to erect hoarding and scaffolding. Shortly afterwards the foundation-stones were laid ; the first by the bishop, the second by Sir Francis Windebank, one of the Principal Secretaries of State, the third by Sir Henry Martin, a judge, and the fourth by Inigo Jones. The work was carried on for nine years, and was completely finished except the steeple. It was intended to take down the remains of the old tower, and to rebuild it on stronger pillars in proportion to the church ' with a spire of stone suitable thereto '. The scaffolding for the purpose was actually erected, but the whole work was stopped owing to the disturbed state of the times, and we are left to conjecture what kind of design Jones would have produced for a lofty spire of stone under the particular circumstances that confronted him.

# CHAPTER XIII

The Masques—Arrears of Salary—The Pressing of Workmen—
St. Michel-le-Querne—Report on Decayed Stonework—Further
Masques.

THERE seems to be no doubt that about this time—the year 1631 is mentioned—Jones laid out the piazza of Covent Garden, including the church of St. Paul on the west side. There is practically nothing of his work left from which any conclusions can be drawn. The existing arcade on the north side may well be part of the original idea, but the actual work has undergone many vicissitudes. As to the church, it was first repaired by Lord Burlington, and then burnt down in 1795. Hardwick, the architect, rebuilt it on the plan and in the proportions of the original building, but the fidelity of the reproduction is too uncertain to allow it to be regarded as an example of Jones's work. Horace Walpole confesses that he wanted taste to see the beauty either of the piazza or the church. The barn-roof over the portico of the latter had to his eyes little of dignity or beauty, he says ; and in a footnote he gives the origin of the well-known tale about Jones and the barn-like appearance :

Mr. Onslow, the late speaker, told me an anecdote that corroborates my opinion of this building. When the Earl of Bedford first sent for Inigo, he told him he wanted a chapel for the parishioners of Covent-garden, but added, he could not go to any considerable expense ; in short, said he, I would not have it much better than a barn—' Well ! then,' replied Jones, ' you shall have the handsomest barn in England.'

After the lapse of a century or so both the church and the piazza had fallen into a sad state of decay, and in commenting on Pope's lines at the end of the third book of the ' Dunciad '—

> See under Ripley rise a new Whitehall
> While Jones' and Boyle's united labours fall,

the editor of the edition of 1778 says :

At the time when this poem was written, the banquetting-house of Whitehall, the church and piazza of Covent Garden, and the palace and chapel of Somerset house, the works of the famous Inigo Jones, had been for many years so neglected, as to be in danger of ruin. The portico of Covent Garden had been just then restored and beautified at the expence of the Earl of Burlington ; who, at the same time, by his publication of the designs of that great master and Palladio, as well as by many noble buildings of his own, revived the true taste of architecture in this Kingdom.

This view of architecture and of its patronage by Richard Boyle, Earl of Burlington, is characteristic of the eighteenth century. The present day does not take Burlington's architecture quite so seriously as did the past age, and the designs of Jones which he published have already been shown to be mostly the work of Webb.

The incidents recorded in connection with Jones during the years 1635 to 1640 are more numerous than during any period of similar length. He was busy with masques, with matters architectural and with duties incident to the surveyorship and the various Commissions with which he was connected. The masques were more elaborate than ever : new ideas in relation to the scenery were worked out and adopted ; stage effects were heightened and among other devices huge clouds were made to open : a note of Jones against one of his sketches says, ' The Cloud w^{ch} opening Eternity was seene '—a subject not easy to express, and a revelation not easy to contrive.

For the present purpose it would be wearisome to enter into the details of these many masques. It is only their general effect that is of importance, together with a few matters of detail that either illustrate their elaboration or throw some light upon Jones's personality. But the subject is full of interest and has been worked out with great care by the authors of the Walpole Society's book who, among other things, give the sources of inspiration upon which Jones drew, sources for the most part of Italian origin. A perusal of the book and an examination of its illustrations might even lead the student to read the text of the different masques, which, aided by the description of the scenes which often accompanies it, has been of the utmost use in assigning Jones's drawings to their appropriate masques.

The year 1635 saw towards its beginning, on 10th February, Sir William Davenant's production, *The Temple of Love,* to which thirty drawings are assigned, including one for the proscenium, entitled by Jones ' for the Queenes Masque of Indianes 1634 ' (Plate XX), but which agrees exactly with the description in the text of *The Temple of Love.* At its end, on 31st December, it saw *Florimene,* by an unknown author, for which there are eleven drawings. Those for the first of these masques include several of landscape character with rocks and trees, all skilfully rendered ; and one of the scenes shows some ornaments re-used from the *Cœlum Britannicum* of the year before, an act of economy that gave point to one of Jonson's gibes. The drawings for *Florimene* include some dainty and poetical conceptions of scenery (Plate XXI) and go to show that Jones could draw landscape with as much sympathy as the human figure. It is interesting to find that one or two of these drawings were probably worked out by John Webb, and certainly owe their titles to his hand. Webb was now twenty-four years old and had been with Jones seven years. From this time onwards not a few of Jones's reports are also in Webb's handwriting.

In November of this year, 1635, an indication is afforded of the depleted condition of the King's coffers, and it is afforded in a manner that could hardly have been agreeable to Jones and his fellow-officials. Two lists of salaries are given and another one of payments. Of the two lists one appears to show payments made, and the other arrears owing. Of the eleven names mentioned only four are familiar, which, with the amounts concerning them, are as follows :

|  | £ | s. | d. | £ | s. | d. |
|---|---|---|---|---|---|---|
| Inigoni Jones | 45 | 12 | 6 | 91 | 5 | 0 |
| Thome Baldwin | 27 | 7 | 6 | 13 | 13 | 9 |
| Henrico Wicks | 36 | 10 | 0 | 73 | 0 | 0 |
| Nico Stone | 18 | 5 | 0 | 28 | 5 | 0 |
| Eidem | 18 | 5 | 0 | 41 | 1 | 3 |

Some three weeks later the list of payments ' in fees and annuities ' includes :

|  | £ | s. | d. |
|---|---|---|---|
| Inigo Jones . . . . . | 68 | 8 | 9 |
| Nicholas Stone. . . . . | 41 | 1 | 3 |
| Henry Wicks . . . . . | 54 | 15 | 0 |
| Thomas Baldwin . . . . | 13 | 13 | 9 |

These figures, which have a certain ratio with each other, are interesting as showing the salaries paid to the respective officials. It will be remembered that Jones received 8s. a day, plus 2s. 8d. for travelling expenses, and £80 per annum for his ' recompense of avails ', amounting in all to £274 13s. 4d. Therefore the sum of £45 12s. 6d. represents (within a few pence) two months' salary. The arrears amounted to four months'. In the case of Thomas Baldwin the £27 7s. 6d. represents two months' salary at 9s. per day, without any extras, one month being in arrear. Henry Wicks, at 6s. per day, had received three months' pay, and six months' was owing. Nicholas Stone's salary was equal to Wicks', namely, 6s. per day. Of the rest of those on the list four received 6s. per day and three 4s. The subsequent payments must have been in reduction of the arrears. Jones got three months', Baldwin his one month's, Wicks three months', and Stone had one item cleared off, the other remaining in abeyance. Incidentally it may be added that to one of the remaining officials eighteen months' salary was due, and to another more than two years'.

Turning again to the actual figures, it will be seen that Jones, the surveyor, received 1s. per day less than Baldwin, the controller; but Jones had in

addition £80 per year, which made him the more
highly paid official. His salary had not been increased since his appointment twenty years earlier;
and if he be regarded with the eyes of the great
personages with whom he came in contact, what was
the position of His Majesty's surveyor at 8s. a day
in comparison with that of gentlemen willing to give
£10,000 for a peerage or a step in the peerage? It
must have been his own uncommon ability which
brought him the esteem that he undoubtedly enjoyed.

During all this time the work was going on at
St. Paul's (for which Jones declined any reward),
occasionally hindered by the pressing of indispensable
men into work for the Navy. Minor work was also
being carried out at the royal houses of Oatlands,
Greenwich and Somerset House. There are drawings
by Jones for a chimney-piece at Oatlands, a doorway
at Greenwich, and a chimney-piece at Somerset
House. Once more the Navy came in with its
annoying interference, ignoring Jones's certificate of
exemption, and inferring that he was departing from
the strict paths of truth in his statements. On
29th January 1636(–37) Jones issued his certificate
that Thomas James and Richard Durkin, carvers,
were employed by him about special service for the
King at Somerset House (quite possibly on the
carving of the chimney-piece), a business which
required great haste and from which they could not
be absent. To this document the Commissioners of
the Navy added a note on 8th February to the effect
that they were assured by the master carver of the
Navy that the two men had been pressed before

Mr. Inigo Jones employed them, ' yf his information be false we leave him to answere it '. Taking the master carver's view, the Commissioners had committed the men to prison lest their example should induce all others of the same profession to leave their work on the ' Great Shipp now in buildinge at Woolwich '. Thereupon Jones obtained, on the following day, a certificate from Thomas James himself, in which James says that he had been pressed by Mr. Christmas, carver, into work for the Navy out of the Queen's Majesty's work at Greenwich, where he had wrought a year and a half with two other men this last summer, when Mr. Surveyor was out of town. About a month since he had been put by Mr. Surveyor on some work at Somerset House, and when Mr. Christmas heard of it, he sent pursuivants to arrest him and one of his men. This was on 7th February, ' being Tuesday last ' ; the next day they were taken before the Commissioners of the Navy, who committed them to the Marshalsea : the pursuivant, however, allowed them bail in £40 apiece. All this had put them to a great deal of trouble and had hindered the work, which might have been finished by then if they had been allowed to do it.

The Commissioners lost no time in noting on Jones's certificate the decision they arrived at. The outcome of the quarrel is not stated, but in view of Jones's success in similar cases (that of the quarry workers at Portland occurred about the same time), it may be presumed that he prevailed in this as well. But the difficulties he encountered must have been irritating, and here again the fact that all sorts of commissions, appointed for the most part on the

King's own initiative, could send anybody to prison
with whom they fell out, must have done much to
increase the detestation in which the arbitrary ways
of the Court were held.

Two other matters deserving of mention are
connected with the year 1636.   On 24th February
Sir William Davenant's masque *The Triumphs of the
Prince D'Amour* was produced, for which there is
not more than one drawing by Jones—a scene of a
grove with the Temple of Apollo in the middle.   The
office book of Sir Henry Herbert says that the scenery
was the work of ' Mr. Corseilles ', but Jones's drawing, which is undoubtedly by his hand, agrees so
closely with the printed description that even if not
expressly designed for this masque it must have been
re-used from some other.   There is also an architectural drawing dated 1636—the plans and elevation
for the Chirurgeons' Theatre, of which the design
itself may have been Jones's, but the actual drawings
and title are by the hand of Webb.   That hand was
at present immature, for, among other things, it is
difficult to reconcile the connection of the staircases,
which are placed in two external square turrets, with
the levels which they are supposed to serve.   The
building was of an oval plan, with an oval hipped
roof, ' an elliptical cupola ', which must have had
an ugly effect if carried out according to the drawing.
Walpole thinks it was one of Jones's best works, but
as it was demolished at the end of the eighteenth
century, it is impossible now to form an opinion.

In April 1637, the work that had been carried out
at the chapel of Denmark (or Somerset) House some
years before—going back, indeed, as far as the time

when it was built for the Infanta of Spain—was at last paid for.  A warrant was issued to the Queen's treasurer on the certificate of Inigo Jones for £1,050 ' over and above the first estimate '.  What lay behind this grant of a warrant is not disclosed. Whether Jones had difficulty in justifying so considerable a sum for extra work, or whether the accounts went through on his certificate alone, there are no means of judging ;  but he seems to have been able, as a rule, to carry the authorities with him, as he did in the case of the workmen impressed by the Admiralty.

The strength of his influence is shown in another matter which arose just at this time, and one that was referred to him in his official capacity.  The church of St. Michael-le-Querne in Cheapside was being rebuilt, and adjoining it on the east was a mean shop which was not only a disgrace to the street, but interfered with the enlargement of the church, which unless enlarged would not hold much above half the parish.  Accordingly five members of the Commission for Buildings were appointed to inquire into the matter, among them being, in addition to Jones, our old acquaintances Sir Henry Spiller and Laurence Whitaker.  They were to interview the churchwardens and parishioners in order to have the rebuilding stayed, and they or any three of them, ' whereof Mr. Surveyor to be one ', were forthwith to come to terms with the owner of the shop and cause it to be demolished, so that the church might be enlarged and both the church and street might be beautified.  Further, any three of them, including, as before, Inigo Jones, were to view the conduit which adjoined the church and supplied a fountain there, and to give directions for its suitable accommodation for the better beautifying of the church and street.

Compulsory acquisition of property for the purpose of public improvement is well enough known in the present day ; but it is hedged round with safeguards, it has the sanction of Parliament, and it cannot be lightly or easily applied. But compulsory acquisition on the initiative of a Commission responsible only to the King was a much more arbitrary proceeding. Yet, arbitrary as it was, its object was excellent —that of beautifying the city ; and it may be doubted whether at any other period so reverent a care was taken (in official circles) of beauty for beauty's sake.

Some four months passed without much being done, and then, in September, the matter came before the Privy Council, who set themselves to examine a number of designs, some submitted by the parishioners and some by Inigo Jones. This procedure would hardly commend itself to modern ideas —a committee judging an architectural competition without the help of a trained adviser. However, their decision did them credit, for their choice fell upon Jones, and after long debate it was ordered that the parishioners should proceed with the rebuilding according to his plans. He, however, was to provide a door to the parson's house in a specified position, and at the narrowest end of the church he was to contrive a vestry. Furthermore, he was to respect the lights of the adjoining properties as far as could be done without spoiling the design ; and in order to save the pockets of the parishioners, they were to submit estimates of what they were proposing to do so that it might be seen whether Mr. Surveyor's plans or theirs were the cheaper. This was a belated and somewhat disturbing tribute to economy, since they had already selected Mr. Surveyor's design.

The parishioners were obdurate and did nothing, and a fortnight later an order was issued by the King in Council, stating that notwithstanding frequent orders, the house at the east end of the church was still standing, although 'the King expected that it had long since been pulled down . The Lord Mayor was therefore required without further delay to satisfy the owner, to pull down the house and to carry out the orders already given regarding the conduit and fountain.

Whatever the Lord Mayor may have done in compliance with this order, the parishioners themselves, led by one Mr. Binion, a silkman, assumed an attitude of defiance. So much so that Jones approached the King to enlist his support. Either the draft or an unsigned copy of his appeal, drawn up in Webb's hand, states that Jones remodelled his design in accordance with the Privy Council's instructions. This he showed to the parishioners (after they had caused him annoyance by breaking an appointment with him), whereupon Mr. Binion maintained that they might do the work in their own way, an idea which Jones absolutely rejected. They had no intention, it appeared, to make a vestry. When he asked for the return of his plans so that he might get the business despatched because he had much pressing work to do for the King, they

refused, pretending that the plans were lost.  He
had only received a portion of their estimates and
those not until a day or two before, and when he
asked for their plans in order to check their estimates,
they flatly refused to send them.   He had that day,
he goes on, been summoned to attend the Lords at
the Star Chamber to answer a petition against him
for causing delay in the rebuilding, and all this
trouble he believed to be caused by Mr. Binion, who
was resolved, according to report, that the church
should be rebuilt after their own way or not at all.

Jones accordingly desired that His Majesty should
give order to ' some of the Lords to cause this Binion
to desist from his malitious vexation '.   He was
anxious to carry out his orders quickly, seeing how
full of business he was both for the King and Queen
in matters that admitted of no delay ;  and he was
also anxious to finish the only thing he had to do,
namely, to make the estimates so that His Majesty
might see the cost of both schemes.

In this case, as in many others, the record of the
difficulties has survived although their solution has
not.   But whether Jones had influence enough to
get his way or not, it is clear that in all matters of
negotiation, and in arrangements for beautifying the
street, he was to take the lead, and it was his design
that was to be adopted for the new church.   It is
also clear that he could ill spare time from his regular
official duties to bestow upon these outside matters.

While the difficulties at St. Michael-le-Querne were
still giving trouble, another troublesome matter was
thrust upon Jones's attention.   It appears that
people had got into the way of repairing decayed

stonework with lime and hair, instead of going, as propriety would suggest, to a mason to replace the old stone with new. The Commissioners for Buildings had issued two orders prohibiting plasterers from thus poaching on the mason's preserves, but without effect; and the Company of Freemasons now prayed the Commissioners for redress. The Commissioners thereupon appointed out of their number Sir Henry Spiller, Laurence Whitaker, Inigo Jones and Alderman Garway, of whom any two, Mr. Surveyor being one, were to take evidence as to the allegations, and either to reform the abuse or report back with recommendations as to what should be done. Here was another investigation to occupy the time and try the temper of Inigo.

Meanwhile work was proceeding at St. Paul's and at Greenwich. There is a drawing by Jones for the doors on the north and south sides of St. Paul's in 1637. The doors are alike in their design, which is of no great interest, but quite equal to the rest of the work on the south front. There are also drawings for two chimney-pieces at Greenwich, that is, the Queen's House there. One of these is 'for the roome next the bacstaiers above', and the other for the 'Cabinet roome abouve behind $y^e$ round staier'. Both are dated 1637. The design for the cabinet room is the more important, it is drawn freehand and the detail is touched in with Jones's usual grace and freedom. In the frieze of the upper portion he has hastily printed 'Henrietta Maria Regina' (Plate XXII).

The two years 1638 and 1639 produced more evidences of the kind of work that largely occupied

Inigo Jones's time than any others ; the early part
of 1640 affords a little material, but after that year
ensues an almost complete blank, the glimpses
obtained of him being but few and fleeting.   He was
engulfed in the turmoil of events which preceded
and accompanied the Civil War.   The early part of
1638 was devoted to two masques, one certainly
written    by    Sir    William    Davenant,    *Britannia
Triumphans* ;   the   other,   called   *Luminalia*,   being
probably  his  work  as  well :  7th  January  and
6th February were the days on which they were
produced.   *Britannia Triumphans* must have taken
many weeks in preparation, for there are more than
fifty drawings and sketches devoted to it.   Most of
these are of costumes for a great variety of characters,
such  as  a  fiddler  (unkindly  inscribed  ' scraper '),  a
ballad-singer, a vintner's boy, a mountebank, a Zany,
Cade,  Kett,  Jack  Straw,  a  fat  attorney  and  lean
clients, and many others.   But there are also drawings  for  several  scenes,  among  them  one  inscribed
' scenne with London farr off '.   This is of considerable interest because the foreground is composed of
houses   and   the   background   shows   the   city   of
London beyond the river Thames, with houses and
churches surrounding, as a central feature, old St.
Paul's Cathedral with its massive tower, lacking the
ancient  spire.   The  houses  in  the  foreground  are
described  in  the  text  of  the  masque  as  ' English
houses of the old and newer formes ', a phrase that
indicates the growing change in design ;  but it was
the newer forms that came the easier from Jones's
pencil in this as in all his other sketches (Plate XXIII).
These sketches by Jones's own hand were by this

time being supplemented by some of Webb's, and one of them was made on the blank side of a piece of paper which bore on the other an erased address, to ' John Webb, Seruant to his Ma^ts Surveyor of Workes '.

*Luminalia* is noteworthy in that, among its eleven drawings that have been preserved, there are two of Jones's most poetical conceptions. These are scenes of Night, landscapes with stately but sombre trees bordering a river in which the moon is reflected. One of these drawings (Plate **XXIV**) still bears the splashes made by the scene painters in preparing the actual scenery. The source of Jones's inspiration has been found to be a German etching, but he was able, like Shakespeare before him, to throw a poetical glamour over ideas suggested by other persons of more prosaic imagination.[1]

[1] See References and Notes, *post*, for particulars of this identification.

# CHAPTER XIV

Official Reports—Water Supply and Drainage—Report on Brick-
making—Report on Undesirable Buildings—Housing Problems—
Water Supply for the Palace—Further Housing Problems.

D URING this year (1638) Jones was busy with
a variety of duties appertaining to his office.
In April the King's stables, both in London
and at some of his country houses, were reported to
be so decayed that other accommodation had to be
hired for His Majesty's horses. Jones was therefore
instructed to survey them all and to prepare separate
estimates for repairing them. He was then to send
the estimates to the Lord Treasurer, who was thereupon to order the repairs with as much speed as
might conveniently stand with other occasions of
payments for His Majesty's service. It is evident
that grave doubts existed as to whether the royal
purse could stand the strain of doing the whole work
at once, especially as there was another and immediate call upon it in the shape of the payment
for a new lodge at Hyde Park which had cost more
than £1,100, and some repairs to the brick walls and
copings round the court at Hampton Court, which
came to half that sum.

A few weeks later Sir Henry Spiller and Inigo Jones
were instructed to examine into a complaint made
by the Earl of Clare, to the effect that the Earl having
enclosed a piece of his own ground in Clement's Inn

Fields in order to store materials there for a new building on old foundations—and it will be remembered that erecting a new building on new foundations within two miles of Whitehall was forbidden—some one had informed the Board that the enclosure had been erected by night and with a view to a new foundation. Whereupon the Board had instructed the sheriffs to demolish it. The matter was referred to Jones and his colleague to report and recommend a course of action. A second complaint of the Earl was similarly referred. His mansion house was situated in Drury Lane, and adjoining the garden were two stables which had just been converted into dwelling-houses, one by a bricklayer, the other by a hackney coachman. Not only had a wooden dormer been made, but chimneys had been erected from which the smoke, when the wind lay that way, was driven into his lordship's garden and gallery to such an extent as to render them useless to himself or any of his family.

Hardly had this business been disposed of than another called for Jones's attention. The water supply of the palace, it appeared, was liable to pollution, a matter of great importance both for His Majesty's diet and all other necessary uses. Inigo Jones therefore prayed the Privy Council to issue a proclamation, or at least a writing to be read in the churches near the palace, forbidding anyone to erect any building or dig any pit, or otherwise to put the royal water supply in danger of contamination or loss under pain of such punishment as the offence should deserve. This salutary desire to ensure a pure water supply was at that time confined to the King's house, and it was to be obtained by certain restrictions on the liberties of his subjects. But fortunately ideas on such matters have widened, and it is now held that an uncontaminated supply is essential for every one, both the King and his subjects.

Not only was the supply of water in those days a rather casual affair, but another matter deeply affecting health, namely, the disposal of sewage, was equally devoid of system. Once again had Inigo to assist in an inquiry affecting the King's palace. On the west side of St. Martin's Lane, which still retained some of the characteristics of a rural road, was a field called Swan Close, surrounded by a wide ditch and having a deep pond in it. The ditch adjoining the lane received all the water and soil from the St. Giles's district, and when full it overflowed into other ditches and the pond. In fine weather the water evaporated and left the soil dry, which was then periodically dug out and put on the bank, a process which caused no annoyance to the King's house in Whitehall. But my lord of Salisbury built houses along the west side of the lane ; partly on the land occupied by the ditches and pond which were filled up for the purpose. In order then to dispose of the sewage an underground drain or ' vault ' had been laid, but with an insufficient fall. This drain served not only for the houses, which lay much lower than the street, but it took the water from St. Giles's which used to evaporate without harming the King. The new drain soon came to the level of the surface and discharged its contents into channels above-ground which found their way to Charing Cross and so to Whitehall, to which they became a continual nuisance.

Such were the primitive methods of sewage disposal at that time.   The nuisance had been complained of as far back as the time of King James of blessed memory, but nothing had been done and the King was put to great charges in fruitless endeavours to mitigate it, and to prevent the mischief caused by 'several furies of sewers'.

The Commissioners appointed to inquire had not shirked their responsibilities.   They had caused a substantial sewer to be laid from St. Martin's Lane to the Thames, and had assessed the cost upon all householders whose drains did or might issue into it.   But payments were slack and the work had been held up for more than a twelvemonth for want of funds, a great part of which was due from my lord of Salisbury and not paid.   In the meantime much of the nuisance to the King's house still continued.

The report is dated 19th September 1638, and within four days the Privy Council, to whom it was addressed, issued an order stating that having considered the matter and heard Mr. Inigo Jones, surveyor of His Majesty's works, and some of his colleagues, and having perused a schedule of those persons who refused to pay their assessment, a messenger had been appointed to wait upon the recalcitrants and require them to pay at once ; any who refused were to be brought up under a warrant to answer for their refusal.   As to my lord of Salisbury, he averred that the drain put in by his father was adequate, and that any obstruction to it or any nuisance was caused by buildings erected since it was made ; on the other hand, Inigo Jones and his colleagues had certified that the nuisance had existed before the erection of the later buildings, and still continued. Accordingly the Commissioners were to inquire further into the matter; his lordship was to have convenient and timely notice of their meeting and might (if he pleased) send a representative to the inquiry, the doings and proceedings at which were to be reported to the Board before Allhallowtide next, that is 1st November, some five weeks later. It is not without interest to note how far less peremptory was the treatment of my lord of Salisbury than that accorded to the ordinary householder.

But the consideration was ill requited, for in the following June Inigo and his colleagues, Laurence Whitaker, Thomas Baldwin, Peter Heywood and Henry Wicks, reported to the Council that a considerable amount of money was still owing for the sewer, of which £101 8s. was due from ' the Right Hono$^{bl}$ the Earle of Salisbury '. They had sent their messenger several times to speak with his lordship's agent, and even sent him down into the country for the purpose, but the agent had replied that he must have a copy of the order to send down to his lordship in the North, and that he had received no order to pay ; he would, however, call and see the Commissioners—which he had not done.

It is evident that the agent, like others of the fraternity both before and since, was anxious to evade responsibility by any plausible excuse ; but Jones's office kept its eyes open and one day as he was passing it happened that he was observed and was

forthwith waylaid and interviewed in the street.
He was equal to the occasion, however, and made
his escape on the ground that he had nothing to
say to the Commissioners unless he had orders from
my lord of Salisbury.

As to the balance of the considerable sum still
owing, some few householders had paid, but there had
been many changes of tenants and it was difficult
to determine upon whom to fix the payment.    In
two instances houses had been let on lease, and the
Commissioners were of opinion that the two lessors,
a Mr. Trencher and a Dr. Gifford, were liable.
All which they left to their lordships' grave
consideration.

Such were some of the vexatious matters to which
Inigo Jones had to attend.    There are one or two
more on record during this and the following year,
and as they throw some light on his occupations as
well as on the proceedings of the time, they may as
well be recounted before returning to his more
congenial work of architectural design.

In September 1638, a Commission was appointed
to inquire into the abuses of brickmakers and bricklayers, ' the difference and variety between which
hath been an occasion to retard the service '—a
delicate way, it may be presumed, of alluding to
what would now be called a strike.    The Commission
was an important one as it included the Earl Marshal
of England (Earl of Arundel), the Earl of Dorset,
Mr. Secretary Windebank, Sir Henry Spiller, Knight,
Inigo Jones Esq[r], Surveyor of His Majesty's Works,
John Horne, Laurence Whitaker and George Long
Esq[rs], justices of the peace for the county of Middle-

sex. There were to be two commissions, one was to inquire into the abuses of the brickmakers, the other into those of the bricklayers. The true making of bricks and tiles was to be ensured and a reasonable price fixed, but on no account was the duty payable to His Majesty to be impeached or overlooked. Offenders were to be certified to the Board in order that they might receive condign punishment, and His Majesty's subjects be well dealt with.

A small matter claimed his attention shortly afterwards. The tenant of some ground in St. James's Fields, where seven years previously David Mallard had caused trouble through transgressing the regulations, had parcelled the ground out with ditches and railings, and had built a bridge of bricks for the easier access of his carts. This also appears to have been contrary to the regulations, or at any rate to the views of the Privy Council, for that body issued an order for demolishing the bridge and restoring the ground to its former condition. Armed with the order Jones visited the spot, interviewed the tenant and showed him the order. The offender in this case was meeker than Mr. Binion of St. Michael-le-Querne and the parishioners of St. Gregory, for he undertook to have the order complied with by the following Thursday, and at once set workmen on to the demolition. He was a man to whom Jones must have owed some gratitude for saving him trouble and vexation.

On the same day that Jones was able to send this satisfactory report, 26th October 1638, he delivered another on a more complicated matter. The neighbourhood of Covent Garden was partly but not wholly occupied by houses of a good class, and a certain John Ward had started building some small houses on land lying between Covent Garden and Long Acre.   There were to be seventeen houses approached through a covered alley 9 feet wide, which was to lead into another proposed alley of about double the width.   The houses had only two rooms on each floor, and were to have each a little backyard.   There would have been in fact all the making of a slum.   John Ward was proposing to carry his new alley out at one end into Covent Garden through the garden of My Lady Stanhope, and at the other through several other gardens.   But Jones was definitely of opinion that he would not find the owners willing to sell, and consequently this nest of mean houses would have had but one narrow way of access ' and noe other to goe out '.   Whether the pestering of good houses with alleys of houses such as these was against the proclamation, he left to their Lordships' grave wisdom to consider.   After considering it for three months their lordships, altogether disliking the design, ordered the stoppage of the work, and enjoined upon His Majesty's Surveyor and the Justices the duty of seeing their directions punctually observed.

This incident shows how every one felt at liberty to build just what he liked without regard either to the neighbours or the general public ; and how, in London at any rate, a check was now to be put on their activities, a check wholesome enough even if arbitrarily applied.

Another matter of the Earl of Clare's was referred to Jones in May 1639.   The Earl may almost be

looked upon as an old if distant acquaintance, for
it was his father, Sir John Holles, who in the year
1616 was one of those that gave £10,000 in return
for a peerage, and was created Baron Houghton, a
title which after a lapse of eight years he changed
for that of Earl of Clare.   His step into the peerage
and the step upwards had both been taken through
the good offices of the Duke of Buckingham.   He
died in 1637, so the Earl whose concerns involved
Inigo Jones had enjoyed his title some eighteen
months.   The son took after his father in a fondness
for building, and he was now proposing to demolish
some old and mean houses in a place called Reindeer
Yard, and to build better dwellings.   Reindeer Yard
was a main thoroughfare from Lincoln's Inn, Gray's
Inn and Holborn to Westminster, and consisted of
small houses and stables, which rendered it noisome
and such a nuisance to the neighbourhood that a
' general clamour ' might break out at any time.
The inhabitants of the houses were of so poor a class
as to be likely to become a charge on the parish, not
to mention the probability of their starting an
epidemic.   Accordingly Jones was instructed by the
Privy Council to call to his assistance some others
of the Commissioners for Buildings and to submit a
report.   This he did in company with Laurence
Whitaker, and they found that the state of the yard
was as wretched as described ; that the houses were
mean and that some of the coach-houses had rooms
over them occupied as dwellings.   They fully concurred with the idea of rebuilding with fewer houses
' fit for persons of some good quality ' whereby the
place would be made better for decency, for the

health of the neighbourhood and for the conveniency
of passengers. All which they humbly submitted to
the consideration of their Lordships, who, it can
hardly be doubted, were in sympathy with the
sensible wish of the Earl and the sensible advice of
Jones and his colleague supporting it.

One other matter connected with the housing
problem of the time is on record, during 1639. In
September a William Price, one of the grooms of
His Majesty's privy chamber, had got involved with
the Privy Council in connection with his converting
the Antelope Inn in Holborn into dwelling-houses,
so the matter was referred to Inigo Jones and John
Horne to straighten out, and they were instructed to
attend the next sitting of their Lordships.

It is evident from these records which happen to
have escaped destruction, that the state of many
parts of London was deplorable, and that a general
improvement was sought for and indeed achieved.
The machinery for effecting this was clumsy and
was not always tactfully set in motion, but the
authorities were fortunate in having, in the person
of Inigo Jones, an agent of determination and
common sense.

An important commission or committee was
appointed in November 1639, with Jones at its head,
to inquire into the price of lime and sand, two of the
' principal materials for building ', and also of wages
in the building trade. After conference with lime-
burners, bricklayers and plasterers, it appeared that
the price of lime had been much enhanced within
the last few years without any sufficient reason, and
the committee found that lime ought to be delivered

anywhere along the Thames in London and its suburbs, at 6 shillings for 25 bushels. Cartage away from the Thames to be at the rate of 6 pence per mile. The cartage of sand was to be at the same rate; the price of sand at the pit was to be 8 pence for 18 bushels. As to the wages they were carefully and duly published at the Sessions of the Peace, and exhibited at the sessions-house, according to statute. All that was wanted, therefore, was the enforcement of the law, and it would be well to publish the regulations regarding lime and sand in like manner. All which was humbly submitted by the signatories, Inigo Jones, Laurence Whitaker, Thomas Baldwin, controller of the works, Henry Wicks, paymaster, George Longe, Peter Heywood and Edward Roberts, names now familiar in connection with Jones's reports.

A straw showing which way the wind was blowing in relation to the royal demands for financial assistance was stirred in Hampshire in the summer of 1639. Inigo Jones had issued a warrant to one, Thomas Burges, in May, for providing 244 loads of timber for the King's work in the repair of the west end of St. Paul's Cathedral. Burges reported to Jones that he had marked the timber in the woods of the county, and had reported the matter to the nearest Justice of the Peace, in whose presence he had interviewed the owners of the timber and they had undertaken on behalf of the county to bear the cost of delivering the timber at the wharves at Chertsey and Reading, whence it could be brought by water to London. But when, in obedience to the justice's order, he had attended at Quarter Sessions, the justices there assembled absolutely refused that the county should be charged with the carriage of the timber. Such refusal in connection with His Majesty's works was unheard of in the writer's experience, and he desired to know what he should do.

The justices were evidently in a contumacious mood, and did not discriminate between the public work at St. Paul's and the private work of the King —it was all King's work.

The King's requirements indeed were the first consideration. The water supply to the Palace at Whitehall was of great importance, but it was drawn from sources liable to be tainted. Jones had already dealt with one source in a manner likely to be annoying to the ordinary person who owned land adjacent to its course. He was now in June 1639 concerned with a trouble in a supply from ' Picka-dilly '. The water was ' corrupted by reason of the buildings there ' ; a remedy had been devised of which the cost had been undertaken by a Mrs. Baker and Sir James Oxenden. These persons had pressed Jones, he reported, to issue a certificate that the work was completed, in the hope of evading the cost of work not finished and other work not begun. But Jones had obtained a certificate from the King's serjeant plumber and the clerk-of-works at Whitehall setting forth the state of the work, and he enclosed it in his report to the Privy Council in order that they might see the untruths alleged by Mrs. Baker in her last petition, and he prayed the Council to fix a definite date for the completion of the work so that His Majesty might have the use of the water supply.

The certificate certainly bears out the unfitness of the water for drinking purposes, for among the matters still requiring to be done was the filling up of a certain pond which in winter overflowed into the water supply, and as this pond was used for washing diseased horses and dogs, it is not surprising that the serjeant plumber and clerk-of-works were of opinion that 'the water will be of no use to his majesty, but be still subject to be corrupted as formerly it was'. But why the cost of avoiding the corruption should have fallen upon private persons, even if they happened to own property adjoining the supply, is not very clear.

Two or three matters of a technical nature are the last that the State Papers supply. In January 1640 a certain Aquila Wykes was the tenant of a house overlooking the garden of the Dean of Westminster; the building was used as a house of detention, and the Abbey authorities complained that Wykes's prisoners were an intolerable annoyance owing to their looking out into the garden. The matter was referred to Inigo Jones, together with his frequent colleagues, Whitaker and Baldwin, and they had suggested building the windows up as far as the transome (a cross-piece at about two-thirds of the height of the window). This was objected to by Wykes and his adviser on the ground that it would make the rooms utterly void of all light; but the complainants denied this, and moreover said that the nuisance would still remain unless the windows of the two upper stories were likewise built up. The Privy Council concurred in this view and ordered the windows to be built up accordingly until Wykes or his adviser could satisfy them that they should not remain so blocked, in which case their Lordships would order them to be opened again.

With this decision Mr. Wykes had to be satisfied ; but how long it remained in force, in view of the changes brought about by the Civil War, is a matter upon which there is no information.

In June of the same year a certain Alderman Grundy petitioned to be allowed to pull down some ruinous houses in St. Lawrence Lane and build four new ones in their stead. The matter was referred to Sir Henry Spiller and Inigo Jones, who recommended that the petitioner be allowed to build two houses ' fit for merchants or others of good quality, which will have fit light and air '. The recommendation goes to show that Jones gave enlightened consideration to such matters, and did what he could to prevent overcrowding. In the following August he dealt with another case of much the same kind, and a few days later he submitted an estimate for some repairs at the Tower of London.

These are the last records of Jones's official duties that the State Papers supply. They are, it is true, of a commonplace nature, but they throw a little light on the local government of the time, such as it was ; and they clearly indicate that much of his time was taken up with work that offered no scope to his artistic abilities.

# CHAPTER XV

Temple Bar—Kirby Hall—The Last Masque—Loan of Money to the
King—Fall of Basing House—Death of the King—Coleshill—Death
of Inigo Jones—His Will.

FROM these troublesome details of water
supply, drainage, insanitary areas, building
regulations and persons who set themselves
to thwart the beneficent intentions of the King and
his faithful surveyor, it is a relief to turn to matters
of architectural design, even if these were of no great
magnitude. It was about this time or perhaps a
little earlier that Jones designed a screen for Winchester Cathedral, of which the drawing is preserved
at the Royal Institute of British Architects (Plate
XXV). Work had been done at the Cathedral either
by Charles I or in his honour, of which the date is
determined by an inscription as 1634. Jones's screen
may have been built at the same time, but it was
probably a little later, for he witnessed a contract
entered into by the sculptor, Hubert le Sueur, to
make two statues, one of King James and the other
of King Charles, which, there can be no doubt, were
to be placed in the two niches of the screen. The
contract is short and is of sufficient interest to be
given in full : it is dated 17th June 1638 :

I Hubert le Sueur Sculptor have bargained with the
Kinges Ma^tie of great Bretaine to cast in brasse two statues
of 5 footes and 8 inches high. One that representeth our

late Souveraine Lord Kinge James, and the other our Souveraine Lord Kinge Charles for the summe of 340$^{ll}$ of good and lawfull money of England to be paid in this manner viz$^t$ 170$^{ll}$ before hand and the other 170$^{ll}$ when the worke shalbe finished and delivered to the surveyor of his Ma$^{ties}$ workes in March ensuinge. And the said Hubert le Sueur is to receive the aforesaid summes w$^{th}$out paying any Fees for the receipt thereof.

HUBER LE SUEUR.

I was present and wittnes to this bargain.

INIGO JONES.

In the restoration of the cathedral the screen was removed, but the statues were preserved and placed at the west end.

Jones's design was simple, solid and dignified, but, like all work of that time, it was intentionally Classic in character, and had no affinity with Gothic surroundings.

The passing generation will remember Temple Bar, which stood at the point where the Strand becomes Fleet Street, and where it sadly blocked the traffic. It was the work of Wren, and had been familiar to every Londoner for two centuries. But it is not generally known that Jones had made a design to answer the same purpose in 1638. There are several drawings of the scheme preserved at the Royal Institute of British Architects, one of which is a ' purfill ', or section, dated 1638, and signed by Jones. This agrees generally with the sketch elevation which is neither dated nor signed (Plate XXVI). The carved panels on this drawing evidently did not satisfy Inigo, for there are alternative sketches more neatly drawn (Plate IV) in which the oblong panels present the same subjects as those on the elevation, while the circular panels are filled with maritime subjects which would have been less easily legible than the single figures of ' Lœtitia ' and ' Hylaritas ' originally intended.

Another design dated in this year is one for a front of Somerset House, that was never in fact carried out. The drawing is by Webb and it bears the characteristics of his treatment as distinguishable from those of Jones. But this distinction is not always easily or certainly to be made, and it is beyond question that Jones was making architectural designs at this period and consequently was in a position to be the real author while Webb was merely the draughtsman. Were it not for this possibility the character of the design and drawing would undoubtedly point to Webb as the author.

Jones had a free but sure touch, and he seems to have avoided as far as possible the help of mechanical appliances in his drawing. This is apparent in the design for two houses, or, it may be, two alternative designs for the same house, which are among the few of his house-designs that have been preserved (Plate XXVII). The general proportions, the relations of voids to solids and the restrained but interesting variety of treatment show the hand of a master, and stir a feeling of regret that more work of this kind is not to be found among his drawings.

Tradition has always connected Jones with some of the work at Kirby Hall in Northamptonshire, a large house built by a Sir Humfrey Stafford in 1570 with the help of John Thorpe. No sooner was it finished, however, than it was bought by Sir Christopher Hatton, Elizabeth's dancing Chancellor, who had himself built an even larger house at Holdenby in the same county. In course of time Kirby descended to another Christopher Hatton, the son of a cousin of the Chancellor. This gentleman was in high favour with Charles I and was made a Knight of the Bath at the coronation. He was a devoted adherent of the King, he was created Baron Hatton of Kirby in 1643, and subsequently became Comptroller of the Household, when already the Household was more or less in a fugitive condition. He was so much in the confidence of Charles as to be chosen a Joint Commissioner for the King at the Uxbridge Conference in 1645. After the royal cause became hopeless he retired to France, but after the Restoration he enjoyed the countenance of the new king as much as that of the old. It is clear that before the storm-clouds had gathered and while the King and his friends still walked in security, he resolved, in 1640, to do something to modernize his house of Kirby. One front, the north, was recased in what was called a more 'regular' fashion. Several new windows, doors and other features were inserted, designed in the true Italian way, and a handsome gateway was built into the balustraded wall of the outer court (Plate XXVIII). All this new work is ascribed to Inigo Jones, and although there is no direct evidence that he was employed, the character of the work is consistent with that idea, and the tradition satisfies one of the tests presently to be indicated as being desirable of application in such cases, namely, that Hatton was a person of great influence at Court, and one for whom the services of the King's surveyor might be available. Further than that it would be unwise to go, but this at least may be said, that Jones would have no cause to disclaim the authorship of the gateway, and that the gateway itself harmonizes with the series of similar designs that are undoubtedly from his own hand.

But there is one more achievement of Inigo that demands attention, for it was the culmination of his wonderful work in stagecraft. This was Sir William Davenant's masque *Salmacida Spolia*, produced on 21st January 1640 and again on Shrove Tuesday. The labour of devising the costumes and designing the scenery must have been enormous. There are thirty-nine drawings of costumes at Chatsworth, and at the British Museum there are the ground-plan of the stage and scenery and a section showing the stage and machinery. These are described as ' for the King and Queen's Ma^{tie} Masque of Salmacida Spolia in the new masquing house Whitehall 1640 '. The title is in the handwriting of Webb, which accounts for the conventionality of the spelling. The Chatsworth drawings are full of vigour so far as the figures are concerned, while those for the scenery include a rough sketch for ' Storm and Tempest ' which admirably conveys its intention and contrasts notably with the second scene, a peaceful avenue of stately trees beyond which is seen a distant city. Both the King and Queen took part in this masque, and there are several sketches for their costumes. Those for the King are given a conventional beardless face, with no attempt at portraiture (Plate **XXIX**). Another scene is one of architectural character and shows a street lined with Classic buildings leading towards a monumental bridge across which are pass-

ing vehicles and persons. It is quite possible that
this was one of the last drawings of architecture
that Jones produced.

The masque itself was the last of the magnificent
series that began in 1605, a series that owes its ever-
growing splendour to Inigo Jones : and as his first
notable effort in design was the *Masque of Blackness*,
so his last, or almost his last, was the masque of
*Salmacida Spolia*. The exception, if exception it
be, was the work at Wilton in Wiltshire. But before
dealing with this in any detail it will be well to trace
Jones's movements during the war so far as the
scanty information allows.

It seems certain that *Salmacida Spolia* was produced in January 1640 ; the title-page of the quarto
edition confirms this, and yet Jones's drawings for
it are dated by him as 1640, which according to his
invariable custom of dating would include the first
three months of 1641. All his other drawings for
masques to be performed in January or February
of a certain year are dated the year before, in
accordance with the reckoning of the time, which, as
already said, ended the year in March instead of the
previous December. It is not easy to account for
the discrepancy, but in this instance he may perhaps
have departed from his usual custom, for not ónly
does the printed copy of the masque give the date
as January 1640, but during the early months of
1641 the King must have been too deeply absorbed
in his conflict with Parliament and the unhappy fate
of Strafford to be in the mood for masques.

Indeed the unrest of the times seems to have
invaded the Court and its recreations, for the writer

of a letter two days after the first performance of *Salmacida Spolia* says ' the mask was performed last Tuesday night, myself being so wise as not to see it. They say it was very good, but I believe the disorder was never so great at any.' To the King, however, the disorder, even if it were part of the general unrest, carried no significance, for yet another letter written on the 14th February, but by a different hand, says, ' Their Majesties, with their royal children, are in perfect health, and for their recreation intend to dance again their mask this Shrovetide ; the joy of her majesty being enceinte again, advancing rather than hindering that pastime.' But the years of joy and pastime were soon to close.

It has been already pointed out that after the year 1640 the State Papers afford no information as to Jones's official duties, but from other sources it appears that his reports, or those of his deputy, Webb, came before Parliament until March 1643. But his life must have been an uneasy one at this time. In December 1641, as already said, he had to appear before the Lords to answer the charge in respect of St. Gregory's church, and early in the following January the King, whose interests had been for many years his chief concern, and for whom he had devised so many brilliant spectacles, left White-hall for the last time as a free agent. There were to be no more masques ; the old days of supremacy and happiness were over.

In due course, but at some indeterminate date, Jones must have left London to follow his master, and have appointed Webb as his deputy. On the 28th July 1642, the King and Court were at Beverley in Yorkshire (Charles being engaged in an abortive attempt to obtain possession of Hull), and Inigo Jones was with them ; for on that day the King gave him a receipt for £500 lent by Inigo Jones, Surveyor of Works, which he promised to satisfy again.    Bearing in mind subsequent events, it is very improbable that the debt was satisfied during the King's lifetime ;  and it is more than likely that Jones never saw the money during his own, for a clause in his will speaks of the debt (of which the amount is not stated) owing to him for his entertainment and service to the late King and Queen, whereof he bequeathed £50 to the Paymaster of Works to be paid within one month of the debt being discharged.    Whether this inducement was sufficient to move the Paymaster under the Commonwealth to obtain the money, unhappily does not appear, but the Paymaster was Henry Wicks, no doubt the same Henry Wicks who had been Paymaster in the old days and intimately associated with Inigo Jones. Although the amount of the royal debt is not stated in the will, it would appear from Webb's Petition that £1,500 was due as arrears of wages, ' besides £500 ', which may have been the money lent at Beverley.

On the 22nd of August 1642, Charles raised his standard at Nottingham and the country was enveloped in the clouds of civil war.    Into those clouds Jones disappeared and no trace of him can be found until three years later, when he was at Basing House on the occasion of its capture by Cromwell.

The storming of the house was announced to the

Speaker of the House of Commons by Cromwell himself in a letter written from Basingstoke on the day of the assault, 14th October 1645. The place had been surrounded with artillery and before six o'clock in the morning the storm broke. Although it had baffled other commanders so often as to be regarded as almost impregnable, it soon fell before the fury of Cromwell's onslaught, and that without much loss to the besiegers. It was almost battered to pieces, and what escaped the cannon was destroyed by a great conflagration caused by the neglect of the garrison to quench an early fire-ball. Much of the rich and costly furniture and hangings was saved only to be plundered by the soldiery, who helped themselves to whatever they could lay hands on, and forthwith sold it to anyone who would buy. The very lead was stripped off the roofs and hardly a single gutter was left. The house consisted of an Old House and a New House, either of them according to Mr. Hugh Peters, who reported the capture to the House of Commons, ' fit to make an emperor's court '.

By the end of the day the whole place was an empty ruin ; the works of art and costly plenishings of the owner, the Marquis of Winchester, were scattered over the countryside, and he himself was a prisoner. So too were Inigo Jones and (according to Vertue) Hollar the engraver. Among the slain was ' Robinson the Player ' who had angered the Parliamentary soldiers the day before by mocking at them and their Parliament.

Through this scene of carnage and plunder (there were nearly a hundred of the defenders slain) moved

Inigo Jones, roused, it would appear, at that early hour from his bed, for he was clad only in the scantiest of attire. How could he escape, an old man of seventy-two, stricken, as we must believe, with infirmities, and dim of sight ? He could not, and he did not. His capture gave the liveliest satisfaction to his enemies, in whose minds still rankled his high-handed treatment of the parishioners of St. Gregory's. One news-sheet, published during the week of the taking of Basing House, says, ' There was the famous Surveyor and great Enemy to St. Grigory, Innico Jones, who was carried away in a blanket, having lost his cloaths '—left behind, presumably, in his hurried rising from his bed. Another sheet calls him ' the King's Surveyor, and Contriver of Scenes for the Queen's Dancing-Barne'. Thus contemptuously did they speak of his masterpieces of the scenic art produced in his beautiful Banqueting House. Other sheets speak of him as a Knight, ' Sir Indico Jones ' ; and yet another sheet, in reporting Cromwell's letter to the Speaker, adds a list of the prisoners taken, of whom the first three were the Marquis of Winchester, Sir Robert Peake and ' Inago Jones '. Clearly he was a well-known and cordially hated malignant.

No doubt he was sent by Cromwell, along with the Marquis and other notable prisoners, to the Parliament in London, but there is nothing to say if he were committed to prison, nor, if so, for how long. But he had to pay for his loyalty to the King, as did many others of his companions. His estate was sequestrated, but he made application to the Committee for Compounding, urging that he had never borne arms against the Parliament, nor given information to the enemy. Within a few months his affair was settled on payment of a fine of £545 and a further sum of £500 for his ' fifth and twentieth part '. In July of 1646 his pardon was confirmed by the Lords and his estate restored. He may have thought himself lucky in getting off so lightly, and must have felt that it would not be wise, nor incumbent on him either at his age, to take any further active part in the struggle. Webb seems to have escaped even better, for apparently his estate was not sequestrated, although he had given information to the enemy. According to his own account he ' sent to the King at Oxford his designs of all the fortifications about London, their proportions, the number of guns mounted on them, how many soldiers would man them, how they might be attempted and carried and all particulars relating thereto in writing '. He did more than this, for he ' carried his majesty's jewellery in his waistcoat through all the enemy's quarters unto Beverley in Yorkshire, which being afterwards discovered, Mr. Webb was plundered to the purpose, and a long time kept in prison being close prisoner for a month '. The luck which let Mr. Webb off so easily attended him further, for throughout the time of the Commonwealth he appears to have carried on his work as an architect without molestation.

Walpole in referring to the fine imposed upon Jones mentions an incident that was not uncommon in those troublous times :

Whether it was before or after this fine I know not, that he and Stone buried their joint stock of ready money in

Scotland-yard ; but an order being published to encourage
the informers of such concealments, and four persons being
privy to the spot where the money was hid, it was taken up
and reburied, in Lambeth-marsh.

Where, for anything known to the contrary, it may
still lie, although it would hardly be worth while to
institute a search for it.

This brief appearance of Jones on the stage of the
war is all that can be told of his movements during
its continuance.  Apparently he did not resume his
duties as surveyor ; Webb was still acting as his
deputy after a fashion, and receiving the King's
commands to design a palace at Whitehall.  From
somewhere he must have watched with sad eyes the
failure of the cause with which he was bound up.
In some retreat he must have heard of the ' unfortunate calamity ', as Webb phrases it, which befell
his royal master, with whom he had worked so long
for the beautifying of London, and whose arbitrary
disposition was so much in harmony with his own.

The end came with the death of the King on the
30th January 1649, a time of the year which in the
old days had been marked by so many of Inigo's
triumphs in scenic design.  The end came ; further
struggles were useless ; and Jones, accepting the
situation, appears once more to have turned his
attention to architecture in a fitful way.  Philip,
Earl of Pembroke, brother to Inigo's early patron,
was engaged upon alterations of his house at Wilton
in the later months of 1649, and both Jones and
Webb gave him assistance.  Pembroke had made
his peace with the new Government, and there is
nothing surprising about the employment of Webb,

who was quite ready to work for supporters of the
Parliament. But the case was somewhat different
with Jones, who can only have been an ardent
Royalist. He was, moreover, an old man, suffering
from infirmities. There are, however, drawings for
some ceilings at Wilton dated 1649, and to this period
may also be assigned with much probability the fine
work in the Double and Single Cube rooms. The
drawings of the ceilings have, as to six of them, their
titles in Jones's hand ; the other two have Webb's
writing, including the finest of the series (Plate XXX).
But this particular drawing must surely owe its
vigour and directness of expression, not to mention
the charm of its design, to Jones. Others of the
series are entitled by him ' ceeling of yᵉ countes of
Carnarvon's bedchaber ' and ' ceeling of Countes of
Carnarvons with-drawing roome '. These go some
way to confirm the idea that they were prepared in
the year 1649, for the Countess was a daughter of
Earl Philip, and as her husband had been slain in
the moment of victory at Newbury in September
1643, it would appear that she came back to her old
home where she had her own suite of rooms. The
drawing must therefore have been made subsequent
to 1643. There are no drawings for the noble apart-
ment, the Double Cube room (Plate XXXI), but there
is one of the exterior of the front of which it forms
part. Of the various dates put forward in connection
with the work at Wilton, the evidence points on the
whole to this year of 1649 ; and it also points to
Jones as the designer, in spite of his age and his
probable dimness of vision.

Coleshill in Berkshire is a fine house that has always

been attributed to Inigo Jones, largely on the strength of a tablet in the house definitely assigning it to him ; but in recent years the note-books of Sir Roger Pratt and a diary of Sir Mark Pleydell have combined to put the matter in a different light. Coleshill belonged to the Pleydells, but was bought by a Sir Henry Pratt, who died in 1647, and was succeeded by his son, Sir George. Shortly after Sir Henry's death, the house was burnt down, and Sir George started to build a new one. His relative, Roger, who was afterwards, as Sir Mark Pleydell says, architect to his cousin, Sir George, ' in friendship to him ', went to Coleshill in company with Inigo Jones, either in 1649 or 1650, and so much did they dislike the site of the house that had been begun, that although it was already one story high, they persuaded Sir George to start afresh, and the new house was built, with Pratt as the architect. He took the advice of Jones from time to time and visited the place on several occasions with him. He consulted him in particular about the ceilings. But beyond giving advice to Pratt, Jones could have had very little to do with Coleshill. It must always be remembered that he was now an old man of seventy-six or seventy-seven—a great age for that period ; and it was just at this time, namely on the 22nd July 1650, that he made his will, in which he says he is ' in perfect health of mind, but weake in body '.

He had, indeed, less than two years to live, for on the 21st June 1652 he died at Somerset House in the Strand. Nothing is known of his last years nor of his dying hours, but it is easy to believe that his devoted pupil Webb, and Webb's wife, his kinswoman, were assiduous in their care of him to the last. And so, as Webb says, 'through grief, as is well known, for the fatal calamity of his dread master', passed away one of the most brilliant figures that have adorned the history of English art.

His will shows that although for many years he had moved among the noblest and even most august personages in the realm, he still remembered his old friends and his kinsfolk, humble though they might be. There were no death duties payable in those days, and consequently there was no valuation of his estate, but he was not a poor man when he died. He left £100 for his funeral expenses, and £100 for a monument, ' to bee made of white marbele '. To Richard Gammon, who married his kinswoman, Elizabeth Jones, he left £500 and half his wearing apparel ; to Mary Wagstaffe, his kinswoman, £100 ; to her five children £100, to be equally divided between them ; to John Damford, carpenter, £100 ; to Stephen Page, for his faithful service, £100 ; to Anne Webb, his kinswoman, £2,000 ; to her five children by John Webb, £1,000 ; of the debt already mentioned as owing to him for his entertainment and service to the late King and Queen, he left £50 to Henry Wicks, paymaster of the works, to be paid within one month after the debt had been received, and the remainder to be equally divided between his executor (Webb) and Richard Gammon. To the poor of St. Martin's parish he left £10, and the like sum to those of St. Bennet's. Finally he appointed John Webb, of the parish of St. Martin-in-the-Fields, who married his kinswoman, Anne Jones, the executor of his will, and two other persons to be the overseers of it, all of whom were to have £10 each. The will was proved by John Webb on the 24th August 1652.

His specific legacies amounted to £4,150 and half his apparel, as well as what may have been realized from the royal debt.   The residue, of which nothing is known except that it included the other half of his wearing apparel, would fall to be divided among his blood-relations.   It is perhaps not without significance that in the year after Jones's death, John Webb bought the estate of Butleigh in Somerset from the owner, Thomas Simcox, and that he established himself there as a country gentleman, who, however, still pursued his calling as an architect. At Butleigh he was buried on 4th November 1672, twenty years after the death of his great master, and there he was succeeded by three generations of his descendants.   Although he bought the estate soon after Inigo Jones's death, it is quite possible that the old tag, *post hoc ergo propter hoc,* may not apply ; but the fact of the purchase remains.

# CHAPTER XVI

Jones primarily the King's Surveyor—Tests for His Works—His Character as a Man—His Attitude in Money Matters—Ben Jonson— Quarrel with Ben Jonson.

THE question of what buildings were designed by Inigo Jones has always aroused considerable interest and will probably continue to do so, and no good purpose would be served by trying to prove or confute the numerous claims that have been set up on his behalf. The process would be both tedious and futile. It is almost impossible to prove a negative ; all that can be done in regard to cases where no actual evidence is available, is to indicate the kind of test it would be reasonable to apply.

It will have been gathered from the foregoing pages that although Jones had a decided preference for architecture among the arts of design which he studied, yet no reliable evidence has come to light to connect him with actual building operations before his appointment as surveyor to Prince Henry in the year 1611. From that time onwards his official duties became his chief concern, and more particularly was this the case when he obtained the more arduous post of surveyor to the King. This was now his life's work, and so far as such restrictions applied in those days, it was a ' whole-time ' appointment. That he had plenty to do as surveyor must have become apparent from the number of cases which, even at the risk of inspiring tedium, have been cited at some length, and yet not out of proportion to the amount of his time which they occupied. He himself sometimes became impatient at delay in these matters, especially when caused by obstinate persons, like Mr. Binion, because it hindered him from pushing on with urgent work for the King and Queen. By the world at large he was not thought of instinctively as 'the great architect, Mr. Jones', but as 'the King's Surveyor'. It is true that among his intimates he was looked upon and publicly acclaimed as a great architect, but even so late as the fall of Basing House, the public prints identified him as the 'famous surveyor' and the 'King's surveyor'.

The opinion of his intimates is right : he was a great architect, but not one open to be employed by anyone desiring his services. All his principal works—the Queen's House, the Banqueting House, the refacing of St. Paul's Cathedral, the laying out of Lincoln's Inn Fields, the royal chapels—were either ordered directly by the King, or by commissions appointed by him. When he was engaged upon the Lincoln's Inn scheme, and the benchers wanted him to design their chapel, they arranged for an old friend of his to 'move' him thereto, not to go in the ordinary way of business and obtain his services.

This being the case, it will be found that nearly all, if not actually all the work which may be called private, was done for great nobles influential at Court, such as Buckingham, Pembroke, Arundel and

Bedford, or for persons of standing there, such as
Lionel Cranfield and Francis Crane.

One of the tests, therefore, to apply in a doubtful
case is this : Was the client a man of such influence
at Court as to be likely to obtain the services of the
King's surveyor ?

Then there is the more debatable question of style,
and here the weight of evidence is all against the
conclusion that Jones ever designed a building in
what is known as the Elizabethan or Jacobean style.
From his youth upwards, or at any rate from his
early manhood, he had studied at first hand the
architecture of Italy, and chiefly under the guidance
of Vitruvius and Palladio.  He set himself to purify
English architecture of what he held to be the
shortcomings of English designers who had not been
able to draw their inspiration from the fount itself.
England was full of buildings of charming and
original design in which the influence of Italy was
apparent, but mixed with much that was not truly
Classic, and handled in a manner that was not
' scholarly '.  It was this kind of design that Webb
had in mind when (as already mentioned) he said
to Dr. Charleton in regard to Inigo, ' for I must tell
you that what was truly meant by the Art of Design
was scarcely known in this Kingdom until he . . .
brought it in use and esteem among us here.'
Jones's own drawings bear out this estimate of his
aims.  His architecture has the much desired
' scholarly ' touch, and although some of his ornament
has affinity with that of the Jacobean designers, it is
much more austere and restrained than their ordinary
and somewhat exuberant work.  The few plans of

his that have survived are simple and severe and
show none of the ingenuity and playfulness displayed
in many of those in the Thorpe collection.

Taking the evidence into account, and arguing
from the known to the unknown, it appears to be
to the last degree unlikely that Jones designed
Chilham Castle, for instance, or any of the buildings
in Oxford that have been attributed to him.   Recent
researches in regard to the latter reveal nothing to
connect him with them.   On the contrary, such
evidence as there is points to Stone as the designer
of the Gateway of the Botanical Gardens, and an
examination of the authentic work of Jones removes
not only this but the porch of St. Mary's Church and
the work at St. John's College from the sphere of
probability that Jones designed them.

Another test to be applied, therefore, in uncertain
cases is this : Is the general conception, is the handling of the detail, and are the proportions such as
Jones would have adopted ?

Leaving conjecture and coming down to hard facts,
there is Webb's list of his works which he adduced
in support of the pre-eminence of Jones as an
architect :

What should I say of his works for sacred uses, and the
honour of his country, since the Cathedral of St. Paul owes
its magnificence to his studies ;  and St. Paul's in Covent
Garden, with the royal chapels at Denmark House, and St.
James's were of his design ?   What of those buildings of his,
for ornament and necessity, since the Banqueting House of
his majesty's palace of Whitehall, his majesty's royal house
at Newmarket, and the Queen Mother's new building at
Greenwich were ordered by him ?   What of his Masques,
etc.

The list is not a long one, and it is hardly likely, Webb's object being to extol Jones, that he would not have made at least a general reference to other notable buildings if they had been numerous. In this connection it is not without significance that Roger Pratt, when speaking of architecture, says that the only remarkable buildings in England are the Banqueting House and the Portico of St. Paul's, to which he adds elsewhere the Queen's House at Greenwich. Webb's silence with regard to other important buildings, such as Somerset House, which are attributed to Jones but of which the drawings are by Webb, is also not entirely without significance, nor is the fact that on Jones's monument, erected by Webb, the only two works of the *architectus celeberrimus* that are mentioned are the building at Whitehall and the restoration of St. Paul's Cathedral.

It is probable that Webb's list includes the most important of Inigo's works, but his exceptional powers of design were employed on many smaller matters in the way of special features and embellishments, such as gateways, chimney-pieces, ceilings, fountains, doors and windows. A few houses are known to be by him, such as one for Lord Maltravers in Lothbury, 1638, ' Sir Peter Killigrew in yᵉ blackfryers Mr. Surveyors desygne ', and one or two others of which the drawings are preserved. But it must never be forgotten that his skill in architecture was displayed over and over again, and with great advantage, in the scenery of his masques.

Looking at his designs and drawings as a whole, Webb's encomium is fully justified when he said, ' Mr. Jones was generally learned, eminent for architecture, a great geometrician, and in designing with his pen (as Sir Anthony Vandyke used to say) not to be equalled by whatever great masters in his time, for boldness, softness, sweetness, and sureness of his touches.' This testimony has often been quoted as that of Vandyke, but the reference to Vandyke within the brackets and the general trend of Webb's discourse point to Vandyke as being responsible for the phrase ' designing with his pen ', rather than for the testimonial with regard to the touches.

It is unfortunate that so little material exists for forming an opinion of Inigo Jones as a man. There are two sets of testimony, neither of which is rich in detail, and both of which must be taken with caution. One is that of his friends, expressed in such matters as dedications of books, in references to him as a collaborator in producing masques, and, so far as Webb is concerned, in emphasizing the high lights of his portrait as an architect. The other is that of Ben Jonson after their quarrel, in the numerous opportunities he took of venting his spleen.

The laudatory mention of him by the poets of the masques may owe something of their praise to the fact that Jones was a person of influence at Court. The dedication of George Chapman's ' Musœus ' in 1616, although perhaps tinged with the high colouring appropriate to the purpose, is handsome enough.

### THE EPISTLE DEDICATORY

To the Most generally ingenious, and our only Learned Architect, my exceeding good Friend Inygo Jones, Esquire ; Surueiguer of His Majesties Workes.

Ancient Poesie, and ancient Architecture, requiring to

their excellēce a like creating and proportionable Rapture,
and being alike over-topt by the monstruous Babels of our
Moderne Barbarisme ; Their Uniust obscurity, letting no
glance of their trueth and dignity appear but to passing
few : To passing few is their left apparance to be presented.
Your selfe then being a Chiefe of that few by whom Both
are apprehended ; and their beames worthily measur'd and
valew'd.   This little Light of the one, I could not but object,
and publish to your choise apprehension ; especially for your
most ingenuous Love to all Workes in which the ancient
Greeke Soules have appeared to you.   No lesse esteeming
this, woorth the presenting to any Greatest, for the smalnes
of the worke ; then the Authour himselfe hath been helde
therfore of the lesse estimation : having obtain'd as much
preseruation and honor, as the greatest of Others :   the
smalnesse beeing supplied with so greatly-excellent Invention and Elocution.   Nor lacks even the most youngly-
enamor'd affection it containes, a Temper grave enough, to
become, both the Sight and Acceptance of the Gravest.
And therefore, howsoever the mistaking worlde takes it
(whose left hand ever receyn'd what I gave with my Right).
If you freely and nobly entertaine it, I obtaine my End :
your Iudicious Love's continuance, being my onely Object :
To which I at all partes commend

Your Ancient poore Friend<br>
GEORGE CHAPMAN.

This is the only intimation there is that Jones was
interested in Greek literature and, possibly, knew
something of the language, but ' learned ' though he
was, he was not a scholar such as Chapman was in
Greek, or Ben Jonson in Latin.

Chapman intimates that Jones was of a grave
disposition, an opinion which his portraits confirm,
as also do his few and rather heavy incursions into
the regions of humour.

He was not niggardly nor grasping in money

matters,—for he undertook the work at St. Paul's
without payment, and he seems to have borne long
arrears of pay without grumbling.   Indeed, according to Webb, he was generous to a fault in respect of
his salary at the outset of his official duties.   The
Office of Works having contracted a great debt in
the time of his predecessor, amounting to several
thousand pounds, he was consulted by the lords of the
Privy Council as to how the situation could be met,
as the exchequer was empty 'and the workmen
clamorous'.   He at once offered to forego every
penny of his salary until the debt was discharged,
and not only did he do this, but he persuaded his
fellow officials, the controller, Baldwin, and the
paymaster, possibly Wicks, to join in the renuncia-
tion, and thereby the whole arrears were absolutely
cleared.

The story certainly gives food for thought ;  for
Jones's salary was £275 a year, at which rate it would
have taken some ten years to clear the debt.   With
the help of his friends, who would contribute some
£300, the requisite time would have been about five
years ;  and how the three of them were to live, unless
they had ample unacknowledged perquisites, it is
difficult to understand.   But after making due
allowance for Webb's over-emphasis, there would still
remain a considerable residue of self-sacrifice on the
part of Jones and his friends.

Very little light is shed on his recreations.   The
only known fact is that he belonged to one or more
companies of choice spirits—they would be called
' clubs ' in the present day—who met at a tavern
and promoted mirth and conversation by copious

drinking. Ben Jonson, who wrote some rhymed 'Rules for the Tavern Academy', and therein set up a standard that was not always attained, indulged freely in this stimulant; Jones followed him at a long distance, and although he admits to having been drunk in his company, he was probably an abstemious person according to the notions of the time, and there is no reason to suppose that his liking for wine ever interfered with his work or his intercourse with his patrons.

There is no doubt that he was of a domineering and arbitrary temper. Jonson refers to him as 'Dominus Do-all'; the parishioners of St. Gregory's said that he insisted upon being 'Sole Monarch' in dealing with that church. His letters show him to have been impatient at being thwarted; in fact, he shared to the full the arbitrary disposition which marked the royal circle from the King downwards. But against all his shortcomings must be set the fact that he retained the affection of Webb to the last; and Webb, being his pupil and assistant, was exposed to more annoyances and trials than any other person.

He moved among the best intellects of the time. Many of his friends have already been mentioned; they were all men of mark. He also knew Vandyke, although it is not possible to say how intimately; Mr. Secretary Windebank consulted him in August 1633 about a house for Vandyke, and Jones sat to him purposely for a portrait to be given as a present to Webb. George Chapman, of 'Homer' fame, was an intimate friend, as Jones himself records on a monument which he placed (in the form of a Roman

altar) in the churchyard of St. Giles-in-the-Fields.
' In honour of sound learning,' says the Latin
inscription, ' he caused this monument to be erected
at his own expense to his familiar friend.' It has
been suggested that he knew Shakespeare, and was
able to give enough information about Italy to
account for the local colour in the plays having their
scene in that country. But altogether, apart from
the observations that Shakespearian students might
make, it is certain that no evidence has so far come
to light to support the conjecture.

Ben Jonson was, of course, for many years, one
of his intimates, and the quarrel between them adds
nothing to the credit of either of them. But as it
goes to show the failings of each as apparent to the
other, it cannot be entirely ignored.

If Jones was domineering, so too was Jonson after
his fashion. His friend, Drummond of Hawthornden, sums him up at the end of the ' Conversations '
of 1619 :

> He is a great lover and praiser of himself, a contemner
> and Scorner of others, given rather to losse a friend, than
> a Jest, jealous of every word and action of those about him
> (especially after drink, which is one of the Elements in which
> he liveth) . . . he is passionately kynde and angry, carelesse
> either to gaine or keep, Vindicative, but if he be well answered,
> at himself.

Being thus impulsive, he laid himself open to dis-
comfiture, and it is not surprising that Jones had
the better in the conflict caused by the attempted
licensing of the *Tale of a Tub*. Thenceforward
Jonson was not slow to take advantage of an opportunity of girding at his antagonist and laying bare the

failings and foibles that he saw so clearly, and indeed had seen for many years.   He had spoken of him to Drummond as the ' greatest villain in the world ' and as an ' arrant knave '.   After the final break he reflects upon his honesty in his ' Expostulation with Inigo Jones ' :

> Live long the feasting-room ! and ere thou burn
> Again, thy architect to ashes turn ;
> Whom not ten fires, nor a parliament, can
> With all remonstrance, make an honest man.

These accusations point to some serious weakness in Jones's character, which, even if known to Jonson and not merely imagined, has never been revealed or even touched upon by anybody else, and they may well be regarded as the outbursts of a petulant and angry man.   Jonson piqued himself upon his own honesty ; ' of all styles,' says Drummond, ' he loved most to be named honest, and hath of that ane hundreth letters so naming him.'   The word had a wider signification in those days than an expression of rectitude in money matters.   It meant frank and straightforward ;  and in the manœuvres of a life at Court Jones may well have thwarted others as well as Jonson.   The reflection on his honesty just quoted, however, follows upon an innuendo that Jones received full payment for scenery that had been re-used, a circumstance which, even if true, would hardly have excited general indignation in those days.   Jonson's other gibes are aimed at foibles rather than at serious defects of character, and while exciting a smile, add no lustre to the poet's reputation.   Webb's ' great Geometrician ' becomes with Jonson ' an architect able to talk of Euclid '.

The ' generally learned ' man is twitted for his bad Latin.   In the *Tale of a Tub* In-and-In Medlay the joiner—a part aimed at Inigo—says :

> I have a little knowledge in design
> Which I can vary, Sir, to *Infinito*.
> TUB.  *Ad infinitum*, Sir, you mean.
> MED.  I do.
>   I stand not on my Latin, I'll invent,
>   But I must be alone then, joined with no man.

Medlay's insistence upon doing everything himself is touched upon elsewhere, for another character says of him :

> He'll do't alone, Sir, He will join with no man,
> Though he be a joiner : in design he calls it
> He must be sole Inventor : *In-and-In*
> Draws with no other in's project, he'll tell you
> It cannot else be feasible or conduce :
> Those are his ruling words.

Medlay, that is Jones, was in fact a Dominus do-all. So the fun goes on throughout the play, but unless the audience knew Jones and his foibles, his masterful spirit and his favourite phrases, more than half the point must have been missed.

Jonson aimed other barbs at Jones, but enough of his attacks have been cited to show that to him at least Jones's character offered vulnerable points. His serious accusations must, however, in the cautious words of the Scottish version of acquittal, be held to be ' not proven '.

Jones was not passive under these attacks ; he entered the lists with the same weapons as his opponent, but wielded them with a less skilful hand. He wrote the epigram already quoted which is to be found among the Harleian MSS. in a book that belonged to a Thomas Crosse, as is shown by 'an acrostic on my name' written on an early page. Herein Crosse has transcribed many pieces of verse, culled from books (and possibly other sources) of the seventeenth century. Among them are two of Jonson's invectives against Jones, 'Mr. Johnson to Inigo Joanes Marques Wouldbe' and the epigram ending 'Thy forehead is too narrow for my brand', and this one by Jones against Jonson, entitled 'To his false freind mr. Ben Johnson'. It would be interesting to learn whence Crosse obtained it, as most of the other pieces in the collection are from printed sources. Jones's diction is confused and obscures his meaning, the confusion being increased by what must be errors of transcription. But the gist of the complaint appears to be that Jones was expecting from Jonson, in reliance on his honesty, some meed of long overdue thanks. This he had not received and the neglect had turned what might have been the language of love into that of hate. He wonders that Jonson dare inveigh against the manners of the age when the ills with which he had charged Jones were imaginary. But in such inaccuracies lay the storehouse of Jonson's plots :

> thou hast writt
> of good and badd things not with equal witt:
> The reason is, or may be quickly shewne,
> The good's translation, butt the ill's thyne owne.

Jones had never been to Scotland on foot (as Jonson was fond of proclaiming that he himself had), but he had heard Jonson's tedious story of his journey until he had got as tired as ever the traveller was.

Besides I have been druncke with thee, and then
Satt still and heard the rayle at other men,
Repeate thy verses—

and had done all that might be to seal their friendship.  He had preferred him in his choice ' before
greate Lords ', and yet by this neglect Jonson had
earned the disrespect here charactered to the life.
Jones sums up in the last two lines :

From henceforthe this repute dwell with the, then—
The best of Poetts, but the worst of men.

It so happens that in his epigram Jones touches upon
some of the very failings that Drummond had noticed
in Jonson—his pride in being honest, his egotism,
his jealousy of others, and his love of liquor.

The angry passages between these two great men
appear to have had but little effect upon their
fortunes.  Jonson's invectives did nothing to injure
the position of Jones ; indeed Jonson was warned
by a friend that they were likely to do himself harm.
And Jonson had no reason to dread the result upon
the public of a battle of wits with Jones.

But let these wranglings pass :  they do nothing
to lessen the value of the work which either
antagonist did.  Rather let us take leave of Jones
as we see him in his portraits, grave and high-
spirited yet refined.  Let us dwell on his memory
as ' generally learned ', constant always to the learning he had imbibed in Italy.  Although his record
may have to be shorn of much that old admirers wove
into it, although students may be curbed in their
eagerness to found theories upon his style, yet a large
residue remains of his actual buildings, his charming

drawings of architecture and decoration, and above all, those for his masques ; a residue ample enough to show how great he was in design, and how much he did to ennoble the art with which his name is chiefly linked.

# REFERENCES AND NOTES

P. 9. *The decree of the Court is dated 18th October 1589.* The text of the decree, from the Book of Orders and Decrees of the Court of Requests, preserved in the Chapter House at Westminster, is printed in Appendix A of the *Life of Inigo Jones*, by Peter Cunningham.

P. 11. *the statement made by his earliest biographer.* In the 'Memoirs relating to the Life and Writings of Inigo Jones Esq:', prefixed to *Stone-Heng Restored*, fol. 1725.

P. 11. *Horace Walpole says of it.* In *Anecdotes of Painting in England.*

The picture mentioned by Walpole now hangs at Chatsworth. It represents a hawking scene, with two men and several dogs. One of the men is mounted and both carry hawks. The colouring is conventional, including the blue distance, and it is doubtful whether Walpole would obtain universal support in his opinion of the trees. To use a modern term, the picture looks like a 'pot-boiler', and has little of the vigour and grace of his later drawings.

P. 17. *but reputed to have over valued, etc.* Introduction to the 1725 edition of *Stone-Heng Restored.*

P. 27. *'the fame of his presence'.* Allan Cunningham's *Life of Inigo Jones.*

P. 28. *'In any other court of Christendom besides?'* Webb's *Vindication*, p. 119.

Pp. 30, 31. The Earl of Arundel's letters are printed in the *Life of Thomas Howard, Earl of Arundel*, by Mary Hervey, pp. 42, 43.

P. 33. *published in pamphlet form.* See *Leland's Collectanea* (*Iohannis Lelandi Antiquarii De Rebus Britannicis Collectanea*), 1770, vol. i, pt. 2, p. 626.

P. 41. *himself took a hand.* Peter Cunningham, p. 7.

Pory's letter is quoted from the Cotton MSS. in Brit. Mus. by J. Payne Collier in his *History of English Dramatic Poetry . . . and Annals of the Stage*, 1831, i, 366.

P. 42. *commissioners appointed to inquire.* See *Complete Peerage*, vol. v, p. 144.

P. 42. *to see the King's face again.* See *A Genealogical History of the Kings of England*, by Francis Stanford, 1677.

P. 43. The letter of April, 1616, is in the *State Papers* (*Dom.*) *James I*, vol. 86, f. 132.

P. 43. for Edmund Bolton, see *Dict. of Nat. Biography*.

P. 46. *to cost them £300 a man.* Peter Cunningham, p. 8.

P. 46. *the longer liver of them.* See *Complete Peerage*, vi, 534.

P. 46. *Masque of Queens.* Twenty of the drawings are in the Chatsworth Collection : the 'House of Fame' is in the Burlington-Devonshire Collection at the Royal Institute of British Architects. See the Walpole Society's *Masques*, p. 37.

P. 50. For John Donne, see Walton's *Lives*.

P. 52. For Jones's expenses, see Peter Cunningham's *Revels at Court*, p. xxxix ; for Spenser's, p. xxx.

P. 52. *with all suitable officers.* See Stanford's *Genealogical History*, as before, p. 528.

P. 52, last line. Walpole Society's *Masques*, p. 42.

P. 53. Daniel's tribute to Jones is quoted by Peter Cunningham, p. 12.

P. 54. For Prince Henry's expenses, see *Revels at Court*, pp. x–xv.

P. 55. '*Inigoe Jones devyser*'. See *Revels at Court*, p. ix.

P. 56. The estimate for the Islands at Richmount is in the *S.P. Dom. Jas. I*, vol. 63, fol. 85.

P. 59. Coryat's verses are in the *S.P. Dom. Jas. I*, vol. 103, f. 33.

P. 61. *such casualties as that stirring age should afford.* See *Temple Newsam Papers*, pub. by Hist. MSS. Comm., 1913.

P. 66. For Jones's fees, see *Revels at Court*, pp. xv, xvi.

P. 66. The Reversion is in the *S.P. Dom. Jas. I*, ' Docquett, 27 April 1613. The office of Surveyo[r] of his Ma[ties] workes w[th] all ffees and duties thereunto belonging for Inigo Jones during his Life in Revertion after Simon Basill who now enioyeth the same. P'cured by S[r] Thomas Lake. K. Gall.'

P. 67. The historian is Stanford, in his *Genealogies*, p. 531.

P. 67. *The Lords Maske.* Campion says :—' the starres moved in an exceeding strange and delightfull manner, and I suppose fewe have ever seene more neate artifice than Master

Innigoe Jones shewed in contriving their motion, who in all
the rest of the workmanship which belonged to the whole
invention shewed extraordinarie industrie and skill.' *Progresses of King James I*, 558.

P. 68.   Chamberlain's letter to Alice Carleton, *S.P. Dom. Jas. I*,
vol. 72, 30 ; that to Dudley Carleton, vol. 89, 17.

P. 69.   The cost of the masque is given in Peter Cunningham's
*Life*, p. 16.

P. 71.   For Carleton's letter to Chamberlain, see *The Life
of Thomas Howard, Earl of Arundel*, by Mary Hervey,
p. 74 ; and the same book for other references to Lord
Arundel.

Pp. 85, 86, 87.   The details of Jones's salary, etc., are given by
Peter Cunningham, pp. 18, 46, 48.

P. 88.   Webb's observation is on p. 19 of his *Vindication*.

Pp. 88, 91.   The letters to Carleton are in the *S.P. Dom. Jas. I*,
vol. 86, 132 ; vol. 88, 9 ; vol. 89, 67.

P. 89.   The warrant is mentioned by Horace Walpole in his
*Anecdotes of Painting*, under ' Inigo Jones '.

P. 91.   The warrant in respect of the dramatic entertainment
is given in the *Revels at Court*, p. xliv.

P. 92.   In regard to the consignment of pictures, see *S.P. Dom.
Jas. I*, vol. 90, 145 ; and Miss Hervey's *Life of Lord Arundel*, p. 131.

Chamberlain's letter of 22nd June is in the *S.P. Dom.
Jas. I*, vol. 92.

P. 95.   The drawings of Smithson and Jones are at the Royal
Institute of British Architects.   Compare Smithson, Sheet
19, with Jones, Drawer 3, No. 5 ; Smithson, Sheet 72, with
Jones, Drawer 3, No. 1 ; and Smithson, Sheet 54, with Jones,
Drawer 3, No. 10.

P. 96.   Sherburn's letter.   *S.P. Dom. Jas. I*, vol. 95, 10.

P. 97.   Jones's sketches for windows ; R.I.B.A., Drawer 1,
Nos. 8–10.   The fountain is at Worcester Coll., Set 1,
..No. 29.

P. 98.   Chamberlain's letter.   *S.P. Dom. Jas. I*, vol. 103, 33.

P. 105.   The estimate is in the *S.P. Dom. Jas. I*, vol. 108, 55.

P. 107.   The warrant is quoted in *Revels at Court*, p. xlv.

P. 108.   Webb's Brief is in the *S.P. Dom. Chas. II*, vol. 5,
74, 1.

P. 111.   Webb's Appointment is printed in full in the Appendix,
Peter Cunningham's *Life*, p. 48.

P. 114. See Peter Cunningham's *Life*, pp. 21, 22.

P. 115. The Declared Account is quoted by Cunningham, p. 21.

P. 116. The *Conversations* with William Drummond are printed in *Ben Jonson, ed. by C. H. Herford and Percy Simpson,* 1925, vol. i.

P. 117. Gate-house at St. Albans. *S. P. Dom. Jas. I*, vol. 107, 4.

P. 118. *conveyed with much pomp to Westminster Abbey.* Stanford's *Genealogies*, p. 526.

P. 118. The payment for the hearse is in the *Accounts of the Treasurer of the Chamber,* quoted by P. Cunningham, p. 19.

P. 118. For the Lincoln's Inn Fields Commission, see Rymer's *Fœdera*, xvii, 119–21.

P. 119. For the building of Lincoln's Inn Chapel, see *Records of the Hon. Soc. of Lincoln's Inn (Black Books, etc.)*, vol. ii.

P. 122. *Workmen were pressed into the service of the Crown.* P. Cunningham's *Life*, p. 22.

P. 123. For Inigo Jones's letter, see Miss Hervey's *Life of the Earl of Arundel*, p. 168. ' Hā Courte ' is Hampton Court.

P. 124. Repairs at Ely House, P. Cunningham's *Life*, p. 19. Ely House had been the town residence of the Bishops of Ely. Sir Christopher Hatton (Elizabeth's Chancellor) obtained a grant of the site and built a house, known as Hatton House, on the garden and orchard. This descended to his nephew, William Newport, who took the name of Hatton. His wife was Elizabeth Cecil, daughter of the first Earl of Exeter ; she outlived him and married, secondly, Sir Edward Coke. Smithson has a drawing of ' My Ladye Cookes House in Houlborn '.

Ely House, which adjoined, was prepared as a residence for the Spanish Ambassador, Gondomar, and fears were entertained that indignation would be aroused at the prospect of having Masses said in a Bishop's chapel. Gondomar, in fact, wanted a back way to his house in order to admit Catholics privately to worship, but Lady Hatton would not agree. She appears to have had an awkward temper, and quarrelled with her second husband. In 1622–3 Charles Stuart, Earl of Lennox (shortly afterwards created Duke of Richmond), obtained a grant of Ely Place, and in April 1624 his body lay in state for six weeks in Hatton House. He had probably been in treaty for its purchase, but his widow and Lady Hatton quarrelled over the sale, and it did not come off.—Wheatley and Cunningham's *London, Past and Present*, II, 11–12.

Inigo Jones made a drawing in 1622–3 of a gateway ' for my lo. Stuard at Hatton House '. (See p. 128.)

P. 125. The Report on Sir Robert Manfield's glass is in the *S.P. Dom. Jas. I*, vol. 113, 53.

P. 126. For the Gateway at Beaufort House, see *Some Architectural Works of Inigo Jones*, by H. Inigo Triggs and Henry Tanner, Jun., p. 14.

P. 126. The *Masque of Augurs*. See Walpole Soc. *Masques*, p. 50.

P. 127. Chamberlain's letter. *S.P. Dom. Jas. I*, vol. 133, 24.

P. 128. ' *for my lo. Stuard* '. See note as to this, p. 124.

P. 129. The gossiping letters. *S.P. Dom. Jas. I*, vol. 137, 27. J. Payne Collier's *Hist. of English Dramatic Poetry, etc.*, vol. i, pp. 438–9.

P. 130. For Charles's first sight of Henrietta Maria, see Stanford's *Genealogies*, p. 539.

P. 130. Stow says that Somerset House was granted by James I to his Queen, Anne of Denmark, in 1616, and that he commanded it to be called Denmark House.

P. 130. *The Savoy Chapel, likewise, shall be converted.* Chamberlain to Carleton, May 5, 1623. *S.P. Dom. Jas. I*, vol. 144, 11.

P. 130. The laying of the foundation-stone is mentioned in a letter to the Rev. Joseph Mead, printed in *Court and Times of James I*.

P. 131. Chamberlain's letter is to Carleton, 14 June 1623 ; *S.P. Dom. Jas. I*, vol. 146, 85.

P. 135. Jones's letter is at the Soane Museum and is printed in Inigo Triggs and Tanner's *Inigo Jones*.

P. 136. Payment for the ' Maskes '. *S.P. Dom. Jas. I*, vol. 164 (docquets 12).

P. 137. Chamberlain to Carleton. *S.P. Dom. Chas. I*, vol. 2, 55.

P. 138. The Commission of 30 May, 1625, is given in Rymer's *Fœdera*, xviii, 97.

P. 141. For the French Pastoral, see Walpole Soc. *Masques*, p. 52 and Pl. X.

P. 141. Refusal to pay for highways. *S.P. Dom. Chas. I*, vol. 32, 112.

P. 142. The Stove. *S.P. Dom. Chas. I*, vol. 67, 26.

P. 144. For Buckingham's assassination, see Stanford's *Genealogies*, p. 542.

P. 146. Report on Sir Kenelm Digby's building. *S.P. Dom. Chas. I*, vol. 149, 35.

P. 147. Report by Justices as to the plague. *S.P. Dom. Chas. I*, vol. 175, 3.

P. 149. Pory's letter is printed in Gifford's *Memoirs of Ben Jonson*, p. clx.

P. 152. Report on Scipio le Squyer's building. *S.P. Dom. Chas. I*, vol. 193, 76.

P. 153. Report on William Cooke's building. *S.P. Dom. Chas. I*, vol. 192, 67.

P. 154. Report on David Mallard, *S.P. Dom. Chas. I*, vol. 206, 68.

St. James's Field was the open space now occupied by St. James's Square and the adjoining streets.

Pp. 155–8. The reports, etc., as to St. Gregory's Church are in *the same*, vol. 213, 8a, 9, 11, 19a ; vol. 211, 80.

P. 158. The subsequent history of the St. Gregory's affair will be found in *An Important Collection of the Great Affairs of State*, by John Nalson, LL.D., 1683, vol. ii, pp. 728–9. Also in the *Commons' Journals* for 1641–2 and the *Dict. Nat. Biog.*

P. 160. King's Coins. *S.P. Dom. Chas. I*, vol. 183, 1.

P. 163. Illumination of Banqueting House. Walpole Soc. *Masques*, p. 65.

P. 163. Jones's drawings for Somerset House are at the R.I.B.A., Drawer 1, Sheets 21, 18.

P. 163. Footnote. Wheatley and Cunningham in *London, Past and Present*, iii, 270, give 14 September 1632 as the date of laying the first stone. A letter is quoted from Garrard to Wentworth (*Strafford Letters*, vol. i, p. 305) :—
' January 8, 1636. This last month the Queen's Chapel in Somerset House Yard was consecrated by her Bishop ; the ceremonies lasted three days, massing, preaching and singing of Litanies, and such a glorious scene built over their altar, the Glory of Heaven, Inigo Jones neer presented a more curious piece in any of the Masques at Whitehall; with this our English ignorant papists are mightily taken.'

P. 163. Application for *The Tale of the Tub*. See Collier's *Annals*, footnote, p. 53.

P. 166. The drawing of the Proscenium is at the R.I.B.A.

P. 167. Sir Henry Herbert's note is quoted in the Walpole Soc. *Masques*, p. 19, from Malone's *Variorum Shakespeare*, 1821, iii, 236–7.

P. 171. Resolution as to St. Paul's. *S.P. Dom. Chas. I*, vol. 232, 14.

P. 173. Pressing of workmen. *S.P. Dom. Chas. I*, vol. 352, 57 ; vol. 354, 12, 18.

P. 174. Webb's *Vindication*, p. 27.

P. 175. *According to Dugdale.* Sir Wm. Dugdale's *History of St. Paul's Cathedral in London*, 1658, p. 135. This edition has Hollar's plates.

Pp. 180, 181. The lists of salaries are in *S.P. Dom. Chas. I*, vol. 301, 9 ; vol. 302, 94.

P. 182. Jones's drawings are at the R.I.B.A., Drawer 1, Sheets 20, 23, 34, 35.

P. 182. In connection with Jones's position, it is not without interest to learn that when he stayed at Hampton Court he was lodged on the topmost floor, in a garret, as he calls it. There is a sketch of his at Chatsworth (*Designs by Inigo Jones*, vol. 4, fol. 65), the landscape seen from his window, with a wall in the foreground, beyond which are some trees, and in the distance a hill with a windmill. It is entitled in Jones's writing 'Ham Court out of my garrett window, 1636'.

P. 183. Pressing of men for the Navy. *S.P. Dom. Chas. I*, vol. 346, 69, 71.

P. 184. The drawing for the Chirurgeons' Theatre is at Worcester Coll. Set I, 7.

P. 185. Warrant for the Chapel, Somerset House. *S.P. Dom. Chas. I*, vol. 352, 12.

P. 185. Church of St. Michael-le-Querne. *S.P. Dom. Chas. I*, vol. 356, 143 ; vol. 367, 83 ; vol. 370, 16.

P. 189. Report on decayed stonework. *S.P. Dom. Chas. I*, vol. 367, 202.

P. 189. Jones's drawing for doors at St. Paul's, R.I.B.A., Drawer 1, 52. Those for chimney-pieces, Drawer 1, 36, 38.

P. 191. Footnote. Mr. C. H. Bell has kindly supplied the following note :—

After the publication by the Walpole and Malone Societies of their volume on *Inigo Jones's Designs for Masques and Plays at Court*, Mr. Henry M. Hake, now Director of the National Portrait Gallery, discovered that the beautiful

scene of Night for ' Luminalia ' is copied very closely from
an etching by Hendrik, Count Goudt (1613) after a picture
by Adam Elsheimer (Dutruit, *Manuel de l'Amateur*, iv,
321, No. 3 ; H. S. Reitlinger in *Print Collectors' Quarterly*,
viii, 1921, 291).   The subject of this is the ' Flight into
Egypt by Moonlight '.   Inigo has taken about a third of
the background on the left, no doubt from the print, as
although Charles I possessed a painting of moonlight by
Elsheimer, ' St. Christopher and the Child Christ ', now at
Welbeck Abbey, the ' Flight into Egypt ' belongs and always
has belonged to the Gallery at Munich.   It is most probable
that Jones owed his acquaintance with Elsheimer's work to
Rubens, whose profound admiration for and study of the
German artist's pictures is recorded in his letters and
elsewhere.

P. 192.   The king's stables.   *S.P. Dom. Chas. I*, vol. 388, 25 ;
vol. 390, docquets v, 17.

P. 192.   The Earl of Clare and Clement's Inn Fields.   *S.P. Dom.
Chas. I*, vol. 390, 107.

Pp. 193–4.   Matters of water supply and drainage.   *S.P. Dom.
Chas. I*, vol. 393, 1 ; vol. 398, 10, 130 ; vol. 424, 41.

P. 197.   Abuses of brickmakers.   *S.P. Dom. Chas. I*, vol.
399, 43.

P. 198.   Regulations in regard to St. James's Fields.   *S.P.
Dom. Chas. I*, vol. 400, 99.

P. 199.   John Ward's buildings.   *S.P. Dom. Chas. I*, vol. 400,
100 ; vol. 410, 132.

P. 200.   Reindeer Yard.   *S.P. Dom. Chas. I*, vol. 420, 27 ;
vol. 424, 70.

P. 201.   Antelope Inn.   *S.P. Dom. Chas. I*, vol. 429, 60.

P. 201.   Commission on price of lime.   *S.P. Dom. Chas. I*, vol.
432, 58.

P. 202.   Timber from Hampshire.   *S.P. Dom. Chas. I*, vol.
426, 11.

P. 203.   Water supply to Palace.   *S.P. Dom. Chas. I*, vol.
424, 76.

   ' Pickadilly.'—Robert Baker of St. Martin in the Fields
appears to have been the owner of Pickadilly Hall, which
stood at the corner of Windmill and Coventry Streets.
His widow, Mary Baker, subsequently sold it to Col. Panton
(whence Panton St.).   The district became known as Picka-
dilly, and on Feb. 7, 1638, the Star Chamber ordered all the

houses there, which had stood since 1615, to be demolished. ' They are found to be great nuisances and much foul the springs of water which pass by those houses to Whitehall and the City.'—Garrard, *Strafford Letters.* vol. ii, p. 150, quoted in Wheatley and Cunningham's *London*, iii, 85, 87.

P. 204. Aquila Wykes's house in Westminster. *S.P. Dom. Chas. I*, vol. 442, 2.

P. 206. Hubert le Sueur's agreement. *S.P. Dom. Chas. I*, vol. 393, 26.

There are sketches by Inigo Jones for these statues at Chatsworth (*Sketches and Masques*, vol. i, 129). They are freely but carefully drawn and are slightly coloured. Le Sueur followed them in the main, but varied both the pose and the costume a little in each case.

P. 212. The letters are from Robert Read to his cousin, Thomas Windebank, *S.P. Dom.*, Jany. 23, 1640 ; and from Secy Vane to Sir Thomas Roe, *S.P. Dom.*, Feb. 14, 1640.

P. 213. Jones's loan to the King. *Calendar, State Papers,* July 28, 1642.

P. 215. The news-sheets referred to are *The Moderate Intelligencer*, Oct. 9–16, 1645 ; *Mercurius Britannicus*, Oct. 13–20, 1645 ; and *The True Informer*, Oct. 11–18, 1645.

P. 216. Sequestration of Jones's estate. *Cal. Committee for Compounding Dom.*, p. 112. *Lords' Journals*, 1646, viii, 342a, 344a, 350b, quoted in the *Dict. Nat. Biog.*

P. 216. Webb's account of his services. *S.P. Dom. Chas. II*, vol. 5, 74, 1.

P. 219. Date of Jones's death. P. Cunningham, in his *Life*, p. 37, says that he had examined the Register of St. Bennett's and found that Inigo Jones was buried 26 June, 1652.

P. 220. Jones's will is printed at length in Appendix E of P. Cunningham's *Life*.

P. 225. Webb's list is in the *Vindication*, p. 119.

P. 229. The foregoing of his salary by Jones is mentioned in Webb's *Vindication*, p. 119.

P. 230. Jones's sitting to Vandyke is mentioned by Vertue. *Brit. Mus. Add. MSS.* 23069.

# APPENDIX A

## INIGO JONES'S COPY OF VITRUVIUS'S
## *I DIECI LIBRI DELL' ARCHITECTURA*

The copy of Vitruvius mentioned by Vertue is now in the Chatsworth Library. It was published at Venice in 1567 (not 1568, as Vertue says). In the bottom margin of the ornamental title-page Jones has written the same motto as in his sketch-book, ' Altro diletto che Imparar non trovo '; and at the side is his signature, scratched through with a pen. Such erasures occur in many of his books and may perhaps point to an attempt on the part of those who sold them (contrary to Webb's expressed wish) to hide their identity. On the last page is a note in Lord Burlington's writing and signed by him : ' This book belonged to Inigo Jones and the notes are of his hand writing.' On the title-page is the name ' W^m Barry Lond 1714 '.

The marginal notes are not so numerous as those in his *Palladio*, nor do they include so many personal touches. For the most part they indicate in English the matter of the Italian text. There are a few of Jones's own comments, as when he says, ' Methinks Vitruvius might as well prefer the gramarian to the philosopher as the mathematition to the Architect.' The only dates he gives are that mentioned in the text (p. 52), 1609, when he was in Paris, and 1614, when he was at ' Pottigiolo ', or ' pottiolo ', as he calls it elsewhere [probably Cape Pozzuoli, near Naples], and where he saw a temple of marble. He mentions his ' noatbook of Architecture ', his ' noat booke A ', twice, and his ' second noat booke '; but these references can hardly be to the only note-book known to have been preserved, which is now at Chatsworth. He makes one or two comments on the change of scene in theatres. Beyond these few matters nothing of personal interest seems to emerge except the conclusion that he was an earnest and acute student of classic architecture.

The marginal note referring to the year 1609 runs thus : ' being in Paris the yeare 1609 a Provancall maad a triall to make a Perptuall mociō but did not Reusire ' (succeed). The date when these notes were made does not transpire, but from their general tenor they would seem to be subsequent to his Italian visit of 1614.

## INIGO JONES'S BOOKS AT WORCESTER COLLEGE, OXFORD

Inigo Jones had (for that age) quite a considerable library. Most of his books are preserved in the library at Worcester College, but one or two, including his *Vitruvius*, are at Chatsworth. Those at the College were presented, along with the Jones-Webb drawings, by Dr. George Clarke. They are of a solid character and include no light literature ; they are nearly all of Italian publication. Not a few of them have annotations by Jones, but some are so clean as to suggest that they were not often consulted.

Mr. C. H. Wilkinson, librarian of the College, contributed a full account of the Worcester College Library to the *Proceedings and Papers of the Oxford Bibliographical Society* (vol. i, part iv, 1926), and included a complete list of Jones's books now in the library : with his permission the list, together with his notes, is here reprinted ; but his note regarding the famous *Palladio* is omitted, as its substance has been dealt with in the foregoing pages. As already indicated, Jones's signature was usually scratched through with a pen, and the cases in which this has occurred are marked in the list thus, †. Those in which the books have notes by Jones are marked thus, *.

1. *†*Herodoto Alicarnaseo Historico delle guerre de Greci & de Persi, Tradotto . . . per il Conte Mattheo Maria Boiardo.* Venice, 1539. 8vo.

2. *Torelli Saraynae Veronensis Leg. Doct. De Origine Et Amplitudine ciuitatis Veronae.* Verona, 1540. fo.
   Note on title-page : ' Inigo Jones. Venetia 30 Juli 1614 2$^{11}$¼.'

3. †*Opera di Andrea Fulvio delle antichità della Città di Roma, . . . Tradotta . . . per Paulo dal Rosso.* Venice, 1543. 8vo.

4. †*Lucio Floro de Fatti de Romani . . . Tradotto . . . per Gioan Domenico Tharsia di Capo D'Istria.* Venice, 1546. 8vo.

5. \*†*L'Opere Morali Di Xenophonte Tradotte per M. Lodovico Domenichi.* Venice, 1547. 8vo.
   With this is bound in contemporary vellum *I Sette Libri di Xenophonte,* 1347, by the same translator and printer.

6. \*†*Dione Delle Guerre de Romani. Tradotto Da M. Nicolo Leoniceno.* Venice, 1548. 8vo.

7. \*†*Vegetio Dell' Arte Della Guerra, Tradotto da Francesco Ferrosi.* Venice, 1551. 8vo.

8. †*Appiano Alessandrino Delle Guerre Diuili et Esterne de Romani.* Venice, 1551. 8vo.
   There are three title-pages in this volume, and Jones's signature appears again on the third of them where it is not scratched out.

9. \*†*L'Ethica d'Aristotile Tradotta . . . per Bernardo Segni.* Venice, 1551. 8vo.

10. \*†*La Republica di Platone, Tradotta . . Dall' Eccellente Phisico Messer Pamphilo Fiorimbene da Fossembrone.* Venice, 1554. 8vo.

11. †*Q. Curtio de' Fatti D' Alessandro Magno, Re De' Macedoni. Tradotto Per M. Thomaso Porcacchi.* Venice, 1559. 4to.

12. †*La Geografia di Claudio Tolomeo Alessandrino, Nuouamente tradotta . . . Da Girolamo Rvscelli.* Venice, 1561. 4to.

13. \*†*La Prima Parte della Geografia di Strabone . . . Tradotta . . . De M. Alfonso Buonacciuoli.* Venice, 1562. 4to.
   The Second Part, printed at Ferrara, 1565, is bound up with the first. The signature on the title is very effectively scratched out, but 'es' is legible. On the back of the title is a note and below it in the same hand 'De' Libri di Vincentio Scamozzi'. The marking throughout the two volumes and some notes in Italian are, perhaps, by Scamozzi. English notes on II, 145, 289–90, are by Jones.

14. \**L'Architettura di Leon Batista Alberti, Tradotta . . . da Cosimo Bartoli.* Monreale, 1565. fo.

15. *L'Architettura di Pietro Cataneo Senese.* Venice, 1567. fo.
   This volume can be identified as having belonged to Jones by the architectural drawing inside the cover.

16. \**Le Premier Tome de l'Architecture de Philibert de l'Orme* Paris, 1567. fo.
   The signature in this volume is untouched.

17. *†*Delle Vite de' Piv Eccellenti Pittori Scultori et Architettori
. . . Giorgio Vasari . . . Prima Volume della Terza Parte.*
Florence, 1568. 4to.

> On the fly-leaf there is a pen-and-ink drawing of two heads.
> On the last leaf after the colophon Jones wrote his name again
> and it is not scratched out. On p. 247 he writes a ' noote ' in
> reference to Fra Jacondo's ' remedy agaynst the Stopynd of yᵉ
> lagune of Vennis ' . . . ' that now at my being at venice 1614
> The Brenta is all opened, but all will not searue '. This life
> and that of Antonio da Sangallo are the most fully annotated.

18. *Le Antichita della Città di Roma . . . Bernardo Gamucci da
San Gimignano.* Venice, 1569. 8vo.

> This book is included on the rather slight evidence afforded by
> some figures.

19. **Ditte Candiotto Et Darete Frigio Della Gverra Troiana,
Tradotti Per Thomaso Porcacchi Da Castiglione Arretino.*
Venice, 1570. 4to.

> There are two notes in Jones's hand on pp. 89 and 92.

20. *†*Della Institvtion Morale di M. Alessandro Piccolomini.*
Venice, 1575. 4to.

21. †*De Gli Elementi D'Euclide.* Urbino, 1575. fo.

22. †*Dell' Epitome Dell' Historia D'Italia . . . Guicciardini.*
Venice, 1580. 8vo.

23. *†*Le Mechaniche Dell' Illustriss. Sig. Gvido Vbaldo De'
Marchesi Del Monte: Tradotte . . . dal Sig. Filippo
Pigafetta.* Venice, 1581 4to.

> Folios 43–8 are supplied in MS.

24. †*La Militia Romana Di Polibio, Di Tito Livio, e di Dionizi
Alicarnaseo. Da Francesco Patricii Dichiarata.* Ferrara,
1583. 4to.

> This book has the signature ' W. Ralegh ' as well as that of
> Inigo Jones on the title-page, and across the top is written,
> in what I take to be Raleigh's hand, ' Amore et virtute '.
> Raleigh's signature, as well as that of Jones, has been scratched
> through with a pen, but is easily legible. I am able to quote
> so eminent an authority as Dr. W. W. Greg in favour of the
> genuineness of Raleigh's signature.

25. **Le Cose Merauigliose Dell' Alma Citta' Di Roma.* Venice,
1588. 8vo.

> On sig. O 1 there is a second title *L'Antichità di Roma di M.
> Andrea Paladio.* The only evidence that the book belonged to
> Jones is furnished by a note in his hand on the fly-leaf.

26. †*Ragionamenti Del Sig. Caualiere Giorgio Vasari.* Florence,
1588. 4to.

27. †*Descrittione Di Tutta Italia, Di F. Leandro Alberti Bolognese.* Venice, 1588. 4to.

28. *De Rebus Praeclare Gestis A Sixto V Pon : Max.* Rome, 1588. 4to.

This is one of the most interesting of the collection. The book was presented to Inigo Jones by Edmund Bolton, and on the fly-leaf is the following inscription : ' Tertio Calendas Januar. M.DCVI Styl. Angl. Arrham, tesseramque amicitiae, futurae cum Ignatio Jonesio sempiternae, Edmundus Bolton do libellum hunc. Ignatio Jonesio suo per quem spes est, Statuariam, Plasticen, Architecturam, Picturam, Mimisim, omnemque ueterum elegantiarum laudem trans Alpes, in Angliam nostram aliquando irrepturas. MERCURIUS IOVIS FILIUS.'

29. *\*Della Architeturra di Gio. Antonio Rusconi.* Venice, 1590. fo.

Contains notes in Jones's hand on pp. 49 and 55.

30. †*Le Imagini De Idei De Gli Antichi, . . . Raccolte Dal Sig. Vincenzo Cartari Reggiano.* Venice, 1592. 4to.

31. *\*I Quattro Libri Dell' Architettura Di Andrea Palladio.* Venice, 1601. fo.

This is the well-known copy of Palladio which Jones had with him during his visit to Italy in 1613–15. Dr. Clarke bought it, says Mr. Wilkinson, not with the rest from Mrs. Webb, but from Michael Burghers on March 3, 1708–9. Burghers purchased it on April 21, 1694, but he does not say from whom he obtained it.

32. †*Historia Della Citta E Regno Di Napoli, di Gio. Antonio Summonte Napolitano.* 2 vols., Naples, 1602–1603. 4to.

Both volumes—in the second the signature has not been touched— are dated ' Napoli 1 mayio 1614 : 14 Carlini 2 voll '.

33. †*Geometria Prattica dichiarata da Giovanni Scala.* Rome, 1603. fo.

34. *\*Le Fortificationi Di Buonaiuto Lorini.* Venice, 1609. fo.

Inigo Jones read this book with great care. Many of the margins are filled with translations and notes, even drawings. Some of the plans in the earlier part of the volume are covered with translations of the explanatory part of the text. The signature has not been scored through.

35. *\*†Opuscoli Morali, di Plutarcho Cheronese ; . . . Tradotti . . . Dal Sig. Marc' Antonio Gandino, e da altri Letterati.* Venice, 1614. 4to.

36. *\*†L'Idea Della Architettura Vniuersale, Di Vincenzo Scamozzi.* Venice, 1615. 2 vols. fo.

Inigo Jones annotated this book, particularly the second volume, very fully. On the title-page he gives the date March 25, 1617.

His known difference of opinion with Scamozzi as to the merits
of Palladio finds expression in such notes as ' see Palladio frõ
whom Scamozi take it ' (ii. 18). ' Scamotzio erres for the Dorik
tēpels of yᵉ greeke had no bases expressing a naked foote of a mã,
and bases imitate a soccolo or sliper ' (ibid.). ' This Palladio
took frõ yᵉ tēpel of Ioue and is to avoyde small mēbers being high
frõ the eye so scamzo contradicte himself ' (ii. 20).

37. *I Commentari Di C. Giulio Cesare, . . . Fatte da ANDREA
PALLADIO. Venice, 1618. 4to.

38. *†L'Architettura Militare Di Gabriello Busca Milanese.
Milan, 1619. 4to.

39. *Della Architettura Di Gioseffe Viola Zanini Padouano Pittore,
Et Architetto. Padua, 1629. 4to.

40 and 41. Both I Acta Mechmeti I Saracencium Principis, 1597,
and Arthur Hopton's The Topographicall Glasse, 1611
(which lacks the title), have some figures at the end which
seem to have been written by Jones.

---

A few more of Jones's notes from the Palladio, in addition to
those already mentioned, will be of interest.

Hales [halls] for festes triamfeo playes maskes and weddniges,
and therefor must be larger then the rest to resceve many people.

This capitell was carved by Palladio his owne hands as yᵉ masons
at Vicensa tould mee.

The gentellman that owneth this house yoused [used] me exiding
kyndly and himself went with me all aboute.

All thes observationes Scamotzio, da bragadotio, makes his own.

From other notes, as well as that about the ' gentellman ', it
is evident that Jones made a very considerable tour of the
buildings connected with Palladio.

The earliest date after his return to London appears to be
January 18th (1615)—a day earlier than that mentioned in
the text.

# APPENDIX B

INIGO JONES'S PANEGYRICK VERSES IN CORYAT'S
' CRUDITIES '

*See the text*, pp. 58, 59, 63

Odde is the Combe from whence this Cocke did come,
That crowed in Venice gainst the skinlesse Jewes,
Who gave him th' entertainment of Tom Drum ;
Yet he undaunted slipt into the stewes.
For learnings cause ; and in his Atticke rage
Trod a tough hen of thirty yeares of age.

Enough of this ; all pens in this doe travell
To tracke thy steps, who Proteus like dost varie
Thy shape to place, the home-borne Muse to gravell.
For though in Venice thou not long didst tarrie,
Yet thou the Italian soule so soone couldst steal,
As in that time thou eat'st but one good meale.

For France alas how soone (but that thou scornedst)
Couldst thou have starch'd thy beard, ruffl'd thy hose ?
Worne a foule shirt twelve weekes, and as thou journedst,
Sung Falaliro's through thy Persian nose ?
For faces, cringes, and a saltlesse jest,
And beene as scab'd a Monsieur as the best.

Next to the sober Dutch I turn my tale,
Who doe in earnest write thee Latin letters,
And thou in good pot paper ne're didst faile
To answere them ; so are you neither debters.
But sympathize in all, save when thou drink'st
Thou mak'st a crab-tree face, shak'st head, and wink'st.

Last, to thy booke the Cordiail of sad mindes,
Or rather Cullis of our Od-combe Cocke
Sodden in travell, which the Critique findes
The best restorer next your Venice smocke.
This booke who scornes to buy, or on it looke,
May he at Sessions crave, and want his booke.

## INIGO JONES'S LINES
## IN THOMAS CROSSE'S MS. COLLECTION OF VERSES

*See text*, p. 234

### TO HIS FALSE FREIND MR. BEN JOHNSON

Sixe daies are done with endlesse hopes since I
had, with expectance of thy honesty,
thought of my thankes to bee delivered free,
which soe longe I have travail'd for with thee ;
but thy neglect hath channgd the happier fate
and made thy birth abortive turne to hate,
whose language like thy nature now must prove
and blame itt not you might have thought itt love.
I wonder howe you ever durst invay
In satire, epigram or Libell-play
against the manners of the tyme on men
in full examples of all mischeifes, when
no ill thou couldst soe [staske dwells ?] not mee
and there the storehouse of yo$^r$ plotts we see,
for thou that hast in thee soe many waies
of practizd mischeif, hath begott thy bayes
in readinge of thy selfe, tickling the age,
stealinge all equall glory from the stage,
that I confesse with like forme thou hast writt
of good and badd things, not with equal witt :
the reason is, or may be quickly shewne,
the good's translation, butt the ill's thyne owne.
for though with tired pace and sweaty feete
I never went to Scotland, nor did meete
thee att returne my selfe alone, or with
my freinds, but soe far of(f) a(s) Hamersmith,
yett I ofte unto yo$^r$ Jurnes glory
with patience heard you tell the teadious story

of all you in that trafficke suffered, thoughe
I was as tyr'd as thou couldst bee to goe.
besides I have beene druncke with thee, and then
satt stille and heard the rayle at other men,
repeate thy verses, and done all that might
to make my succession to thy heart be right :
and t'other daie I gave thee stile and woords,
preferd thee in my choise before greate Lords,
but thou hast proved nowe by this neglect
lesse worthy then that groome my disrespect
heere charected unto the life, for hee
deceivd no trust which murthered is by thee.
   from henceforthe this repute dwell with the then
   the best of Poetts but the worst of men.
             Inigo Jones.

# CHRONOLOGY

1573. July 15. Inigo Jones born.
1589. Law case between father and Richard Baker.
1597. Father died. Will proved 5th April.
1601. Date (of purchase in Italy ?) in his ' Palladio '.
1603. ' Henygo Jones picture maker.'
1605. Jan. 6. 'Masque of Blackness.'
1605. May. Probably in Italy.
1605. Aug. Entertainments at Oxford : described as a ' great traveller '.
1606. Jan. 6. 'Masque of Hymen.'
1606. Dec. 30. Edmund Bolton presents book.
1608. Shrove Tuesday. Masque, ' Hue and Cry after Cupid '.
1609. Feb. 2. 'Masque of Queens.'
1609. Before June. Carries letters to France.
1610. May 30. Prince Henry created Prince of Wales ; Masque, ' Tethys' Festival '.
1610. Christmas. Masque, ' Love Freed, etc.'
1611. Jan. 1. Masque, ' Oberon the Faery Prince '.
1611. Jan. 13. Appointed Surveyor to Prince Henry.
1611. May 17. Gives estimate for work at islands, Richmond.
1611. Sept. 2. Coryat's Philosophical Feast.
1611. Coryat's *Crudities* published ; Panegyric Verses by Jones.
1611. John Webb born.
1612. Nov. Prince Henry died.
1613. Feb. 14. ' The Lords' Masque.'
1613. Feb. 15. ' The Lawyers' Masque.'
1613. April 27. Grant in reversion of office of Surveyor to the King's Works.
1613. Sept. 23. At Vicenza. His principal visit to Italy.
1614. In Italy during the whole year.
1615. Jan. Returned to London.
1615. Sept. Simon Basil died, and Jones succeeded to the Surveyorship, his pay commencing on Oct. 1.

1616. Drawing for entrance to a Jacobean house.

1616. Correspondence as to pictures for Lord Arundel.

1617. March. King James's Progress to Scotland. Improbable that Jones accompanied him.

1617. June 22. Queen's House at Greenwich begun now or a little later.

1618. Jan. Masque, ' Pleasure Reconciled to Virtue ' ; causes disappointment.

1618. Jan. 27. Lincoln's Inn Chapel, resolution to move Inigo Jones to supply ' model '.

1618. April. Drawing, study for windows.

1618. Oct. Visit to Ware Park, pleased with grapes and peaches.

1618. Nov. 16. Commission for laying out Lincoln's Inn Fields according to a plan by Jones.

1619. Jan. 12. Old Banqueting House burnt down.

1619. March 2. Queen Anne died. Her hearse.

1619. March 5. Report on Gatehouse, St. Albans.

1619. April 19. Estimate by Jones and others for new Banqueting House.

1619. Drawing for great door at Banqueting House.

1619. Drawing for ' window of ye Modell ' (Banq. Ho.).

1619. June 1. New Banqueting House begun.

1620. March 29. Certificate as to Sir Robt. Mansfield's glass.

1620. Aug. 17. Letter to Lord Arundel.

1620. Dec. 31. Payment for work at Ely House.

1620. Instructed to examine and report on Stonehenge.

1621. Gateway at Beaufort House.

1622. Jan. 6. ' Masque of Augurs.'

1622. March. Banqueting House completed.

1622. Sept. 5. New Hall being altered.

1622. Drawing ' for my lo. Stuard at Hatton House 1622–23 '.

1623. Jan. 19. Masque, ' Time Vindicated, etc.'

1623. May. Chapels for the Infanta.

1623. June. Lincoln's Inn Chapel consecrated.

1623. Stable at Theobalds.

1623. York House Water-gate about this time.

1624. Twelfth Night. Masque, ' Neptune's Triumph, etc.'

1624. May. Settlement with Jones for previous masques.

1625. Jan. 9. Masque, ' The Fortunate Isles, etc.'

1625. March 27. King James died. His hearse.

1625. May 30. Commission for Buildings ; Jones a member.

1626. Feb. A French Pastoral.
1626. July. Refuses to pay for mending highway.
1627. June 1. Drawing for Clock-turret at Whitehall.
1627. June 16. Certificate as to dangerous stove.
1627. Drawing for doorway, St. James's Park.
1628. John Webb goes to Jones as his pupil.
1628. Aug 23. Duke of Buckingham assassinated.
1629. Sept. 10. Certificate as to Sir Kenelm Digby's buildings.
1629. By this time Jones had been made a Justice of the Peace for Middlesex.
1630. Nov. 2. Report by Justices (including Jones) as to the Plague.
1630. Nov. 24. Report as to the dearth of grain.
1631. Jan. 6. Masque, ' Love's Triumph, etc.'; cause of outbreak of quarrel with Ben Jonson.
1631. Feb. 22. Masque, ' Chloridia', the last in which Ben Jonson collaborated.
1631. May 28. Report as to Wm. Cooke's building.
1631. June 13. Report as to Scipio le Squyer's building.
1631. June 14. Report as to St. Gregory's Church and its effect upon St. Paul's.
1631. Report as to David Mallard.
1631. Layout of Piazza, Covent Garden.
1632. Jan. 8. Masque, ' Albion's Triumph '.
1632. Jan. 21. Appointed to examine the King's coins.
1632. Feb. 14. Masque, ' Tempe Restor'd '.
1632. Feb. 25. Report on St. Gregory's Church.
1632. Drawings for Somerset House.
1633. Jan. 8. Masque, ' The Shepherd's Paradise '.
1633. May. Ben Jonson seeks to license ' The Tale of a Tub ', but the character, Vitruvius Hoop, to be struck out.
1633. About this time the house at Stoke Bruerne was built.
1634. Feb. 3. Masque, ' The Triumph of Peace '.
1634. Feb. 4. Jones appointed Surveyor for the renovation of St. Paul's.
1634. Feb. 18. Masque, ' Cœlum Britannicum '.
1634. May 12. George Chapman died. His monument erected by Jones.
1635. Feb. 10. Masque, ' The Temple of Love'.
1635. Dec. 31. Masque, ' Florimene '.
1636. Feb. 24. Masque, ' The Triumphs of the Prince D'Amour '.

1636. Drawings for the Chirurgeons' Theatre, Chimney-pieces at Oatlands and Somerset House, doorway at Greenwich.

1637. Difficulties in connection with pressing of workmen.

1637. May and onwards. The matter of the Church of St. Michael-le-Querne.

1637. Investigation as to decayed stonework.

1637. Drawings for the doors at St. Paul's, and Chimney-pieces at Greenwich (Queen's House).

1638. Jan. 7. Masque, 'Britannia Triumphans'.

1638. Feb. 6. Masque, 'Luminalia'.

1638. April 24. Jones to survey the King's stables.

1638. April. New Lodge at Hyde Park.

1638. May 18. Jones to view land of the Earl of Clare.

1638. June 15. Water-supply to Whitehall Palace.

1638. June 17. Hubert le Sueur's agreement for statues (for Screen in Winchester Cathedral).

1638. Sept. 18. Report on sewage disposal.

1638. Sept. 30. Order as to abuses of brickmakers.

1638. Oct. 26. Report on irregularities in St. James's Fields.

1638. Oct. 26. Report on John Ward's buildings.

1638. Drawings for Lord Maltravers's house, Temple Bar, and Somerset House.

1638. Kirby Hall alterations.

1639. May and June. Survey and report as to Reindeer Yard and the Earl of Clare.

1639. June 21. Report as to a new sewer.

1639. June 27. Report on water-supply from Piccadilly.

1639. July. Hampshire Justice and supply of timber.

1639. Sept. 29. Directed to report on the Antelope Inn.

1639. Nov. 15. Directed to report on prices of lime and sand.

1640. Jan. 15. Report on Aquila Wykes's house.

1640. Jan. 21. Masque, 'Salmacida Spolia,' the last of the series.

1640. June 15. Directed to report on Alderman Grundy's proposed rebuilding.

1640. Aug. 19. Report as to conversion of old buildings for housing purposes.

1640. Aug. 28. Estimate for work at the Tower of London.

1640. Kirby Hall alterations.

1641. Dec. Cited to appear before the Lords concerning St. Gregory's Church.

1642. July 28. Lends the King £500.
1645. Oct. 14. Fall of Basing House. Jones taken prisoner.
1645. Hides his money.
1649. Jan. 30. Death of King Charles.
1649. Work at Wilton.
1649. About this time visits Coleshill and gives advice.
1650. July 22. Makes his will.
1652. June 21. Inigo Jones died.
1655. John Webb published *Stone-Heng Restored.*

# INDEX

ABIGAIL E. WEEKS MEMORIAL LIBRARY
UNION COLLEGE
BARBOURVILLE, KENTUCKY